THE SITCOM

In this new Routledge Television Guidebook, Jeremy G. Butler studies our love–hate relationship with the durable sitcom, analyzing the genre's position as a major media artefact within American culture and providing a historical overview of its evolution in the USA.

Everyone loves the sitcom genre; and yet, paradoxically, everyone hates the sitcom, too. This book examines themes of gender, race, ethnicity, and the family that are always at the core of humor in our culture, tracking how those discourses are embedded in the sitcom's relatively rigid storytelling structures. Butler pays particular attention to the sitcom's position in today's post-network media landscape and sample analyses of *Sex and the City*, *Black-ish*, *The Simpsons*, and *The Andy Griffith Show* illuminate how the sitcom is infused with foundational American values.

At once contemporary and reflective, *The Sitcom* is a must-read for students and scholars of television, comedy, and broader media studies, and a great classroom text.

Jeremy G. Butler is Professor of Creative Media at the University of Alabama. He has published book chapters and articles on the sitcom in *Journal of Film and Video* and *Cinema Journal*. He is the author of *Television: Visual Storytelling and Screen Culture* and *Television Style*.

ROUTLEDGE TELEVISION GUIDEBOOKS

The Routledge Television Guidebooks offer an introduction to and overview of key television genres and formats. Each guidebook contains an introduction, including a brief history; defining characteristics and major series; key debates surrounding themes, formats, genres, and audiences; questions for discussion; and a bibliography of further reading and watching.

SCIENCE FICTION TV
J.P. Telotte

POLITICAL TV
Chuck Tryon

LIFESTYLE TV
Laurie Ouellette

REALITY TV
Jonathan Kraszewski

THE SITCOM
Jeremy G. Butler

THE SITCOM

Jeremy G. Butler

NEW YORK AND LONDON

First published 2020
by Routledge
52 Vanderbilt Avenue, New York, NY 10017

and by Routledge
2 Park Square, Milton Park, Abingdon, Oxon, OX14 4RN

Routledge is an imprint of the Taylor & Francis Group, an informa business

© 2020 Taylor & Francis

The right of Jeremy G. Butler to be identified as author of this work has been asserted by him in accordance with sections 77 and 78 of the Copyright, Designs and Patents Act 1988.

All rights reserved. No part of this book may be reprinted or reproduced or utilised in any form or by any electronic, mechanical, or other means, now known or hereafter invented, including photocopying and recording, or in any information storage or retrieval system, without permission in writing from the publishers.

Trademark notice: Product or corporate names may be trademarks or registered trademarks, and are used only for identification and explanation without intent to infringe.

Library of Congress Cataloging-in-Publication Data
A catalog record for this title has been requested

ISBN: 978-1-138-85094-1 (hbk)
ISBN: 978-1-138-85096-5 (pbk)
ISBN: 978-1-315-72445-4 (ebk)

Typeset in Perpetua
by Deanta Global Publishing Services, Chennai, India

Printed and bound by CPI Group (UK) Ltd, Croydon, CR0 4YY

CONTENTS

List of Illustrations		vi
Acknowledgments		ix
	Introduction: Comedy Genre, Humor Theory	1
1	Understanding the Sitcom	13
2	A Critical/Cultural History of the Sitcom	57
3	Comedy, Family, and Small Towns	95
4	Comedy, Sex, and Gender Identity	127
5	Comedy, Race, Ethnicity, and Religion	163
6	Comedy, Televisuality, and Convergence	197
	Questions for Discussion	243
	Videography	246
	Bibliography	249
	Index	252

ILLUSTRATIONS

Figures

1.1	In *Arrested Development*, a dejected George Michael walks past a dog and doghouse	35
1.2	Jerry's living room in *Seinfeld* is almost as familiar to us as our own	38
1.3	Director Richard Donner stages a *Gilligan's Island* scene in depth, with the Skipper and Gilligan in hammocks in the foreground and the Professor visible in the back of the set. The next shot …	41
1.4	… cuts to a camera positioned inside the set, about where the hammocks were in the previous shot	42
1.5	Director of *The Carmichael Show*, Gerry Cohen frames actors Jerrod Carmichael and Amber Stevens West in an eye-level medium shot	45
1.6	Even when shot alone, West is framed in a medium close-up, which allows the camera operators to keep her in frame when she gestures and dances	46
1.7	The camera dollies backward, away from AJ Michalka, Hayley Orrantia, and Alex Jennings as they walk confidently through a high school hallway in *The Goldbergs*	48
1.8	The single-camera framing of Orrantia is tighter than what we saw in *The Carmichael Show* and a shallow depth of field blurs the space to either side of her head	49

1.9	An entire episode of *Modern Family* was shot as if it were appearing on Claire's laptop screen	51
1.10	Note the bent position of Amber Stevens West's arms at the end of this shot from *The Carmichael Show*. At the start of the following shot ...	52
1.11	... her arms are now at her side—a tiny continuity error that indicates that two shots from different takes of the same scene have been spliced together	53
3.1	Actresses who played mothers on sitcoms appear in a self-reflexive episode of *Roseanne*: from left, June Lockhart, Isabel Sanford, Roseanne Barr, Barbara Billingsley, Pat Crowley, and Alley Mills	100
3.2	Andy and Opie Taylor stroll down a country road, while accompanied by a whistled song ("The Fishin' Hole"), during the homespun credits for *The Andy Griffith Show*	114
4.1	Jack comments on his "healthy" waitress in *Three's Company*, a show that titillated network-era audiences before nudity and franker sexual humor became common on HBO and other premium-cable channels	131
4.2	On *2 Broke Girls*, Max uses her sexuality to dominate men, jokingly calling herself 'Death Bitch'	134
4.3	Jerry, an actor that Samantha is dating on *Sex and the City*, performs in the nude. The next shot ...	155
4.4	... shows her gazing lustfully at him	156
4.5	Jerry becomes a public spectacle when Samantha, as his publicist, gets him a vodka Times Square billboard in which a bottle serves clearly phallic symbolism	157
5.1	An episode of *Girlfriends* raises the issue of colorism within the black community when darker-skinned Toni ...	177
5.2	... accuses lighter-skinned, mixed-race Maya of not being able to understand the struggles of African Americans with darker skin tones	178

6.1	While standing outside the set of *The George Burns and Gracie Allen Show*, George looks in on his wife	204
6.2	Shattering the fourth wall, Garry Shandling shows his diegetic date around the set of *It's Garry Shandling's Show*	205
6.3	As *The Simpsons'* 25th season started, Bart was still in detention	236
6.4	On the occasion of *The Simpsons*'s parent company being acquired by Disney, Homer cheerfully proclaims, "I for one salute our new corporate overlords!"	238
6.5	The Frinkiac service makes it easier to construct memes and GIFs from *The Simpsons* images	239

Tables

1.1	Evan S. Smith's list of sitcom predicaments and character mixes	27
1.2	Multicam vs. single-camera mode of production	36

ACKNOWLEDGMENTS

I must first thank Erica Wetter at Routledge for her patient persistence in seeing this book through to completion, despite several delays on my part. One would think a short book would be quicker to write than a long one, but, no, no it is not. I am grateful to Marysia Galbraith, Kristen J. Warner, Robin Means Coleman, and Lang Thompson for reading portions of the manuscript and to Nick Buzzelli for tireless assistance in manuscript preparation. I relied on director/producer/writer Ken Kwapis's copious knowledge of television comedy for an insider's perspective. Tom Cherones and Tom Azzari have also been generous with their time and allowed me to interview them on several occasions. I dedicate this book to my 15-year-old son, Ian, who, as far as I know, has never watched an entire sitcom episode—he being of the YouTubian generation. Nonetheless, he has managed to become a fan of both Monty Python and the songs of Tom Lehrer. This gives me cause to think there is still hope for his generation.

INTRODUCTION
Comedy Genre, Humor Theory

Everyone loves the sitcom genre. Each generation of TV viewers defines itself by beloved sitcom characters, catchphrases, and theme songs that become deeply buried in their memory banks. American viewers can't help but remember catchphrases such as Sheldon Cooper's "Bazinga!," Screech's "Zoinks!," and Fonzie's "Ay!" And theme songs like *The Andy Griffith Show*'s whistling introduction, *Friends*' "I'll Be There for You," and *I Love Lucy*'s jaunty tune are as familiar to us as the most popular pop song. And yet, paradoxically, everyone hates the sitcom, too. Critics decry its laughs as fake and its humor as inauthentic—unsupportable without a fabricated laugh track. And they deride its storylines as repetitive and sophomoric. Viewers, too, disdain the humor of most programs, aside from their own favorites, and are perplexed that anyone could find *that show* funny. And even enthusiastic fans of programs eventually tire of their favorites as the seasons go by and showrunners run out of fresh ideas. It is not surprising that "jump the shark," the colloquial phrase for a past-its-prime TV program, comes from a sitcom—a *Happy Days* episode in which Fonzie literally waterskis over a shark. Many actors are embarrassed to appear in sitcoms as well. Tom Hanks, for instance, clearly does not believe that *Bosom Buddies* was the peak of his career. And stand-up comics, most of whom lust after their own sitcoms, are still wary of being seen as sell-outs who have lost their comic edge should they actually get one.

Despite viewers', critics', and actors' love–hate relationship with sitcoms, there is no denying that they comprise television's longest-lived narrative genre—outpacing Westerns, medical shows, soap operas, science-fiction programs, and even its closest competitor in longevity, the crime drama. Moreover, the American sitcom existed well before television was a mass medium. It was born on radio years before TV's post-World War II growth spurt. And, remarkably, the sitcom continues to persist during the current age of media disruption and convergence, as conventional broadcast-network television becomes less and less of a mass medium. Comedies like the Netflix production, *Grace and Frankie*, are now binge-watched on-demand, but they're still fashioned as 30-minute episodes with many sitcom conventions intact. The mere fact of the sitcom's longevity in a medium known for its transience encourages us to account for the cause of its enduring popularity. Moreover, there can be little doubt that during its long history the sitcom has often contributed to national discourses about identity politics, about what it means to be an American, a woman, a man, African American, Latinx, rich, poor, pro-war, anti-war, gay, straight, conservative, liberal, and more. In short, there is no denying that the sitcom is a significant cultural phenomenon.

Notes on Terminology: "Situation Comedy" and "Sitcom"

The ambiguous and varying uses of the terms "situation comedy" and "sitcom" by critics, scholars, industry insiders, and viewers necessitate that I clarify how I apply them in this book and, indeed, what forms of television comedy I address and which I exclude. In the chapters that follow, I have cast a fairly wide net and include all half-hour comedies *that base their humor in narrative situations*. In so doing, I am relying on an early 20th-century definition of "situation comedy." In silent film before 1927 and radio broadcasting during its golden age of the 1930s, comedians sought to distinguish humor rooted in the interaction of characters from humor sparked by short, isolated, verbal, and physical gags. Today, verbal gag comedy is still going strong in stand-up comedy specials and talk-shows' monologues. And physical humor can be found in its purest form in the pratfalls—e.g., skateboard crashes—captured on cell phones and uploaded to YouTube and *America's Funniest Home Videos*. In the gag comedy form, the comedian fires off joke after joke or presents pratfall after pratfall, with little connection among them. A story is unnecessary. Situation comedy, in contrast, tells us a story and we become amused by the predicaments of the characters and their dialogue. Individual verbal jokes or slapstick incidents may occasionally punctuate or even interrupt those stories, but they are not central to sitcoms' amusement value. We watch *Modern Family*, for example, expecting amusing storylines with characters in embarrassing or humorous situations, but we also laugh at Phil's (Ty Burrell) pratfalls.

I recognize that relying on "situation comedy" and "sitcom" as *descriptive* labels instead of pejorative judgments of value runs contrary to common parlance among TV critics and scholars and even everyday viewers—all of whom attach a certain stigma to the word, "sitcom." Much like the phrase "soap opera," "sitcom" has become a term of opprobrium, shorthand for indicating the humor in a TV program is unearned and inauthentic. However, these judgments of quality and taste are particularly unhelpful in discussions of television humor and how it functions culturally and aesthetically. And, further, they are very difficult to sustain in a logical fashion. For example, some critics contend that *Louie*, the program based on the edgy comedy of Louis CK, is *not* a sitcom, because its humor is "realistic" and "authentic" and arises "organically" out of Louis CK's life as a comic (which included, it was revealed in 2017, instances of sexual harassment). But when I watch it, I find Louis CK's performance to be forced and highly constructed—a character that he is obviously performing for the camera. In short, it does not seem authentic to me in the least. This is why a reliance on authenticity as a criterion to separate "quality" TV comedy from the lowly sitcom does not stand up as a logical method of categorization. It relies too heavily on taste as a criterion of value. In contrast, categorizing TV comedy as either narrative (situation comedy) or non-narrative (gag comedy) is logically consistent and can be historically tracked back into older comic forms.

Theories of Humor

Some introductory comments on theory are in order, because the presumptions I make about comedy and humor in the pages that follow are built on the unsteady infrastructure of humor theory. I say "unsteady" because, despite a history that can be traced all the way back to Plato and Aristotle in the 4th century BCE, there is still much disagreement among philosophers about its basic tenets. Typically, the three competing camps of humor theory are classified as superiority, relief (aka, release), and incongruity. At the risk of overly simplifying the complex, subtle thinking about the topic, I will summarize these approaches in the next few paragraphs. And to illustrate the applicability of each theory, an episode of *Modern Family*—titled "Under Pressure," from January 15, 2014—has been chosen largely at random as a test subject. If a humor theory is truly useful, it should apply to virtually any form of comedy. The specific example is almost irrelevant. This episode's main storyline follows two sets of parents as they attend an open house at their children's high school—sitting in on each of their classes and experiencing the "pressures" of being a student. A second storyline pits Mitchell (Jesse Tyler Ferguson) and Haley (Sarah Hyland) against a new neighbor (Jesse Eisenberg) who claims to be more environmentally responsible than Mitchell is.

Superiority Theories of Humor

I begin with superiority theories of humor, which take a rather dim view of humanity and of what makes people laugh. They contend that laughter is evoked principally when people note the weaknesses of others and abruptly feel they are better than them. Seventeenth-century philosopher Thomas Hobbes writes that we take a "sudden glory" when we apprehend "some deformed thing in another" and that we "suddenly applaud" ourselves for our superiority and break out in laughter. Laughter comes from condescending scorn for the butt of a joke and, consequently, is a rather cowardly act—"a sign of pusillanimity," in Hobbes's words! His contemporary, René Descartes held a similar view, arguing that laughter arises from "perceiving some small evil in a person whom we consider to be deserving of it; we have hatred for this evil, we have joy in seeing it in him who is deserving of it; and when that comes upon us unexpectedly, the surprise of wonder is the cause of our bursting into laughter."[1] Thus, for Hobbes, Descartes, and others subscribing to superiority theories of humor, laughter stems from derision, from "making fun" of someone.

Although early theorists discussed superiority in terms of one individual's feelings about another, inferior individual, it's easy to see how derisive humor also underpins the jokes and funny narratives that dominant social classes tell to ridicule, exploit, and subordinate minority populations. Unsurprisingly, narratives trading on unfavorable stereotypes about minorities are commonly found in sitcoms. For example, some critics argue that *Modern Family*'s Gloria, played by an actress from Colombia (Sofía Vergara), embodies the racist identity of the hypersexual, loud, "hot-blooded" Latina. And, true to form, in "Under Pressure" Gloria wears an inappropriately sexy dress to her son's high school open house and gets into a brawl with another parent. Non-Latinx, racist viewers might laugh at Gloria, and feel that her dress and her actions confirm their condescending prejudices toward Latinas. The undergirding attitude of humor based in superiority is "*We* are better than them."

Relief or Release Theories of Humor

Relief and/or release theories of comedy take a different, but not mutually exclusive, tack toward explaining the mechanics of humor. They contend that humans are naturally restrained or, in Freudian terms, repressed, and that we hide forbidden emotions and desires deep below the surface of our psyches. Sigmund Freud gathered his theories of humor into an exceedingly influential book titled, *Jokes and Their Relation to the Unconscious*. In it, he contends that suppressing taboo ideas requires psychic energy, with the superego struggling to contain the impulses of the id. However, like the title of our *Modern Family* episode, living "under pressure" can be emotionally debilitating and stressful. Humor, then, is a way to relieve that pressure, to express thoughts that society (and the superego) deem unacceptable, reprehensible, and disgusting. Humor does so in a way that is safe to both the individual psyche and society at large. For Freud, societal taboos are rooted in violence and aberrant sexuality—as can be seen in his emphasis on the Oedipus complex, where a man murders his father and has sex with his mother—but relief and release theories of humor more generally expect humor to make us less anxious and more at ease with things that are disturbing. Hence, the jokes that appear after every major tragedy can be seen as relieving tension about that event.

Modern Family does not rely heavily on this form of humor, although early in its run it did make fun of Phil's Oedipal desire for his stepmother-in-law, Gloria. And the "Under Pressure" episode does not derive humor from dangerously taboo subjects, but it does explore the topic of how high school students are expected to repress "normal" human desires in order to succeed at school. Alex (Ariel Winter), the Dunphys' over-achieving daughter, has a meltdown at the start of the episode—cracking under the pressure to excel on college entrance exams. The excessiveness of her response to exams is played for laughs as she destroys her own birthday cake and, the following morning, the rest of the family discusses who she would murder first if she imploded and went on a killing spree. However, the rest of the episode does not present her meltdown as excessive and, in a departure from the program's typical tone, when Alex goes to see a psychologist her scenes with him are played straight, with little humor. Afterward, at a high school open house where Alex's mother, Claire (Julie Bowen), is placed in Alex's position, Claire tells Alex, "Wow. So intense. I had no idea the kind of pressure you were under. Honey, I was just you for two hours. I could barely hold it together. I don't know how you don't have a meltdown every day." Alex hugs her tightly and the scene's sentimentality is presented as genuine and not laughable. Thus, the "Under Pressure" episode starts by illuminating how humor can be used as a release valve for social pressure—the pressure put on young people to succeed in school and career—but ends with a sentimental homily of parents coming to understand their children's struggles.

Much like the superiority theories of humor, relief/release theories may be first understood in terms of individuals, but then can be generalized to the societal level. As I examined above, superiority theories explain how minorities are derided and suppressed by social classes that are in positions of power. It is one way that hegemony is maintained. Release theories, in contrast, see comedy as disruptive of the status quo and its laws, conventions, and mores. They presume that humor provides a release or an escape from these conventions and allows us to indulge in normally forbidden thoughts. Comedians are allowed to say things that disturb hegemony, that indulge in carnivalesque excesses, as philosopher Mikhail Bakhtin might say. Bakhtin writes about medieval festivals (carnivals) where social boundaries break down and authority figures may be questioned and ridiculed. Thus, in relief/release theories such as this, humor can be seen to be socially liberating—in contrast to superiority theories where humor aids the social repression of minority voices. Sketch comedies on the order of *Key & Peele* and *Saturday Night Live* contain some of the sharpest critiques of persons in power, but sitcoms such as *Black-ish* can also contain carnivalesque elements, although they have less freedom to do so. ABC allowed *Black-ish*'s showrunner, Kenya Barris, to create episodes that were critical of mainstream white society's treatment of African Americans—including white persons' appropriation of the N-word. However, when Barris shot an episode that was supportive of athletes kneeling during the national anthem, he ran into interference from ABC executives. Citing "creative differences," the episode was shelved and never shown.

Incongruity Theories of Humor

Our third category of humor theories, incongruity, finds amusement in situations where one element is a mismatch for another. For example, in "Under Pressure," Jay (Ed O'Neill) offers Phil (Ty Burrell) a drink from a flask while they are at the open house. The setting of the school room, with notes on a whiteboard and rows of school desks, is clearly incongruous with two grown men squeezed into those desks, drinking alcohol. And from that incongruity arises amusement. This approach to humor can be traced back at least to philosopher Francis Hutcheson in the 18th century. Surveying the history of humor theory, Noël Carroll argues persuasively that incongruity theories offer the most broadly applicable strategies for understanding humor.[2] He explains, "Incongruity is a comparative notion. It presupposes that something is discordant with something else. With respect to comic amusement, that *something else* is how the world is or should be."[3] In my example above, the viewer quickly and without much conscious thought compares Jay and Phil's behavior with how the world of a classroom should be and finds it discordant—hence the humor of the situation. Further, the discordance between the children's realm (the school) and their parents' realm (adulthood) is the central theme of this episode. The parents are all placed in situations where they act like or are treated like children, winding up in the principal's office at the episode's conclusion. They revert to the social roles they played in high school—e.g., Phil as a member of the AV Club—and humor is derived from the incongruity between their immature behavior and their adult bodies.

Incongruity can be instantaneous, as when you see adult men in a funny, incongruous circumstance; but equally significant to the sitcom is incongruity based on a sequence of events. Incongruity can thus occur over time—over the course of a half-hour story or during a 30-second narrative joke. Incongruity arises when we viewers expect one thing to happen, but instead something else occurs. *Modern Family*'s dialogue is filled with quick little surprises that provoke humor by twisting the logic of how the narrative is progressing. For instance, in "Under Pressure," Gloria prepares for the school open house by wearing a sexy dress while her significantly older husband, Jay, dresses casually. This short exchange between Jay and his dryly humorous stepson, Manny (Rico Rodriguez), transpires before they leave for the school:

Jay: "Why do you [Gloria] look like that when I look like this?"
Manny: "My friends say it's because of your money."
Jay: "No, I'm just saying why is she all dressed up for a school open house?"

Jay's question, as he clarifies, is why Gloria is dressed up, but Manny answers a different question: why is a young, sexy woman married to an older, not particularly handsome man? There is a disjunction, an incongruity, between Jay's question and Manny's answer, which the viewer may find humorous. This form of incongruity differs from the shot of Jay and Phil in the school desks because it occurs *over time*. It has a set-up (Jay's line) followed by a punchline (Manny's rejoinder).

Sequential incongruity such as this is embedded in one of comedy's most often-cited premises, the so-called "rule of three." The basic concept is that a comedian (1) sets up a joke, (2) builds anticipation for something humorous, and then (3) delivers a punchline that is incongruous with steps one and two. The pattern might be described as A-A-B. For some, this form of joke-building is old-fashioned and hackneyed, although it certainly persists in much television comedy. *Modern Family* generally avoids the setup-anticipation-punchline structure, but we can see it in operation in the scene in "Under Pressure" where Manny and Luke go on a double date with twin girls. The date is not going well, because each girl's interests don't match the boy she is with. And so Manny suggests they switch partners (set-up). Luke agrees with Manny (anticipation): "Let's just switch dates and get this party started!" But the girls defy the boys' expectations and incongruously express their interest in staying with their dates (punchline). The first girl, with Manny, says, "I've got a thing for Latin men" (punchline one). And the second confirms her interest in Luke by saying, "I like 'em dumb" (punchline two). Neither the boys nor we viewers expect the girls to say this and thus the incongruity in this instance arises solely from the girls' comments coming after the boys' dialogue, from the defeat of expectations that the narrative has built for the viewer.

Carroll covers three additional forms of incongruity in his discussion, all of which appear frequently in the sitcom. First is "emotional incongruity," which obtains when a character is perceived to be either too emotional or not emotional enough.[4] *Modern Family*'s Cameron (Eric Stonestreet) often exemplifies the former, as when he becomes overly excited about organizing the parents into a game of dodge ball; and his daughter, Lilly (Aubrey Anderson-Emmons), deflates his excitement with withering, understated comments. Second is the violation of "standards of grace and taste," which through exaggerated "clumsiness and vulgarity can provoke comic amusement."[5] In "Under Pressure," Mitchell (Jesse Tyler Ferguson) and Haley (Sarah Hyland) spill a boxful of Styrofoam packing peanuts, and their clumsy attempt to recover them is played for humor. Further, Luke often makes blissfully vulgar comments. A final form of incongruity that Carroll details involves mismatched narrative knowledge—when the spectator knows something that the character does not:

> In comic narratives ... it frequently happens that certain characters misperceive their circumstances; they may think they are speaking to a gardener when in fact they are speaking to the master of the house. The audience is aware of this and tracks the spectacle under two alternative, nevertheless conflicting interpretations: the limited perspective of the mistaken character and the omniscient perspective of the narrator. Inasmuch as these viewpoints effectively contradict each other, the incongruity theory counts them as further instances of incongruous juxtaposition.[6]

Although this form of character misperception is not central to the "Under Pressure" episode, it would not be difficult to find entire episodes of more conventional sitcoms—say, *I Love Lucy* or *The Andy Griffith Show*, discussed later—that are built on it.

My quick summary of three categories of humor theories and their application to a *Modern Family* episode is far from a comprehensive consideration of the topic, but I hope it illustrates how these theories can help explain how sitcoms function. In the chapters that follow, I will incorporate this theoretical infrastructure into explanations of how the genre is inscribed with American cultural values constellated around family, gender, and race. I hope also to express the pleasure that the genre can provide, despite the low regard in which it is sometimes held. This guidebook will not survey the "greatest sitcoms of all time" for you, but it will offer you insights into how those sitcoms have come to have such a significant position within American culture of the past 70 years.

Sitcom Characteristics, History, and Case Studies

This book is predominantly concerned with the sitcom as it engages with cultural discourses, choosing to focus on the family, gender, and race because of their centrality to American culture. Individual chapters explore each discourse and then drill down to one specific program as exemplary of it: *The Andy Griffith Show* and family; *Sex and the City* and gender; and *Black-ish* and race. Before addressing these specific discourses, however, I will analyze the sitcom as a narrative form, one that is virtually unique to television. In what other medium are 30-minute humorous stories told with recurring characters that work through similar narrative structures every week for 15 or 20 times a year? Naturally, this form did not spring fully formed from the head of a sitcom showrunner, and so we must also consider the history and pre-history of the genre—looking at its roots in radio, vaudeville, and beyond. Chapter 1 explicates the sitcom form. Chapter 2 maps out the genre's critical/cultural history and describes how television's first major sitcom, *I Love Lucy*, came to establish a format that inspired so many shows after it. Chapters 3 through 5 cover crucial discursive topics. And Chapter 6 considers how well the sitcom is surviving in the 21st century. This concluding chapter unpacks sitcoms that play with the conventions of the genre, sometimes threatening to implode it. *The Simpsons* provides a key example of a program that can corrode the conventions that make up the genre, despite being phenomenally successful and the longest-running narrative program of all time. The final chapter will offer some tentative thoughts about the sitcom's situation in the post-network era of convergence and cord-cutting. Many aspects of convergence culture are volatile and unpredictable, as one might expect of media in chaotic transition. How will a genre so thoroughly entwined with the network-television model fare in this new age? No one really knows, but I will position the sitcom within the current chaos and suggest a few ways that it might survive.

Notes

1 Thomas Hobbes and René Descartes are quoted in John Morreall, "Philosophy of Humor," *The Stanford Encyclopedia of Philosophy*, https://plato.stanford.edu/archives/win2016/entries/humor/, accessed May 31, 2018.
2 Noël Carroll, *Humour: A Very Short Introduction* (Oxford: Oxford University Press, 2014), 1.
3 Carroll, 18.
4 Carroll, 26.
5 Carroll, 26.
6 Carroll, 24.

1

UNDERSTANDING THE SITCOM

Television genres rely on a flexible, ever-changing, and generally unspoken contract between industry professionals and audience members. Showrunners and viewers alike share certain presumptions about a genre's conventions. The showrunners—operating in concert with an intricate television apparatus of producers, writers, directors, network executives, and government regulators—exploit genre conventions to construct programs that are both comfortably familiar and innovatively unfamiliar. Viewers are typically drawn to programs evidencing some degree of familiarity, but not to the extent that they perceive genre conventions as annoyingly tired and worn out. A virtual rule book or a shared code, one might say, of a genre is established over time. And here is where the study of genre becomes essential to media studies and to all cultural critics. The shared, conventionalized stories of a genre are inevitably overlaid with the values of a particular time and place. Thus, examining these stories provides insights into American ideology—particularly in the second half of the 20th century, when network television became our preferred medium of entertainment.

I wish to emphasize, however, that a society's dominant ideological values are seldom uncontested or monolithic and that preferred readings are often countered by against-the-grain and negotiated readings (as suggested by cultural critic Stuart Hall). Even in seemingly homogenous times when hegemony appears to be total—America in the 1950s, to choose a common example—there are always discursive undercurrents and rip tides that can result in anti-hegemonic interpretations of television. One of the great virtues of network-era television's wide appeal to its vast audience's many constituencies was that it supported a certain multiplicity of interpretations, a polysemy, although that was not always obviously true. With the fragmentation of broadcast-network markets through, first, cable television and then the internet, *broad*casting has become *narrow*-casting and programs are now able to appeal to smaller and smaller demographic segments. For 21st-century sitcoms, this has meant that their humor can have a relatively limited ideological range and their storylines can speak to narrowly defined niches of viewers.

This chapter charts the general characteristics of the situation comedy. Here, I will be focusing on the sitcom's undergirding framework, particularly its distinctive narrative and stylistic conventions. I will mostly leave the interpretation of the genre's discourse to later chapters. My initial goal is to establish the remarkably resilient, prototypical attributes of the television situation comedy as it evolved in the 1950s and continues to the present day. However, as explained in the Introduction, I have taken the liberty to include all narrative, "scripted" comedy on American television in this book—extending beyond what is commonly called "situation comedy" or "sitcom" to comedies such as *Modern Family* (2009–), *Veep* (2012–2019), and *The Simpsons* (1989–), which some television observers are loath to label "sitcoms." It's tempting to call this later wave of sitcoms *sui generis* (without genre) or "unconventional," but, as we shall see, they do in fact contain conventions. It's just that their conventions are decidedly different from those of the prototypical sitcom. Consequently, as I outline the archetypal sitcom's attributes, I will also consider how TV comedy has altered its narrative structure and style as the network era has been coming to a close.

In popular lore, *I Love Lucy* (1951–1957), which premiered November 5, 1951, is the original TV sitcom from which all others evolved. The true history of the genre is not that neat and tidy, but *I Love Lucy* is undoubtedly a highly influential and significant early-TV sitcom. In Chapter 2's chronicle of the history of the genre, I will highlight the program, its innovations, and its synthesis of radio and cinema production modes. But first, I will establish the genre's distinguishing features in its current incarnation as a mature genre in a medium that is in upheaval. In this context, we must understand the structure of the individual sitcom episode, the grouping of episodes into seasons, and the multiple-season persistence of successful series over years or decades.

Sitcom Storytelling

Episode, Season, Series

There are really only two absolutely essential attributes of sitcom storytelling as it has evolved during the broadcast-network era: (1) the series must have a *repeatable* premise and (2) individual episodes must be segmented to allow for commercial interruptions. Everything else about sitcom narrative then and now is essentially up for negotiation. The repeatability of a sitcom is established early on in the production process—at the pitch session where show creators advocate for their concepts with network executives. It's not enough to pitch a potentially successful sitcom idea for an initial pilot episode. The show creator must also establish how that concept can be repeated and kept fresh over dozens of episodes. Sometimes show creators are even asked to explain what the program's potential "100th episode" might be like. Where will the characters be 100 episodes down the road? Will the show sustain an audience for 5 or 6 seasons of 13 to 22 episodes per season, or at least for enough shows to qualify for syndication?[1]

The TV industry mandates that each program has a hook, a fundamental premise that might be boiled down to a "logline," a concise one- or two-sentence description of that premise. For instance, *I Love Lucy*'s logline might have been something like, "A madcap woman, married to a Cuban bandleader, is caught up in screwball situations as she attempts to break into show business herself." The logline has a practical purpose. It's used for selling TV and film scripts. But it also can be seen as encapsulating a TV show's recurring "narrative problematic," as scholars such as Mick Eaton and John Ellis have put it. One might think of a series' problematic as the question it poses each week. Four of the five shows highlighted in this book can each be summarized in this manner: will Lucy break into show business? Will an outside force disturb the bucolic calm of Mayberry in *The Andy Griffith Show* (1960–1968)? Will Carrie and her girlfriends find romantic and sexual satisfaction in *Sex and the City* (1998–2004)? How will the family of *Black-ish* (2014–) cope with the challenges to their racial identity? (*The Simpsons*' genre-busting makes it difficult to boil down to a single question.) As you can see, a series' problematic is its constant; it does not change. Or, as Ellis writes, "The basic problematic of the series, with all its conflicts, is itself a stable state."[2]

In its purest state—as exemplified by series like *I Love Lucy* and *The Andy Griffith Show*—the problematic does not change significantly from episode to episode. Each week, a specific conflict based on the series' problematic is posed and that one conflict is resolved during the course of the episode, while the sustaining problematic remains. For example, in the "Crime-Free Mayberry" episode of *The Andy Griffith Show* (November 20, 1961), two men come to town ostensibly to honor Mayberry for having the lowest crime rate in the country—an attribute associated with small-town life and its traditional values of honesty and the golden rule. It's soon revealed, however, that these out-of-towners are frauds who intend to rob the Mayberry Security Bank. Thus, they bring urban, big-city values of greed and criminal activity that disrupt Mayberry's crime-free environment. Fortunately, Andy sees through their ruse and outwits them—yet another victory for the small-town sheriff and his way of life. Despite coping narratively and ideologically with this particular intruder, *The Andy Griffith Show*'s recurring problematic remains strong and stable as other interlopers with their modern ideas will arrive in subsequent weeks.

A sitcom's problematic is played out through a narrative form that is rigidly segmented in network television. The diegetic time contained within the sitcom's half-hour time slot is apportioned in a highly conventionalized fashion, typically falling into four discrete parts. In prototypical shows, the TV industry identifies these parts as:

1. Teaser or cold opening
2. Act I, consisting of one or more scenes
3. Act II, consisting of one or more scenes
4. Tag

The teaser and act I are separated by the main titles; and a commercial break is inserted between acts I and II. The tag is the shortest and most disposable component of this structure and is often deleted to make room for more commercials during broadcasts in syndication, or it might display in a minimized window while the end credits quickly run. This basic broadcast structure—necessitated by the need to accommodate commercials—challenges the sitcom scriptwriter: how can one tell a humorous story within the constraints of a segmented narrative and a strictly delimited running time (approximately 21 minutes, excluding commercials)?

The solution, as has been codified in numerous "how-to" scriptwriting books, involves narrative techniques that modify the standard, Aristotelian, five-act dramatic structure of exposition–conflict–resolution into a framework suitable for commercial television. We can best see this in action by highlighting an episode from *The Big Bang Theory* (2007–2019) that follows the genre's prototypical structure. In particular, I've selected "The Vartabedian Conundrum" (November 17, 2008), based on a story by showrunner Chuck Lorre and Steven Molaro and written by Bill Prady and Richard Rosenstock (the script is available online).[3] First, I should point out that the episode is built on the series' stable problematic, which, in colloquial terms, might be posed as: Will the cast's physicists and engineers stop being so nerdy? In this episode from the show's second season, the main story—or what scriptwriters call the "A" story—tracks physicist Leonard Hofstadter's (Johnny Galecki) continuing romance with Dr. Stephanie Barnett (Sara Rue), which he feels is progressing too quickly. The secondary "B" story details the hypochondria of Sheldon Cooper (Jim Parsons), Leonard's fellow physicist and roommate. As is typical in the genre, the A and B stories share a contact point. In this episode, it's Stephanie who is having sex with Leonard and who is pestered by Sheldon for medical advice. Also typical of the genre is the way that the episode's A and B stories diverge from that point of contact. That is, Leonard has scenes with Stephanie that do not involve Sheldon and vice versa. In any event, both stories are grounded in the series' problematic. Leonard and Sheldon are presented as eggheads accustomed to living solely in the world of the intellect. When confronted with practical, everyday problems (relating to women, understanding their own bodies), they are baffled—leading to humorous, incongruous conflicts with the "real" world.

This second-season episode presents its beginning, middle, and end in a fashion that typifies the sitcom genre. It starts with a short exposition in the cold opening. It needn't introduce us to Leonard and Sheldon or explain that they're roommates, because we've already seen them in dozens of episodes. Even the recurring role of Stephanie needs no explanation as she had been on two episodes before this one, when Leonard "stole" her from Howard Wolowitz (Simon Helberg). Sitcom-episode exposition is, thus, quite abbreviated when contrasted with a novel or book, which must establish its characters from the ground up. The episode need only particularize the issue or goal for that specific week. Accordingly, "The Vartabedian Conundrum" establishes in the opening that Leonard and Stephanie seem to have begun living together (the A story) and that Sheldon is worried about his health (the B story).

To dig deeper into the sitcom structure used to construct the "middle" of these intertwining stories, we may "reverse engineer" the story, identifying the episode's scenes as they are distributed into act I and act II. In this instance, we're fortunate to have online access to the script and may consult its rundown, which presents a list of acts and scenes in table form. The rundown lists the cold open(ing) and act I's three scenes—labeled A, B, and C. The rest of the rundown then charts the episode's remaining six scenes (in act II) and its tag.

Like most narrative forms, the middle of a sitcom story consists of a cause–effect chain of mounting narrative intensity. That is, the first problem or predicament *causes* the second one. The second one, an *effect* of the first, causes a third and so on: cause–effect, cause–effect, cause–effect, until the pressure within the story rises to a climax that must be resolved. Unlike narrative forms such as the classical cinema, however, the sitcom's cause–effect chain must be modified to cope with an interruption that splits the chain in two—similar to an intermission in a play. This interruption leads sitcom writers to place a mini-climax, a minor cliffhanger, just before the commercial break, with the obvious purpose of luring the viewer into staying tuned in for act II. Television is essentially a medium of distraction where the apparatus must fight to hold onto its viewers' attention. Obviously, that attention tends to drift drastically during commercials. After the break, at the start of act II, the episode may resolve that minor cliffhanger or it may delay resolution a short while to further raise tension. In fact, one way to view narrative form—what narrative theorists call its hermeneutic—is to see it as a series of delaying tactics, holding the viewer from eventual gratification. In any event, the sitcom's cause–effect chain resumes post-commercial and once again begins building toward the climax.

In "The Vartabedian Conundrum," scene C, which ends act I, is wholly devoted to the A story. Leonard, Howard, and Rajesh ("Raj"; Kunal Nayyar) eat lunch in the cafeteria at work, and they tease Leonard about his relationship with Stephanie, which further intensifies the conflict between his desires and hers. Leonard is wearing pants bought for him by Stephanie that are uncomfortably itchy—a "wool, fire ant blend," as he says. Narratively, the pants function as a clear, physical manifestation or objective correlative of the discomfort he feels about her presence in his life. In the last line before the commercial break, Leonard protests, "I don't care what you guys think. Stephanie and I are very happy living together," but then he undercuts that declaration by pleading, "I will give either of you twenty dollars to change pants with me." The ambivalence expressed in this line creates a small cliffhanger, hoping to hook the viewer for the duration of the commercial break. Are Stephanie and Leonard going to stay together or will he dump her, just as he yearns to do with the irritating pants? Incidentally, the line as originally scripted was different: "I don't care what you guys think. Stephanie and I are very happy living together. We have a grown-up, mature relationship. (A BEAT, THEN) If we could agree on a new place for my Bat Signal, things would be perfect." It's evident that the scriptwriter designed the scene to end ambivalently, with Leonard declaring one thing and then contradicting it with irony. However, the scriptwriter's original version spotlights Leonard's immaturity and lack of experience with women more than the broadcast version does. Despite the change during the production process, both lines serve the same function: emphasizing ambivalence and raising questions about what will happen next, with both the pants and Stephanie.

In this case, the program's creative team elected to follow the A-story scene with a B-story scene when the narrative resumes after the break. The first post-break scene (scene D) is in the hospital where Stephanie works. Sheldon has snuck inside and wants her to order tests for his imagined malady. Scene D serves two functions: (1) it steps up the tension between Sheldon and Stephanie and (2) it briefly delays our resumption of the A story. We do return to the A story in the following scene (Scene E) where Leonard and Penny (Kaley Cuoco) have a chance encounter in their building's laundry room. He's washing the itchy pants and intentionally ruins them with too much fabric softener, suggesting his desire to separate himself from the person who bought those pants. The A story ratchets up in scene E with Penny encouraging Leonard to express his feelings directly to Stephanie, which is sparked by Penny seeing him destroy the pants Stephanie purchased. Thus, scene E resolves the mini-cliffhanger from scene C (just before the commercial break) by showing us what happens to the pants and it simultaneously delays the answer to the questions about Leonard's decision regarding Stephanie.

In its purest form, a sitcom episode brings its conflict to a peak toward the end of its time slot and then fully resolves that week's conflict. Notably, it does not resolve the program's over-arching narrative problematic as that must remain open in order to support subsequent episodes. To take an example from one of the narrative problematics listed previously, Lucy's attempt to break into show business in any one episode inevitably fails, but it does not fail in such a fashion that she will never be able to make another attempt. It is not, in a sense, a conclusive conclusion or closed ending. The pure sitcom episode provides some modicum of resolution—that is, closing that particular narrative—but keeps the problematic unresolved. And, further, in the pure sitcom series, each week's story is self-contained. What happens one week does not change the characters or their situations. And characters in future episodes will not refer back to earlier episodes. These narrative aspects are what distinguishes the "series" from that of the TV "serial." Sitcom characters are somewhat like the protagonists of *Groundhog Day* (1993) or *Russian Doll* (2019–), forever doomed to work through the same story structure, with small variations during each week's iteration.

Of course, individual sitcoms seldom adhere to this Platonic ideal of a wholly self-contained episode, based on an utterly static narrative problematic. Even the most conventionalized sitcom series involves some continuation of the story from one episode to another and a certain degree of evolution of its characters over the course of a season. My previous example from the mostly conventional *The Andy Griffith Show* (where robbers pose as an FBI agent and a newspaper photographer) is relatively self-contained in that the incident is not mentioned in subsequent episodes, but the program still has *some* narrative development from episode to episode. For example, Andy has a girlfriend (Helen) with whom he becomes increasingly close over the course of several seasons; they eventually get married in the show's spin-off, *Mayberry R.F.D.* (1968–1971). It's quite common in sitcoms, therefore, to have narrative arcs persisting over several episodes or seasons. Many series also have a "bible" that is conceived at the time the show is originally pitched. Show bibles might flesh out a logline with short biographies of the characters, season-long (or longer) story arcs, brief summaries of individual episodes, and even location or budgetary considerations.

Returning to "The Vartabedian Conundrum," we can observe the episode's climax in the final scene of the A story, just before the ending tag. Leonard resolves to dump Stephanie and, following urging from Howard and Raj at the cafeteria, he texts a break-up message to her. He then ruefully states, "It's done. I may never have sex again." The A story appears here to be closed. The question "Will Leonard break up with Stephanie?" seems to have been conclusively answered in the negative. However, this closed ending only lasts a beat. His phone vibrates. He looks at it, comments, "Huh, I guess I was wrong. See ya'," and hastily departs—leaving the disposition of his romance with her in doubt. In typical sitcom fashion, however, Stephanie disappears from the show without additional notice in any later episodes. The actual break-up is never shown or commented upon. Instead, in the following episode, Leonard returns to a story arc begun in the pilot where he romantically pursues Penny, succeeding in marrying her at the start of the ninth season. "The Vartabedian Conundrum" lacks a clear-cut resolution to the Leonard–Stephanie storyline, but the result is functionally the same: after a three-episode story arc, she is eliminated from the program, which allows Leonard to return to his obsession with Penny. And, just like in *The Andy Griffith Show*, characters seldom refer to previous diegetic incidents, unless it is necessary for the development of subsequent episodes.

Leonard's departure from the cafeteria to have sex with Stephanie is not the final scene in the episode. A tag involving the B story comes next: Sheldon remains convinced that his larynx is inflamed, and he communicates with Penny through his laptop's voice synthesizer. In general, tags and cold openings are short bookends to the main narrative. The opening functions to pull the audience in after the break that followed the preceding show and the tag is a small narrative chunk that may provide a little extra story resolution or might just be an unrelated final gag. In "The Vartabedian Conundrum," the tag is rather disposable and might even be deleted in syndication, if additional air time is needed for commercials. It doesn't draw the B story to a conclusion, but, instead, merely offers another humorous variation on the theme of Sheldon's hypochondria.

One final component of the prototypical American sitcom warrants discussion: its length. Originally made to fit into a broadcast schedule's 30-minute time slot, network sitcoms typically have 21 minutes of actual story time (i.e., diegetic time), interrupted by at least one commercial break. "The Vartabedian Conundrum's" total running time is a brisk 21 minutes, including credits. Even as narrative comedies have found new homes on premium cable networks (e.g., HBO's *Curb Your Enthusiasm* [2000–]) and streaming services (e.g., Netflix's *Unbreakable Kimmy Schmidt* [2015–2019]) they have retained that basic time constraint, although now the story time can fill the entire 30-minute time slot. In fact, veteran TV-comedy directors such as Ken Kwapis use that time-based characteristic to identify narrative comedies when they pitch them—referring to them specifically as "half-hour comedies" instead of "sitcoms," because of the pejorative connotations "sitcom" has for some. The length of a program might seem to be a trivial matter as far as aesthetics goes, but the sitcom's 30-minute time limit lends itself to a rather succinct form of story-telling, especially when contrasted with a two-hour theatrical film. And, on the other hand, it can afford to be more expansive than a five-minute YouTube comedy podcast. Just as Elizabethan sonnets constrain the poet to a certain meter and line length, so does the sitcom's time limit force the TV apparatus to construct narratives in certain ways.

"Half-Hour Comedy" vs. "Sitcom": Storytelling and Modes of Production

"Half-hour comedy" shows that resist the "sitcom" label often have strikingly unconventional visual and sound style—as will be discussed shortly—but their narrative structure is not radically different from the prototypical sitcom narrative, although there are some significant exceptions to this. Indeed, shows like HBO's *Girls* (2012–2017) and *Curb Your Enthusiasm* disrupt the conventional sitcom narrative structure to such an extent that they raise reasonable questions as to whether they belong within the comedy genre. For now, however, let us focus on certain shows since the 1990s—distinctive shows such as *The Office* (UK: 2001–2003, US: 2005–2013), *30 Rock* (2006–2013), and *Modern Family*—that are clearly comedies, but which depart in significant ways from the narrative framework outlined previously.

In order to understand the sitcom rule-breaking these shows commit, we first need to identify the two principal ways, or "modes," of TV-show production: single camera and multiple camera (aka, multi-camera or simply multicam). These modes of production are characterized by the camera set-ups, sound stages, and locations they each use, but the differences between the two extend further into full-blown aesthetic systems, with distinct ways of thinking about creating television. In short, single-camera production fashions comedy the way that it is done in the cinema while multicam production inherited its aesthetic from the theater, where the stage is framed by a proscenium arch. Practically speaking, multicam shows, such as *The Big Bang Theory* and *Mom* (2013–) are shot on a sound stage with an audience seated in bleachers—viewing scenes much the way a theatrical audience might. Single-camera shows, such as *Modern Family*, have much greater freedom to shoot on locations and when they are shot on a sound stage it is without an audience. Multicam shows have actors perform scenes straight through in chronological order for the benefit of their in-studio audiences, while four cameras record them. Single-camera shows record their scenes in bits and pieces and in whatever order is most efficient, with just one camera (or sometimes two) recording actors' performances. These bits and pieces are then assembled in the editing process during post-production. Thus, broadly speaking, multicam shows adhere to a "theatrical" aesthetic and single-camera shows are governed by a "cinematic" one. So, how does this difference affect narrative structure?

We have seen how multicamera shows fit into a fairly rigid narrative framework, involving perhaps a dozen scenes of one-to-four minutes each, spread fairly evenly over two acts. Single-camera shows, in contrast, often have a proliferation of very short scenes. For example, a scene analyzed later from *The Goldbergs* (2013–) is a mere 20 seconds long. Moreover, episodes of *The Goldbergs* and other single-camera shows commonly have twice the number of scenes as are in the *Big Bang Theory* episode discussed previously. The abundance of scenes in these shows allows for quicker transitions among scenes and greater complexity in narrative structure. Instead of containing just A and B stories, single-camera shows with large casts can twine together A, B, C, and D stories. Notably, these individual narrative threads are often given equal weight, unlike the multicam sitcom's emphasis on the A story. This can result in a narrative structure that is truly multi-threaded, much like daytime and prime-time serialized dramas— for example, *The Young and the Restless* (1973–) and *Grey's Anatomy* (2005–)—which have large casts and many protagonists involved in numerous narrative threads.

Multiple-threaded, single-camera episodes strain the tidy two-act structure of the multicam show, but, if created for commercial, broadcast television, they still must adapt to that medium's need for segmentation and repeatability. Consequently, we can identify in single-camera, broadcast-TV episodes the narrative fundamentals that they share with multicam episodes: a recurring narrative problematic; exposition that presumes viewer foreknowledge of the characters; a "middle" consisting of heightening tension in a cause–effect narrative chain, although this may be distributed across distinct narrative threads; mini-cliffhangers before the commercial break between acts I and II; narrative closure at the episode's end for the majority of the narrative threads, most of which are quickly forgotten in subsequent episodes; an ending, often with a tag, that does not preclude the repetition of the narrative problematic in the following week; and story arcs that track across episodes/seasons. Thus, differing modes of production allow for some variations of the sitcom narrative structure, but broadcast television's underlying structure ultimately limits the extent of those variations. Those programs on premium channels, such as HBO and Showtime, and streaming services that do not rely on commercials for their business models are permitted more freedom in their narrative design. Since they do not have to accommodate a commercial break between acts I and II, they can be constructed like small, 30-minute movies—building their cause-effect chain without interruption. Of course, since they are not regulated by the FCC, they can also incorporate profanity, bloodshed, and nudity that would not be permitted on broadcast-network television. This leads us to the recurring storylines and character types that comprise the sitcom genre.

Sitcom Storytelling: Archetypal Characters and Recurring Situations

The framework of sitcom storytelling I have just sketched helps us understand the rudiments of the genre, but it does not explain how the sitcom differs from other network-era television shows, including dramas, which also rely on the same framework. To see what distinguishes the sitcom from other genres, we must examine its archetypal characters and recurring situations. We will encounter many of these in the chapters that follow, as we chart the conventions of the sitcom's representation of family, sex/gender, and race/ethnicity; but the genre also contains certain basic characters/situations that separate it from drama and may be clearly identified. Comic characters' lineages can, of course, be tracked all the way back to the 16th-century theatrical tradition of Commedia dell'Arte and even further beyond that to Greek theater in the 6th century BCE. However, for the purposes of this overview, I will limit myself to more contemporary sitcom "tropes"—a term from literary and rhetorical studies that originally referred to various figures of speech (such as metaphors) but which has more recently been applied to literary devices and conventions. Tropes can have a pejorative sense as these devices/conventions often calcify into cliché and stereotype, but I employ it in a more neutral sense to tag narrative conventions of the genre. This recent meaning has carried over into television studies where TVTropes.com, a Wikipedia-like website, has evolved to track television's conventionalized characters and situations. TVTropes.com contains far too many sitcom conventions for us to consider in this short volume, but Evan S. Smith, who has authored a popular book on writing for sitcoms, offers a more manageable list, which is outlined in Table 1.1.[4] He labels sitcom situations as "predicaments" and

Table 1.1 Evan S. Smith's list of sitcom predicaments and character mixes

Predicaments	Character mixes
The big lie	Role reversal
The big secret	Fish out of water
The misunderstanding	Odd coupling
A rock and a hard place	Sex
The surefire scheme	Pretense
Something that rocks the boat	
Time bomb	
Trapped in a space	
Sex	
The dead body	

"character mixes," but both might qualify as "tropes," and most of them may also be found at TVTropes.com.

Smith's labels are somewhat colloquial, but they do accurately account for the plots of numerous sitcom episodes. They are also mostly self-explanatory and do not require additional comment, but I should clarify that "time bomb" is being used figuratively to refer to plots where characters are struggling to meet a deadline. And Smith discusses sex in two contexts: first, when one character is filled with unreciprocated lust for another, which leads to embarrassing encounters; and second, when a will-they-or-won't-they? tension is developed between two characters. Also, by "pretense," Smith identifies so-called "cringe-worthy" comic scenes in which pretentious characters' claims to superior knowledge and skills are revealed to be shams, resulting in their humiliation.

Thus far in this book I have considered two sitcoms in detail: the *Modern Family* episode ("Under Pressure") in the Introduction and *The Big Bang Theory* episode ("The Vartabedian Conundrum") detailed previously. Can we see Smith's tropes in action in them? Certainly.

The "Under Pressure" episode is largely about "role reversal" as the adults are placed in the positions of their children at school. There is also an instance of a "surefire scheme" that goes wrong as Cam creates an elaborate plan of parents playing dodge ball, which leads to pandemonium. Finally, the episode illustrates pretense in characters, as

Mitchell and his neighbor each make pretentious claims of being more environmentally responsible than the other. Eventually, they both get their comeuppance and are shown to be ridiculous and hypocritical. Viewers might cringe at their humiliation.

The Big Bang Theory is similarly built on Smith's tropes. One of the show's central and multiple-season arcs is the troubled sexual/romantic relationship between Leonard and Penny. "The Vartabedian Conundrum" episode uses it as a backdrop, although it is one of the episodes in which they appear *not* to be getting together. The B story of Sheldon's hypochondria fits within the category of pretense as he claims to have medical expertise and then is shown to be a fool. Smith's "odd coupling" trope, which gets its name from the play, movie, and two TV shows titled, *The Odd Couple* (1970–1975, 2015–2017), is also foundational to *The Big Bang Theory*. Even though roommates Leonard and Sheldon are both physicists, the show plays off their different personalities and the friction between them. Sheldon is much more socially awkward and emotionally immature than Leonard—as comes out in this episode in the demands he has placed in the voluminous "roommate agreement," with its "cohabitation rider." Finally, the show employs the "fish-out-of-water" trope by dropping a sexually experienced, intellectually limited young woman (Penny) into the world of virginal male scientists. Although in later seasons, the show does incorporate female scientists, Penny's street smarts still contrast with the scientists' ivory-tower naiveté. The incongruity of her perspective on their culture is often the source of humor. Thus, even in this limited sample of just two sitcoms—one multicam and one single-camera—we can see the function of tropes associated with the genre's narrative structure.

Sitcom Style: Sound and Image

Sitcom narrative structure and the genre's tropes are efficiently and effectively communicated to viewers through stylistic choices made by showrunners, directors, set designers, editors, sound technicians, and so on. And these choices are governed by technological limitations, budgetary considerations, FCC regulations, and common industry or "craft" practices.[5] In short, the television apparatus shapes the way that TV shows look and sound. I've explained previously how a sitcom's mode of production—multicam or single-camera—correlates with variations on the genre's fundamental narrative structure. Mode of production has an even greater impact on sitcom visual and sound style than on narrative, leading to programs that look and sound very different from one another. The multicam mode of production results in programs possessing a "zero-degree of style," in John Caldwell's phrase, by which is meant a style so simple and functional that it serves only to deliver comedians' performances to us and has no significance of its own.[6] This invisible style, it has been argued, is not the source of humor, but only its crude delivery mechanism. Single-camera mode of production, in contrast, enjoys a higher reputation among critics, because its style can be used by TV auteurs to generate humor—through editing, image composition, visual and sound effects, and so on. I have extensively explored the impact of these two production modes on the sitcom in a previous study[7] and space does not permit their full consideration here, but to understand the sitcom genre—especially as it exists in its mature state in the 21st century—it is essential to acknowledge the key distinctions between multicam style and single-camera style. To do so, I will address aspects of sound, mise-en-scene (set design, lighting, costume design, blocking), and cinematography in the two modes.

The overarching principle to be kept in mind when considering the style of multicam productions is that it creates the illusion that the program is being broadcast live and that the viewer is sharing an event with the studio audience in real time, as if in a theater watching a play. Certainly, the viewer intellectually knows that sitcom episodes were recorded sometime in the past, but the viewing experience is one of simultaneity with the production experience. It's as if we are watching while the actors are performing, even if we know on some level that it is only an illusion of simultaneity. The single-camera experience is different and at its extreme—in the animated sitcom, for example—does not rely upon a sense of simultaneity or shared experience or even that viewers are watching actual human experiences. In the outlandish animated series, *Rick and Morty* (2013–), for instance, the protagonists travel through various universes encountering a vast array of alien life and often morph into alternate versions of themselves. Clearly, the illusion of simultaneity and liveness is irrelevant to a show such as this.

Sound Characteristics

The most obvious, and for many the most annoying, characteristic of the multicam sitcom's sound is its laugh track—or, more accurately, its *audience-response* track, which can include applause, sighs, and expressions of disgust in addition to laughter. Nothing distinguishes the sitcom from other narrative-TV genres more than its laugh track. Consider soap operas, police shows, Westerns, horror shows, and murder mysteries. None of them include an audience-response track. On scripted American television, only the sitcom is broadcast with its own audience-response audio. In this regard, it is more closely related to programs with actual studio audiences (e.g., award, game, and talk shows) and sports broadcasts than it is to scripted genres. Laugh tracks have always had their detractors. Many critics, showrunners, directors, scriptwriters, and actors feel they are inauthentic and condescending to the audience. Filmmaker Woody Allen takes pot shots at laugh tracks in *Annie Hall* when a New York-based writer goes to Hollywood where he visits a friend working on the sound mix for a sitcom. The writer is appalled that his friend would add laughs to his show, exclaiming, "Do you realize how immoral this all is?" He then gets physically ill and has to lay down. Considering the disdain they engender, why do sitcoms have laugh tracks? And are there different types of laugh tracks?

Within the TV industry, producers and network executives are the most common advocates for laugh tracks. They argue that laugh tracks elicit a laughter response from viewers and will thus make a show more popular. There is some psychological research that supports this commonsense idea that people feel more comfortable laughing in a crowd and, further, that laughter is contagious, an *automatic* response to hearing others laugh. However, laugh tracks can backfire: if viewers feel they are part of the group that is laughing, then, yes, the laugh track has a positive effect; but if they perceive the laughter as coming from a group to which they do *not* belong, then the laughter can have a negative, even alienating, effect.[8] It can make a program seem less humorous than if there were no laugh track at all. When a viewer does not see the humor of a show, the laugh-track's chuckles and guffaws are perceived as fake, as inauthentic. TV producers recognize the dangers of a cultural mismatch of the laugh track and the viewer at home—to the extent that they will attempt to match the cultural connotations of the laugh track with the cultural values of the target viewers. As sound technician Carroll Pratt stated, with regard to the laugh track on *The Jeffersons* (1975–1985), *a program* designed for African-American viewers: "We have strictly black laughs and 'oohs' [in their repertoire of recorded audience responses]."[9] The risk *The Jeffersons* and similar shows run is that non-black viewers will feel disenfranchised from these so-called "black laughs." Further, Pratt's comment illustrates how laugh tracks are culturally coded and thus are not simply neutral recordings of an audience's reactions.

The mismatch of in-studio audiences and viewers underpins the derisive attitude to shows that are seen to have a hyperactive, unmerited laugh track. *The Big Bang Theory* is a frequent target of such complaints. This has led individuals to remove the laughs from *The Big Bang Theory* segments and post them on YouTube—resulting in very eerie videos of punchlines with no laugh responses. *The Big Bang Theory*'s showrunner, Chuck Lorre, has taken exception to these criticisms and to prove the authenticity of his show's laugh track, he released a photograph of himself and the studio audience with the caption, "We are often accused of using a 'laugh machine' on *The Big Bang Theory*. This [the studio audience] is our laugh machine."

Lorre defends his show's laughs by appealing to their putative authenticity. Because they come from real humans, they must be real. Similarly, other programs with studio audiences proclaim during the credits that the program was filmed before a "live studio audience" as a way of guaranteeing that these are true, earned laughs you're hearing. But claims by industry professionals of laughs' authenticity are rather disingenuous. In the sound editing that is part of every TV sitcom's post-production work, laughs are always "sweetened," in the parlance of the industry. That is, they are augmented for a variety of reasons, including: (1) boosting the laugh level for a joke that received a tepid audience response, (2) covering cuts between different takes of the same scene, (3) compensating for the smaller audience size as the recording session stretches late into the night (audience members tend to get bored and leave lengthy recording sessions), and so on. The laugh response of a studio audience might even be too big, necessitating reducing it to fit the rhythm of a scene. Thus, the laughs we hear once an episode is broadcast are never a wholly accurate, unvarnished record of what went on in the studio that night.

Even if laugh tracks were faithful recordings of the on-set laughs, those laughs themselves are always goosed by the warm-up comedian and other members of the production team. Actor Neil Patrick Harris, a veteran of several sitcoms, explains,

> I find the multi-camera audience incredibly distracting because it's such an inauthentic environment. There's a guy there that's telling them to laugh really loud and saying, 'OK, everybody, this is the fourth time you've seen it, but remember, you've never heard these jokes before, and the louder you laugh the more you'll hear yourself when you're on TV, and here's some chocolate.'[10]

In sum, it is difficult to make a case for *any* sitcom laughter as being "authentic" or spontaneous. Rather, the laughs we hear accompanying sitcom episodes might profitably be thought of as existing on a continuum of authenticity–inauthenticity. On one end of the continuum is the unmanipulated recording of a studio audience captured in the act of purely spontaneous laughter at a humorous event—an ideal that never exists in broadcast television. On the other end is the wholly fabricated laughter that we hear when watching, for example, an animated program like *The Flintstones* (1960–1966). In between these poles is the sweetened laughter of programs recorded before a studio audience. Regardless of where a show resides on this continuum, a laugh track can be said to succeed for a particular viewer when they feel a part of the laughing audience and are enticed to join their state of amusement—momentarily, at least, sharing the feeling of a live broadcast, regardless of the reality of when the show was produced. Even when we watch a 60-year-old rerun of an *I Love Lucy* episode, we can suspend our disbelief of the laugh track's previously recorded nature (i.e., that we know it's not live), connect with the on-screen antics of Lucy and Desi, and feel that we are sharing a studio audience's amusement.

Presenting animated shows and single-camera programs with a laugh track is not often done today, but, as discussed later in my history of the genre, it was quite common during the genre's golden era to do so. In 21st-century television culture, single-camera programs—shot without a studio audience—are more prestigious than their multicam cousins, and the former's lack of a laugh track is one marker of that prestige. Critics argue that shows without laugh tracks demand more active viewers, ones that do not need to be told what is funny by the laugh track's chortles. In this view, the laugh track has become a signifier for all that is wrong about American television comedy, which its detractors characterize as an insulting simulation of authentic amusement. As Inger-Lise Kalviknes Bore summarizes, "The laugh track is seen as a sign of fakery, with prestige being tied to formal innovation and aesthetic experimentation rather than to imitations of liveness."[11] The vituperative attacks on the laugh track illustrate a division between the attitude of cultural critics and the tastes of the TV-viewing public. None of the single-camera, laugh-trackless shows that critics and award shows exalt have had much success in the ratings. Instead, the top-rated scripted comedy show for each year since 2000 has been a multicam sitcom with a very active laugh track: *Friends*, *Everybody Loves Raymond* (1996–2005), *Will & Grace* (1998–2006; 2017–), *Two and a Half Men* (2003–2015), and *The Big Bang Theory*. Single-camera shows from the same time period—such as *Modern Family*, *30 Rock*, and *The Office*—have barely cracked the list of top 20 ranked shows, although they have sometimes had better luck with the desirable 18–35 year-old demographic, which is the major reason they stayed on the air as long as they did.

Single-camera sitcoms, ones that do not rely on the illusion of live sound recorded in-studio, make other distinctive uses of sound. Voice-over (VO) narration is found in several single-camera shows—representing either a character's thoughts (e.g., *Scrubs* [2001–2010] and *Sex and the City*) or a grown-up version of the character looking back at their younger self (e.g., *The Wonder Years* [1988–1993] and *The Goldbergs*). In either case, the VO may be used to create a humorous incongruity between it and what we are seeing/hearing within a diegetic setting. For example, the *Scrubs* episode, "My Life in Four Cameras" (February 15, 2005), begins with a VO by main character, J.D. (Zach Braff): "Things were amazing with Kylie [his girlfriend; Chrystee Pharris], but before I could get more emotionally invested, I needed answers to some questions that were important to me." The VO line builds anticipation that J.D. is about to pose serious questions, but then in the scene itself he says to Kylie, "Name three spin-offs of the sitcom *Happy Days*." The portentous tone of the VO contrasts incongruously with the frivolous nature of the question and thereby generates humor.

In addition to voice-overs, sound effects (SFX) and non-diegetic music can also be used to evoke laughter in single-camera productions in ways that are uncommon in multicam productions. This becomes most obvious in animated comedies where sound frequently contrasts with or comments on the visuals. In live-action sitcoms, SFX and music are generally used more sparingly, but the more "cartoonish" the show, the more extreme the audio can be. *Arrested Development* (2003–2006; 2013–), for instance, has a recurring sound gag where one of the characters walks dejected across the frame and the music track contains Vince Guaraldi's "Christmas Time Is Here," the melancholy tune from the *Peanuts* animated Christmas special. Obviously, the source of the humor is the incongruity between these live-action characters and Charlie Brown. One *Arrested Development* character further signals the incongruous comparison when he mopes past a red doghouse with a dog sleeping on top of it, à la Snoopy on his animated doghouse (see Figure 1.1)! Multicam sitcoms rely less on SFX and music, because their mode of production emphasizes a sense of liveness—an unmanipulated record of a live event—and because their post-production time, when SFX would typically be added, is more limited. There are exceptions to this, but most multicam shows only use non-diegetic music between scenes, not within them, as can be heard in the memorable bass line that *Seinfeld* (1989–1998) features as a bridge between scenes.

Visual Characteristics: Mise-en-Scene

Multicam sitcoms have a very particular visual style that is largely determined by the choice of shooting on a sound stage with an audience on bleachers observing the actors. This is quite obvious and, for the sitcom's detractors, it can be the basis for dismissing the genre as visually simple and functional—stuck at zero-degree style. However,

Figure 1.1 In *Arrested Development*, a dejected George Michael walks past a dog and doghouse—imagery clearly meant to evoke incongruous comparisons with Charlie Brown and Snoopy from the *Peanuts* comic strip.

it's worth considering the connotations of this visual style and exploring how it provides an efficient framework for humor production. I will divide my discussion of sitcom visual style into aspects of mise-en-scène (defined here as set, lighting, costume, and prop design; and blocking), cinematography (aspects of the recording medium itself, which, at the time of this writing, is predominantly digital, high-definition video), and editing. I will first detail the conventions of sitcom multicam production and I will then discuss how single-camera production provides a variation on these conventions, to the point of repeatedly breaking them (summarized in Table 1.2).

To a large degree, multicam set design inherited its aesthetic from live theater, where a proscenium arch frames a three-walled set. In

Table 1.2 Multicam vs. single-camera mode of production

Multicam	Single-camera
Mise-en-scene	
Interior settings (on a sound stage)	Interior and exterior settings (location shooting)
High-key lighting	High- and low-key lighting
Side-to-side blocking (shallow sets)	Side-to-side and deep-space blocking (locations)
Cinematography	
Eye-level camera height (very few high- or low-angles)	Eye-level, plus high- and low-angles
Reliance on medium-shot framing (fewer close-ups and no extreme long shots)	Variable framing: XLS to XCU
Deep focus	Deep and shallow focus
Slightly wide-angle focal length	Variable focal length: wide-angle to telephoto
No subjective shots (i.e., the camera as the "eyes" of a character)	Subjective shots
Zoom shots to "move" closer (rather than dollying)	Zooms and camera movements (including handheld)
VFX only in credit sequences	VFX throughout episodes
Editing	
Longer takes	Shorter takes
Objective camera	Subjective camera
Invisible style	Expressive editing

fact, a typical sitcom sound stage will array three such sets in a row, with audience bleachers running past all of them and a lighting grid above the ceiling-less sets. Four (or three) cameras on dollies capture the action from positions in the floor space between the audience and the sets. This set-up has a major impact on the stories that multicam sitcoms are able tell: they almost all take place indoors on locations that may be repeatedly employed. It's not that multicam sitcoms are unable to build outdoor sets or shoot in front of green screens of city streets and mountains—in fact, they occasionally do—but, rather, that there is an economic disincentive to do so. It costs time and money to build additional sets, add digital effects during post-production, or take a crew outdoors. Plus, it's logistically difficult, if not impossible, to transport an audience to an exterior location with the cast and crew. And so we have sitcoms with interior locations that become as familiar as the rooms in which our own televisions rest: the living rooms of *Seinfeld* (see Figure 1.2), *The Fresh Prince of Bel-Air* (1990–1996), and *All in the Family* (1971–1979); and the workplaces of *2 Broke Girls* (2011–2017), *Taxi* (1978–1983), and *The Mary Tyler Moore Show* (1970–1977). Much like the soap opera, this reliance on interiors strongly shapes the types of stories that may be told in sitcoms. Their situations and predicaments are on a small, personal, intimate scale. They aren't epic adventures out in the world, as we find in Westerns, murder mysteries, and science-fiction shows. Thus, sitcoms lend themselves to stories about interpersonal relationships within families and among workplace colleagues, which often trade on stereotypes of gender, race, and ethnicity.

The single-camera sitcom is not nearly as constrained by interior sets as the multicam sitcom is. Obviously, single-camera shows do still rely on some recurring interior sets, as can be observed in programs as varied as *Community* (2009–2015), *Malcolm in the Middle* (2000–2006), and *M*A*S*H* (1972–1983). But since they are not tethered to a studio audience, they can more easily take the camera to exterior locations. A good portion of *M*A*S*H*, for instance, occurs in the recurring interior sets of the surgeons' living quarters and mobile surgery, but much of it also transpires outdoors—with

Figure 1.2 Jerry's living room in *Seinfeld* is almost as familiar to us as our own. Even though this scene takes place at night, very few shadows are cast and it is lit in high-key lighting.

Southern California locations standing in for Korea. *M*A*S*H* would be a very different and perhaps claustrophobic show if it were all shot on indoor sets and we couldn't see helicopters of wounded soldiers being delivered to the 4077th Mobile Army Surgical Hospital (MASH). Naturally, there are limits of both expense and time to single-camera sitcom production. A weekly half-hour comedy does not have the budget to mount, say, a car chase or a cattle drive or an elaborate gun fight. The financial limitations of the sitcom form force showrunners to develop intimate, humorous scenes on a human level.

After set design, the second aspect of mise-en-scene that characterizes the multicam sitcom is lighting, which is typically broad, bright, and even—in technical terms, "high key." There is a simple reason for this: when shooting with four cameras pointed simultaneously at different parts of the set, a shadowy area might conceal an actor. Almost every scene of every episode of a multicam show is lit this way, using an overhead lighting grid (and so, no shots of ceilings allowed!). Even nighttime scenes are evenly lit, although they might be slightly less bright than scenes set during the day—as can be seen in Figure 1.2, from a nighttime scene. The view outside the window and the illuminated table lamp signify that this is an after-dark scene, but otherwise the lighting design is as flat as earlier scenes. Jerry, the couch, and even the artwork and Mac computer in the background are illuminated at essentially the same level throughout the episode.

Flat lighting such as this may be grounded in budgetary considerations, but it also serves important functions in the production of humor. First, broad high-key lighting showcases the performances skills of the actors, facilitating a certain form of "blocking" (the positioning and movement of actors on a set). Many sitcom stars worked either in stand-up comedy or in improv troupes before coming to television. The very long list of such stars includes (in reverse chronological order) Jerrod Carmichael, Tig Notaro, Tina Fey, Jerry Seinfeld, Ray Romano, Roseanne Barr, Redd Foxx, Don Adams, and, perhaps most notoriously, Jackie Gleason (who disdained any rehearsals for his TV shows). They are accustomed to a theatrical performance style where they can improvise and freely roam across a stage without worrying about falling into a shadow. In a sense, sitcom actors are more restless than those accustomed to single-camera productions where half the job is hitting your mark and being properly positioned relative to the lights and the (one) camera. However, the significance of high-key lighting goes beyond accommodating performers' comfort. It returns us to the notion of zero-degree style, which does not call attention to itself, and it emphasizes the performance of the actors and the dialogue over humor that is generated by the techniques of the medium itself. Thus, the multicam sitcom's humor is rooted in the mise-en-scene more than cinematography, editing, or special effects.

High-key lighting also facilitates directors blocking scenes on sets that must be kept relatively shallow to fit in a sound stage and leave room for the audience bleachers. Most sitcom sets, such as the *Seinfeld* set in Figure 1.2, have very little depth. The *Seinfeld* cast moves side-to-side in front of the cameras—entering from a door on the right—and seldom goes back in the set (toward Jerry's bedroom) or forward toward the camera (where the missing fourth wall would be). This lateral blocking is of a piece with the multicam sitcom's constructed illusion of a theatrical presentation that the viewer is sharing and experiencing, virtually, with the studio audience. Just as theatergoers cannot transgress the proscenium arch and walk into a set, sitcom cameras do not move deeply into the set, maintaining that sense of theatrical distance. And sitcom actors do not come toward the cameras, just as actors in a conventional play do not wander into the audience space (although avant-garde theater has long violated this convention). The multicam sitcom's fourth wall firmly divides performance space and audience space.

Single-camera blocking can explore the depth of its sets to a far greater extent. Even *Gilligan's Island* (1964–1967), a single-camera program that is not known for its elaborate visual style, can illustrate the use of staging in depth. In one evening scene where three of the castaways are shown preparing to sleep in their hut, director Richard Donner places Gilligan (Bob Denver) and the Skipper (Alan Hale Jr.) in hammocks in the foreground and uses them to frame the Professor (Russell Johnson) in the rear of the set (see Figure 1.3). He then cuts to a close-up of the Professor (see Figure 1.4), which would have entailed moving the camera *into* the set, placing it between the hammocks and the Professor (or removing the hammocks altogether). A multicam sitcom rarely stages a scene in depth like this and it would be difficult for a multicam production to get a tight shot of an actor in the back of the set—similar to the inability of an audience member in a theater to walk into the background of a set to examine a detail there. It's not entirely impossible for a multicam show to achieve a shot such as the one of the Professor, but it would have to be done as a pick-up shot, after the main shooting was over. If it were done while four cameras were pointing at the set, then obviously the close-up camera would wind up in another camera's shot. Because it takes extra time and effort to achieve shots blocked in depth, multicam productions, again, have a disincentive to do so, which makes such shots unlikely, but not completely out of the question.

Figure 1.3 Director Richard Donner stages a *Gilligan's Island* scene in depth, with the Skipper and Gilligan in hammocks in the foreground and the Professor visible in the back of the set. The next shot ...

One final function of the genre's high-key lighting is that it is in keeping with the comic tone of the shows. The commonly held notion that comedy must be "light" entertainment is metaphorically connoted by the literally bright, even, lighting design. Very few comedies on stage or TV or in the movies use consistently low-key lighting. Even a multicam show such as *Taxi*, which mostly takes place in a grimy taxi garage at night, relies on high-key lighting. Contrast this with literally dark dramatic shows, such as *Game of Thrones* (2011–2019) or *Buffy the Vampire Slayer* (1997–2003) or the genre of film noir, which employ low-key lighting as a way to visualize the metaphorically dark, morally ambiguous worlds their protagonists inhabit.

The desire to maintain a light comic tone is probably the main aesthetic reason that single-camera sitcoms do not depart dramatically from multicam shows in terms of how they are lit. A single-camera show such as *Cougar Town* (2009–2015), for example, keeps

Figure 1.4 ... cuts to a camera positioned inside the set, about where the hammocks were in the previous shot. The camera has broken through the virtual proscenium to give us a close-up of the Professor.

its interior scenes light and airy. Moreover, it's set in Florida, so that its exterior scenes tend to be bright and pastel-colored, too. Single-camera sitcoms do not share multicam shows' logistical motivations for high-key lighting. That is, the single-camera mode of production does not require that all actors on stage must be simultaneously illuminated by a bank of lights above the stage. Rather, individual actors' lighting set-ups are done on a shot-by-shot basis—permitting lighting design that can be more deliberately crafted for each actor in each situation. Returning to the above scene from *Gilligan's Island* (see Figures 1.3 & 1.4), one can imagine how difficult lighting hammocks above one another would be for a multicam studio with an overhead bank of lights. Shadows would inevitably be cast on the lower hammock. In this particular single-camera set-up, however, lights have been carefully positioned to illuminate all three actors. Note also that when Donner cuts to the Professor in the background, his lighting has been changed. In the first shot, the right side of his face is well illuminated, but in the second shot it is partially in shadow while the left side is brighter. This is a consequence of single-camera mode of production, which can position actors and design lighting on a shot-by-shot basis. The effect is not significantly striking in the instance of the Professor's close-up—serving mainly to signify "nighttime" and convey his thoughtful mood—but it does connote a higher prestige production, linking *Gilligan's Island* with films made for theatrical release instead of live stage productions.

Visual Characteristics: Cinematography

Mise-en-scene is always presented to us viewers through cinematography, through a recording device and through aesthetic choices that may be made regarding framing, camera angle and height, and various other photographic technical properties such as depth of field and focal length. In other words, framing, camera angle, depth of field, and so forth shape how we comprehend what is in the mise-en-scene. In the case of sitcoms, cinematography determines how we may be encouraged to laugh at the comic performances in the mise-en-scene. And as in mise-en-scene design, choosing the multicam or the single-camera mode of production has a significant impact on common cinematographic craft practices. The key difference between the two modes is that multicam cinematography functions to *capture* comic performances of its actors while single-camera cinematography *both* captures performances and potentially generates humor through camera technique. Put in simple terms, if multicam production is zero-degree style, then single-camera production is zero-degree style *plus* humor that calls attention to style itself. John Caldwell, who articulated zero-degree style in TV, employs the term "televisuality" to refer to television style that does not hide itself within a cloak of zero-degree invisibility. Rather, it is "defined by excessive stylization and visual exhibitionism." In its extreme, televisual programs entreat the viewer to look closely at technique and to draw pleasure from its excesses. The humor can become self-reflexive, with television reflecting back on itself *as television*. Most of Caldwell's influential book, *Televisuality: Style, Crisis, and Authority in American Television*, focuses on dramatic programs of the 1980s (e.g., *Miami Vice* [1984–1990]), but I would argue that some single-camera sitcoms of the past 20 years are particularly adroit in their use of "televisuality," which can be observed in shows such as *Modern Family*, *Community*, and, as we will see in detail in Chapter 6, *The Simpsons*.

In sum, then, sitcom cinematography can be beneficially thought of as existing on a continuum from zero-degree style (the camera only serves to record performances in the mise-en-scene) to televisuality (the camera attracts attention to its techniques and those techniques can be used to generate humor). Most programs do not exist on either end of this continuum, but rather reside somewhere in the middle—relying on both zero-degree style and televisuality. To best understand this, we must describe multicam sitcoms' cinematographic conventions and then explore single-camera sitcoms' use, mutation, and violation of those conventions.

Multicam cinematography is principally governed by two of the mode's logistical aspects: (1) the simultaneous recording by four cameras of an episode's scenes *as they play out in entirety* and (2) the need to keep cameras back behind the virtual proscenium arch, outside the fourth wall. Unless an actor substantially flubs a line or some technical mishap occurs, multicam scenes are performed from start to finish without pausing (and typically the scenes themselves are shot in chronological order to avoid confusing the studio audience). As will be elaborated later, single-camera scenes are shot in a very different fashion, with just one (or two) cameras recording individual lines within the scene—in fragmentary fashion and sometimes out of chronological order. Several specific consequences of these two multicam limitations are listed in the left-hand column in Table 1.2. A scene from *The Carmichael Show* (2015–2017)—which began each episode with the announcement, "*The Carmichael Show* is taped before a live studio audience"—can illustrate most of these characteristics (see Figures 1.5 & 1.6; see online video at http://bit.ly/sitcom001).

Figure 1.5 Director of *The Carmichael Show*, Gerry Cohen frames actors Jerrod Carmichael and Amber Stevens West in an eye-level medium shot—a very common framing in multiple-camera sitcoms.

Many of the program's scenes transpire in the typical sitcom setting of a living room (combined with a kitchen area) in the home of the protagonists, Jerrod (Jerrod Carmichael) and Maxine (Amber Stevens West). In Figure 1.6 we can see that director Gerry Cohen—a multi-cam pro whose credits extend back to 1990—chose to record Jerrod Carmichael and Amber Stevens West in the kitchen portion of the set in an eye-level, medium long shot—a framing that is frequently used in sitcoms. That is, the camera seldom retreats back far enough for an extreme long shot that includes the entire set, because it would be difficult to achieve that framing without showing the lighting grid. And the camera also does not get close enough (or the lens zoomed-in enough) in scenes such as this to frame the actors in close-ups that only show their shoulders and heads. Even the individual shot of West does not get any closer than a medium close-up, that is, from the waist up. This scene ends with them kissing on the couch, but there are still no head-and-shoulders close-ups. In general, the camera stays far enough back to loosely contain both actors' frequent gesturing and active movement. West dances in Figure 1.5, and throughout the scene her arms are frequently in motion, as are his. Close, precise

UNDERSTANDING THE SITCOM

Figure 1.6 Even when shot alone, West is framed in a medium close-up, which allows the camera operators to keep her in frame when she gestures and dances.

framing would make it difficult for camera operators to keep the actors in their viewfinders. Figures 1.5 and 1.6 also illustrate the deep focus common to the genre (see also Figure 1.11). We can clearly see the walls and the objects behind Carmichael and West in each shot. A large depth-of-field (i.e., deep focus) is difficult to avoid in multicam sitcoms because of the brightness of the sets and the slightly wide-angle lenses—photographic qualities that generally result in a large depth of field. Consequently, multicam shooting makes it difficult to manipulate focus for specific effects. Instead, almost everything is in focus almost all the time. At the same time, however, multicam sitcoms seldom make use of that deep space for narrative purposes because, remember, their mise-en-scene tends toward lateral movement rather than back-to-front movement.

With these two frames before us (see Figures 1.5 & 1.6), we can see how multicam conventions of cinematography facilitate the capture of Carmichael's and West's performances within the mise-en-scene of *The Carmichael Show*. Framing the two actors at eye-level, "medium" distances—not too close and not too far—provides ample space for their energetic gesturing and makes it less critical for the actors to hit their marks. Also, in terms of aesthetics and TV's common craft practices, super tight close-ups are typically associated with the intense emotions of soap opera and not the "light," comic emotions of the sitcom. Tight close-ups are not that difficult to achieve in multicam productions. After all, daytime soap operas are multicam shows that have used them for decades. But in a comic scene such as this one, an intimate close-up of either character would not suit the mood of the scene. Further, shooting the scene in relatively deep focus simplifies the blocking job for directors like Cohen. He's able to quickly and efficiently position actors on the set without fear of them falling out of focus. Finally, reviewing the aspects of multicam cinematography listed previously, we can confirm that this scene has no subjective shots and only minimal camera movement that merely reframes actors as they move. Thus, in *The Carmichael Show*, budgetary and logistical constraints fit together with aesthetic choices to result in a very distinct, highly conventionalized, zero-degree cinematographic style that showcases the actors' performances and the writer's dialogue—marginalizing the director's job of choosing camera angles and framings. It reinforces the old Hollywood maxim that the cinema is a director's medium while television is a writer's medium. Not coincidentally, Carmichael did not just star in the program that bore his name, he also was instrumental in creating it, was one of its producers, and co-wrote the episode from which these figures were taken.

The single-camera sitcom employs many of the cinematographic conventions of the multicam sitcom. We can chalk up the similarities to the overriding visual aesthetic of television comedy. Even single-camera programs need to showcase the actors' performances and the writers' gags, while keeping the tone light and airy. However, single-camera shows also have opportunities to use cinematography expressively, in ways that may generate humor—as I've listed in the right-hand column of Table 1.2. A 20-second, 8-shot scene from the current sitcom, *The Goldbergs*, illustrates several single-camera cinematographic qualities (see Figures 1.7 & 1.8 and the online video at http://bit.ly/sitcom002). Its director is David Katzenberg and its director of photography (DP) is Jason Blount. In this scene, three popular girls walk down a high-school hallway—from left in Figure 1.7, Lainey Lewis (AJ Michalka), Erica Goldberg (Hayley Orrantia), and Carla Natali (Alex Jennings)—and discuss their plans for a weekend party. Initially, it appears that they will attend a raucous, alcohol-fueled event, but then, incongruously, they prefer instead to have an innocent pajama party with each other.

The most striking thing about this scene's cinematography is that Katzenberg has the camera dolly backward as the girls walk toward it—a combination of camera movement and blocking that would be difficult to achieve in a multicam production. The first shot is also slightly in slow motion, highlighting the girls' confident walk and the bouncing of their perfectly coiffed hair. By having them stride aggressively toward the camera and the camera then keeping pace with them and paralleling their movement, they are thus positioned as assertive, tough mistresses of their high school. For the second shot, Katzenberg keeps the camera moving and places it where the

Figure 1.7 The camera dollies backward, away from AJ Michalka, Hayley Orrantia, and Alex Jennings as they walk confidently through a high school hallway in *The Goldbergs*.

girls are striding—as boys stare at them in awe and unrequited lust. Shot two is a variation on a subjective shot. It's placed where the girls are walking and the camera movement signifies that we have taken their position, but the previous shot indicates that they are *not* looking toward the boys or returning their gazes. They don't even notice the boys and thus this "subjective" shot is not aimed in the direction in which the girls are looking. Rather, they stare straight ahead, in their own confident social bubble. The cinematography expressively emphasizes their power and maturity and so when Erica suggests that they skip a debauched party in order to engage in a childhood ritual, we expect her to be ridiculed. Incongruously, her girlfriends squeal their delight at the idea of an innocent pajama party. The incongruity of their response is what makes the scene humorous.

Other elements of single-camera cinematography may also be identified here. In Figure 1.8, Erica is framed in a head-and-shoulders close-up that is considerably tighter than what we saw in a comparable shot from *The Carmichael Show* (see Figure 1.6), even though this is an emotionally light scene. Additionally, this shot shows how shallow focus

Figure 1.8 The single-camera framing of Orrantia is tighter than what we saw in *The Carmichael Show* and a shallow depth of field blurs the space to either side of her head.

can be used to keep the viewer's eyes on one portion of the frame. *The Goldbergs* is shot in the high-definition TV aspect ratio of 16:9. This slightly wide-angle aspect ratio has the potential for wasted, distracting space on either side of a human face in a close-up. Katzenberg minimizes the distractions by throwing the background out of focus. In regard to one final cinematographic aspect in my list, this scene does not include any true low-angle or high-angle shots—although they may be found elsewhere in this episode—but the angle the camera takes on the girls does result in part of the ceiling being included in the frame, which is seldom revealed in multicam shooting with its overhead lighting grid. This scene from *The Goldbergs* is not fully televisual in that its cinematographic techniques do not brazenly call your attention to themselves. However, it's clear that the cinematography in this single-camera show is not just mechanically recording the performances of the actors. Instead, camera style is expressively helping to create humor.

Truly televisual cinematography can be identified in a variety of sitcoms. When *The Bernie Mac Show* (2001–2006) employs a simple visual effect of text layered over its images, it draws our attention to that humorous text itself. When a *Scrubs* episode titled, "My Life in Four Cameras" (February 15, 2005) and a *Black-ish* episode (May 18, 2016) parodying the 1970s sitcom *Good Times* (1974–1979) break from their single-camera mode of production to present segments in multicam mode, they foreground numerous multicam conventions (including ones drawn from cinematography, mise-en-scene, and laugh tracks) in order to make fun of them. When *Community* transforms most of its cast into animated, video-game avatars ("Digital Estate Planning," May 17, 2012), it creates humor out of the incongruity of the digital world and the "real" world characters. When programs such as *The Office*, *Parks and Recreation* (2009–2015), and *Modern Family* shoot with handheld cameras and include interviews with actors speaking directly to the camera in character, they are mocking the cinematographic conventions of documentary films—to the extent that the neologism "mockumentary" has been coined to label that branch of TV comedy. Furthermore, *Modern Family* presented possibly the most televisual episode in recent sitcom history when it constructed an entire episode

("Connection Lost," February 25, 2015) as if it were a series of video chats and texts appearing on Claire's laptop screen (see Figure 1.9). Eschewing professional, HD cameras, much of the episode was shot with iPhones and tablets. Humor was thus fashioned out of the way that characters used and misused contemporary technology.

Crucially, in each of these instances of televisuality, humor is being produced by taking advantage of television's cinematographic techniques. These are comic bits that do not exist in the mise-en-scene and could not be duplicated on a theatrical stage. They are specific to the medium of television. This is what qualifies humor as televisual. And it is no coincidence that each of these programs uses the single-camera mode of production. Multicam shows pull most of their humor from the performances in the mise-en-scene and the dialogue of the soundtrack. It is only when they borrow techniques from single-camera productions that they can achieve televisual gags. It is not impossible for a program like *The Carmichael Show* to contain televisual humor, but it would be time-consuming and expensive for it to do so and, thus, there are substantial barriers to multicam shows indulging in this form of humor.

Figure 1.9 An entire episode of *Modern Family* was shot as if it were appearing on Claire's laptop screen—including chat screens and Google searches.

UNDERSTANDING THE SITCOM

Visual Characteristics: Editing

The final aspect of sitcom style that I will discuss is how editing may serve television comedy. By now it should not be surprising to read that multicam production relies on rudimentary conventions of TV (and film) editing while single-camera production permits greater latitude in what can be achieved by placing one shot after another.

More specifically, multicam productions typically store the feeds from all four cameras while they capture scenes in a digital format, as the scenes are being performed straight through. The scenes are recorded at least twice—or more if there is some dialogue problem or technical error. In post-production, footage obtained from the four cameras is cut together, often incorporating shots from different takes of a particular line. In *The Carmichael Show* scene broken down above, one can see evidence of the splicing together of different takes in the cut from the 21st shot to the 22nd (see Figures 1.10 & 1.11; see also the previously noted online video). The first shot ends with actor Amber Stevens West's arms up and her elbows bent; and then

Figure 1.10 Note the bent position of Amber Stevens West's arms at the end of this shot from *The Carmichael Show*. At the start of the following shot …

52

Figure 1.11 ... her arms are now at her side—a tiny continuity error that indicates that two shots from different takes of the same scene have been spliced together.

the second shot begins with her arms at her side. It's a small continuity error that would be difficult for viewers to notice, but it does confirm that these two shots are not from the same take. Single-camera productions, in contrast, are recorded shot-by-shot, in fragmentary fashion by one (or sometimes two) camera and then assembled in post-production. Continuity errors can certainly arise in single-camera editing, but because each shot is planned in pre-production this mode of production also has much greater control over each individual shot, which thus allows the editing to be more precise and to have greater expressive impact.

For example, *The Goldbergs* segment discussed previously is succinctly cut together so that the girls' pajama-party plans can be laid out a scene that lasts just 20 seconds (see the previously noted online video). The short duration of the scene is indicative of single-camera productions, which generally tend to have significantly shorter scenes than multicam productions. When a scene is only 20 seconds long, there is not a lot of leeway for communicating story information. True to form, *The Goldbergs*' editor, Peter B. Ellis, efficiently and effectively cuts from medium shots of the three girls to individual close-ups (aka, "singles," in industry parlance) as each girl speaks. In a multicam production, the four cameras would struggle to keep up with the girls' movements. In this single-camera production, it's likely that Katzenberg first recorded a master shot of the girls walking down the hall, then moved the camera into the set in order to shoot singles one-by-one. The medium shots emphasize the girls' solidarity as a clique while the close-ups showcase each girl's emotions. This further enhances the humor when the girls' individual responses to the innocent party (unrestrained glee) contradict what is expected from a presumably mean girl gang. Furthermore, the quasi-subjective shot discussed previously in the context of cinematography requires a certain editing convention to work: cutting from a shot of the girls to a shot of the boys gazing directly at the camera. Point-of-view editing, where one cuts from a person gazing in a specific direction to a shot of that gaze's target (or vice versa, from target to gazer, in this case), only exists through the juxtaposition of two shots and the placement of the camera near or in the position where the gazing actor was positioned. In this case, the girls are not visible in the second shot, and so it is the conventions of point-of-view editing that construct the meaning, "the girls are the target of the boys' gazes." All of these editing techniques taken together indicate a more expressive use of editing than is common in multicam shows.

The editing of sitcoms can tip over from the expressive into the televisual. *The Goldbergs*' episode here discussed opens with a ten-shot montage of pajama-party preparations crammed into six seconds of broadcast time: close-ups of a camping lamp being turned on, three sleep bags rolling out, two snack bags being opened, and make-up supplies being assembled. The quick rhythm of the shots is mildly humorous as it makes it seem as if a major expedition is being mounted when, incongruously, it is just a young girl's party. That is, the party snacks and make-up don't match the camping equipment. And, as with the point-of-view editing, the incongruous meaning of these ten shots ("expedition preparation") is not contained in any of the individual shots, but, rather, only arises from their juxtaposition in quick succession. That juxtaposition is unique to television (and film) and could not be as effectively replicated on stage. It is humor based in foregrounded editing technique and that makes it televisual.

In sum, the sitcom is a genre whose conventions of storytelling and sound-image style work together to amuse us with a variety of incongruities—ideological, narrative, visual, and audio. In its form as it exists in the early 21st century, it has split into two modes of production: multicam and single-camera. There are significant and meaningful differences between the two modes in terms of mise-en-scene, cinematography, and editing; but, generally speaking, they are more alike than different in terms of their narrative problematics and the way they employ TV tropes. These modes of production did not always exist in this form, however. In the next chapter, I'll survey how the sitcom evolved critically and culturally and what position *I Love Lucy* held in that evolution.

Notes

1 The number of episodes ordered by networks for a typical season has steadily declined. During the broadcast-network heyday, a season might run 22 episodes. Today, that number has shrunk to 13 or even 10. And there really is no "typical" number any longer.
2 John Ellis, *Visible Fictions: Cinema: Television: Video* (Boston, MA: Routledge, 1992), 156. See also, Mick Eaton, "Television Situation Comedy," *Screen* 19(4) (Winter 1978), 78.
3 "The Big Bang Theory 2x10 – The Vartabedian Conundrum," *TVWriting*, https://sites.google.com/site/tvwriting/us-comedy/show-collections/the-big-bang-theory, accessed June 12, 2019.
4 Evan S. Smith, *Writing Television Sitcoms*, revised and expanded (New York: Perigee, 2009), 26–36.
5 "Craft practices" is a term used by film scholars to refer to the conventionalized work of numerous "crafts" involved in the production of a film or TV program—including the designing of sets and costumes, cinematography, and editing. See David Bordwell, *On the History of Film Style* (Cambridge, MA: Harvard University Press, 1997).
6 John Thornton Caldwell, *Televisuality: Style, Crisis, and Authority in American Television* (New Brunswick, NJ: Rutgers University Press, 1995), 56.
7 Jeremy G. Butler, "Televisuality and the Resurrection of the Sitcom in the 2000s," in *Television Style* (New York: Routledge, 2010), 173–222.
8 Michael J. Platow, S. Alexander Haslam, Amanda Both, Ivanne Chew, Michelle Cuddon, Nahal Goharpey, Jacqui Maurer, Simone Rosini, Anna Tsekouras, Diana

M. Grace, "'It's Not Funny if They're Laughing': Self-Categorization, Social Influence, and Responses to Canned Laughter." *Journal of Experimental Social Psychology* 41(5) (2004): 542–550.

9 Robert Kubey, *Creating Television: Conversations with the People Behind 50 Years of American TV* (Mahwah, NJ: Lawrence Erlbaum Associates, 2004), 115.

10 Christine Becker, "Acting for the Cameras: Performance in the Multi-Camera Sitcom," *Mediascape*, Spring 2008, 1–11. Also quoted in Inger-Lise Kalviknes Bore, "Laughing Together: TV Comedy Audiences and the Laugh Track," *Velvet Light Trap* 68 (2011), 25–26.

11 Bore, 26.

2

A CRITICAL/CULTURAL HISTORY OF THE SITCOM

> "Lucy, you've got some explaining to do."
> —Ricky Ricardo, *I Love Lucy*

By 1950, television had already begun its phenomenal post-World War II growth spurt. It had severely disrupted radio programming, its broadcasting ancestor; and it had threatened the dominance of the cinema as America's favorite entertainment medium. *The Billboard* magazine was among the broadcasting trade publications that chronicled the rise of television and the fall of radio. Its April 28, 1951 issue had a prescient note: "*I Love Lucy*, a new video situation-comedy featuring Lucille Ball and Desi Arnaz, is being shown around the agencies by Columbia Broadcasting System."[1] *The Billboard* author could not know just how instantaneously significant *I Love Lucy* (1951–1957) would be to the sitcom genre upon its debut six months later and how long-lived its reruns in syndication would prove to be. Lucy would be explaining herself to Ricky for many, many years after the show's original broadcast.

In terms of sitcom history, *The Billboard*'s short blurb is notable because its reference to the "video situation-comedy" signals that the sitcom was already an established genre even though very few television sitcoms had thus far been produced. The first American TV sitcom was *Mary Kay and Johnny* (1947–1950) which debuted on November 18, 1947 as a live, 15-minute broadcast on the now-defunct DuMont network. A few other notable comedies appeared in the years immediately following, but when Arthur C. Nielsen first began rating television programs' viewership during the 1950–1951 season, only two sitcoms were among the top-30 programs: *Mama* (1949–1956) and *The Aldrich Family* (1949–1953). The obvious source of *The Billboard* blurb's sense of a defined genre is the situation comedies that had appeared on radio and had set the basic conventions of the genre.

The Situation Comedy on Radio

Comedy on radio was initially dominated by vaudeville-trained performers rattling off gags, puns, and short jokes instead of presenting character-based humor arising from narrative situations. The first situation comedies reacted against the staccato comic rhythms of vaudeville routines and instead spun gently humorous stories around characters in everyday situations. The earliest and most popular radio sitcom of the 1930s was *Amos 'n' Andy* (1928–1960), which chronicles the misadventures of two friends who run a taxicab company. By the time Freeman F. Gosden and Charles J. Correll brought it to network radio in 1929, they had been producing regional versions of it on Chicago radio stations for three years: first as *Sam 'n' Henry* on WGN (1926–1927) and then as *Amos 'n' Andy* on WMAQ (1928). Essentially, *Amos 'n' Andy* and, thus, the sitcom genre itself, accompanied the birth of American broadcast networks, considering that the program's host network (the National Broadcasting Company or NBC) was created the same year that Gosden and Correll began broadcasting *Sam 'n' Henry* on WGN. Further, *Amos 'n' Andy* was so phenomenally successful that it inspired many people to buy their first radio receivers and thus substantially helped to establish the fledgling medium.

Amos 'n' Andy was foundational to the sitcom because its humor principally arises from its characters' predicaments and not on stringing together individual jokes and gags. As an *Amos 'n' Andy* promotional book put it,

> [The story] is not dialogue in the vaudeville sense. Seldom does it contain what might be called a joke. It if is funny, it is

so because of the *situations* in which the boys find themselves, and the manner in which they meet these *situations*.[2]

The main characters are buffoons who constantly get into scrapes and suffer through misunderstandings; they do not stand around telling conventional jokes. *Amos 'n' Andy* also established how important to the sitcom the superiority theory of humor (outlined in the Introduction) would be to the genre. According to this theory, humor is evoked by the reader or radio listener looking down on comedic characters. Gosden and Correll were white men who portrayed black characters in the radio equivalent of blackface, speaking in a "Negro" dialect that had evolved in 19th-century minstrel shows and subsequently in vaudeville. Amos and Andy were clearly meant to be objects of derision.

Amos 'n' Andy was an unusual and extraordinary success for the genre. During the 1930s, comedy programs dominated the ratings, but most of them were musical-variety comedies based on jokes and short skits—excepting the long-running *The Goldbergs* (on radio, 1929–1946; on network television, 1949–1954), a program that mixed equal parts humor and pathos in its continuing story of a Jewish family. Indeed, narrative programs of both dramatic and comedic form were a very small part of the radio-broadcast day during this time period. In 1925, the year before *Amos 'n' Andy* debuted, narrative programs accounted for only one-tenth of 1 percent of the broadcast day. By 1932, that percentage had risen to 2 percent, but the lion's share of broadcasting was still devoted to music programs (64.1 percent).[3] Of the four or five programs each year that could be called situation comedy, only *Amos 'n' Andy* was regularly in radio's overall top ten—leaving other comedies such as *Lum and Abner* (1931–1954) and *Easy Aces* (1932–1948) far behind. Through most of the 1930s, then, the sitcom was not a significant part of broadcast programming and the genre itself was rather indistinct. As World War II broke out in Europe during the fall of 1939, the sitcom's popularity suddenly ramped up. Two influential and hugely popular programs led the way and inspired a wave of sitcoms during the War years: *Fibber McGee and Molly* (1935–1956) and *The Aldrich Family*.

The creators of *Fibber McGee and Molly*, Jim and Marian Jordan, were particularly aware of the program as a progenitor of the emerging genre of the sitcom. In 1940, as the show came to dominate radio comedy, the Jordans were profiled by the *New York Times*:

> 'As I see it an effective comedy series is one that presents situations that actually happen to everyday folks,' [Jim Jordan] continued. 'That is why we follow *a policy of situation comedy* [emphasis added], in which a sequence is built up, instead of relying on jokes.' Marian added that they were among the first to bring situation humor to the air. 'It didn't go too well at first, either,' she declared. 'People had to be educated to it.'[4]

The phrase situation comedy was thus gaining common acceptance by 1940 and the genre was beginning to acquire characteristics beyond simply being an antidote to vaudeville-style comedy. In fact, sub-genres soon emerged. *Amos 'n' Andy* had established the workplace comedy and *The Goldbergs*, *Fibber McGee and Molly*, and *The Aldrich Family* did the same for the family or domestic comedy.

Settings and recurrent situations are the most noticeable elements of these workplace and family situation comedies, but they share other elements of format and form that would continue into the television era. First, the 1940s situation comedies were mostly 30 minutes long and were broadcast weekly—unlike *Amos 'n' Andy* which began as a daily 15-minute show and only expanded to 30 minutes in 1943 to match competing shows. Second, these 30-minute episodes were customarily interrupted about half-way with a commercial for their sponsors. Although *Fibber McGee and Molly* relied on commercials integrated into the story (known today as product placement), other shows had more distinct commercial breaks. Whether integrated or not, the commercials force the narrative to pause, splitting it into two segments or acts. This segmentation of the narrative is a key component of the sitcom's narrative structure in commercial television to the present day. Third, weekly radio situation comedies broke from the serial format of early shows such as *Amos 'n' Andy* and *The Goldbergs*. Instead, 1940s comedies relied on a repeatable narrative problematic that could inform each individual episode and allow for narrative closure at the end. For example, the narrative problematic of *Fibber McGee and Molly* places Fibber in a predicament of his own devising each week and resolves that specific predicament by the episode's end. The following week's episode then takes no notice of the previous predicament.

A fourth genre characteristic established during the radio sitcom was the laugh track. At the beginning of the genre, comedies were often performed without an audience. Gosden and Correll, for example, initially broadcast *Amos 'n' Andy* from a quiet studio. However, many comedians needed the energy an audience could provide. Popular vaudeville star Ed Wynn craved audience response and after one radio program flopped, he demanded that anyone handy in the studio be gathered together to form a rudimentary audience for the next program, *Ed Wynn, The Fire Chief* (1932–1936), which debuted in 1932. Fellow vaudevillian, Eddie Cantor, so hungered for laughs that even the rehearsals for *The Eddie Cantor Show* (1931–1949) were performed before an audience. Wynn's and Cantor's shows were musical-variety programs with a heavy dose of comedy and not truly sitcoms, but they did establish the general principle of a comedy show incorporating in-studio audience laughter. *Fibber McGee and Molly* inverted that mix by devoting most of the show to narrative situations, but still including at least one musical number per episode. (Some radio historians do not even include it in the sitcom category.) It featured an enthusiastic studio audience that applauded and laughed uproariously through each week's episode. *The Aldrich Family* and other situation comedies were also performed before an audience, incorporating their reaction into the sound mix. Consequently, radio sitcoms provided two models of sound mixes—with an audience and without.

A fifth and final characteristic of the sitcom that found its origin in the genre's radio days is the catchphrase. In radio and TV sitcoms, catchphrases serve a variety of purposes. Most pragmatically, they operate as recurring verbal motifs that programs' authors use as shorthand for quick laughs—as when Ricky scolds Lucy, "You've got some explaining to do." Over time they can become tired clichés, but initially at least they are a comic contract between the writer and the listener, and they come to be expected. Placed in new contexts in each week's episode, they elicit laughs by combining the familiar with the novel. They obviously help establish programs' and specific characters' identities, but when used by audience members themselves they can also allow them to bond in their affection for those programs/characters. As with slang words, catchphrases can establish sub-cultures within society and provide language-based markers for these groups. *Amos 'n' Andy*, *Fibber McGee and Molly*, and *The Aldrich Family* established catchphrases as a nearly essential element of the genre. *Amos 'n' Andy* was first in this regard—relying on phrases in "Negro" dialect such as Amos's "Ain't dat sumpin?" and the Kingfish's "Holy mackerel!" Fibber McGee inevitably told a bad joke or made a terrible pun, leading his wife Molly to scold, "Tain't funny, McGee." And *The Aldrich Family*'s opening was signaled each week by the Aldrich mother calling, "Henry! Henry Aldrich!" and him replying in a cracked, pubescent voice, "Coming, Mother!" Catchphrases can embed themselves deeply in the American vocabulary. For instance, "Holy mackerel!" became such a commonly used phrase in 1930s America that it lost its original association with the Kingfish character. Thus, what begins as a simple comic marker for a program and/or a character can come to have lasting significance to the American lexicon.

After World War II ended in 1945, the radio sitcom peaked. During the 1946–1947 season there were approximately 23 radio sitcoms on the air. A reinvigorated *Amos 'n' Andy* led the pack with a 22.5 Hooper rating. But it wouldn't be long before television disrupted the broadcasting model that had captivated Americans for two decades. Many radio sitcoms of the late 1940s would pivot into the television era, some much more successfully than others. As should be evident from this brief history, the sitcom was well established as a genre form for both broadcasting professionals and audience members during the radio era. Its stock characters, narrative structure, and catchphrases were ready to be launched into the new medium of television. Seemingly, all that had to be added to the radio sitcom was the visuals, but that proved to be more difficult to achieve than one might expect.

The Situation Comedy on Television: Early Missteps and Failures

As noted earlier, the history of the sitcom on American television proper began modestly on November 18, 1947 when a DuMont station in New York City debuted *Mary Kay and Johnny*. Produced, starring, and written by Mary Kay and Johnny Stearns, the show chronicled humorous predicaments of two newlyweds, as the Stearns themselves were. It was transmitted live for 15 minutes weekly, from a freshly built television studio inside the John Wanamaker department store in Manhattan. Although DuMont was assembling its national network at this time, it limited *Mary Kay and Johnny*'s transmission to the New York City area.[5] The show left DuMont in 1948 and in October of that year was picked up by the nascent NBC network, which broadcast it across its expanding web of stations and doubled its time slot to 30 minutes. The sitcom was now officially part of American network television, even if NBC's network didn't yet cover all of the nation.

The original 15-minute incarnation of *Mary Kay and Johnny* was not an auspicious beginning for what now seems to be the genre's inevitable switch from radio to television. Moreover, it was aesthetically a step backward for the sitcom form. Radio sitcoms had settled into a comfortable 30-minute form with relatively elaborate stories aurally crafted specifically for that format. *Mary Kay and Johnny* took place principally on a single living-room set supplied with furniture and props by the department store and captured live by two cameras. Shooting on location was impossible. In contrast, radio could set its stories anywhere its sound effects technicians could create an aural soundscape. Add the sound of waves and suddenly the characters are on a beach. A few car horns and traffic noises and they're on a busy street. Further, 1940s radio shows could create a relatively complex sound mix of dialogue, effects, and music, which could also be recorded on disk for syndication and distribution. Live television in 1948 could not match this level of audio complexity. And its recorded image—in the form of the kinescope—was often a poor reproduction of live-TV's visuals. *Mary Kay and Johnny* was occasionally kinescoped while on NBC, but cost prohibited its daily recording. Consequently, there was no possibility of selling episodes into syndication after the original broadcast, as would be lucratively done by subsequent programs. The live-television sitcoms of the late 1940s were seldom archived. Most of them lasted only a season or two and then vanished into the ether. An efficient, profitable, aesthetically effective mode of sitcom production for television eluded early pioneers. The genre needed a true national hit to establish its viability on television. *I Love Lucy* would be that hit.

I Love Lucy and Sitcom Mode of Production

In 1950, Nielsen steered his market research company toward measuring the fast-growing television audience in the USA. As noted earlier, in the first Nielsen ratings season, only two sitcoms were among the top-30 shows. *The Aldrich Family* had transitioned from radio and *Mama* was based on a popular play and movie (*I Remember Mama*). It is thus particularly remarkable that, in the following season, *I Love Lucy* captured, on average, 50.9 percent of the households that possessed television sets. It was the third most popular show that season, but that was just the beginning of its phenomenal popularity. During the 1952–1953 season, it was the top-rated show, with a massive 67.3 rating. Fully two-thirds of America's TV homes were tuning in to the weekly misadventures of Lucy and Ricky Ricardo that season. *I Love Lucy* remained in that top spot for several years to come, but very few other sitcoms joined it in the top ten during the decade. In fact, the sitcom genre had to wait until the 1960s and 1970s to truly flourish. Thus, *I Love Lucy* was an anomaly during the 1950s, and other programs were unable to replicate its enormous success. However, it was not just astonishing ratings that made *I Love Lucy* important to the genre. More significant are its contributions to the way the genre is produced and distributed and its establishment of the sitcom format.

Lucille Ball and her husband, Desi Arnaz, the stars of *I Love Lucy*, were savvy businesspeople whose Desilu Productions would go on to become a major force in TV production. Ball and Arnaz negotiated aggressively with the program's sponsor (cigarette manufacturer, Philip Morris) and network (CBS) over its production format. They demanded that it be filmed instead of broadcast live and that it be shot in front of a studio audience. CBS balked at the cost and so Ball and Arnaz offered to take a cut in their salaries, under one key condition—that they would own 100% of the show's future use. CBS agreed and thereby lost the rights to some 179 *I Love Lucy* episodes that would prove to be a gold mine in syndication.

Why were Ball and Arnaz so committed to recording on film before a live audience that they were willing to risk losing the deal with CBS? First, recording on film was essential for maintaining the quality of the episodes' look—not just for its first presentation, but for lucrative subsequent uses. It was common practice at the time to record kinescopes from live transmissions and then ship them across the country to play in other time zones beyond the reach of early networking technology, but the kinescope image never looked as good as the original. These same kinescopes could be used to rerun episodes at later dates, but, again, the image was markedly degraded. Filmed originals, in contrast, had a consistent level of quality from the first broadcast to the hundredth. The heightened quality of the filmed originals became a major selling point when a program was offered for syndication on local stations, which, at the time of *I Love Lucy*'s launch, was not as profitable as it would become later. The phenomenal success of *I Love Lucy* during its original run fueled syndication deals that lasted for decades, causing CBS to rue the day it handed syndication rights over to Ball and Arnaz. Indeed, it eventually purchased those rights back from Desilu.

The second ground-breaking component of *I Love Lucy*'s mode of film production was its ability to record a performance in front of a studio audience without pausing to reset the cameras and lights for each shot. Motivating this innovation was Ball's belief that a studio audience was essential for her comic timing and for keeping the energy level high. Although she had become a success as a movie actor performing without an audience, her experience on radio in the *I Love Lucy* forerunner, *My Favorite Husband* (1948–1951), relied heavily on an in-studio audience. There were no true precedents in the sitcom genre itself for this new production mode. Sitcoms were broadcast live like *Mary Kay and Johnny* and possibly kinescoped, or they were shot like short movies, which was the approach being developed by *Amos 'n' Andy* for its transition from radio to television in 1951. However, the game show, *Truth or Consequences* (1950–1988), had developed a system in which three 35-mm film cameras simultaneously recorded the action from different angles while an audience watched and reacted. The footage from the three cameras was then cut together in the editing room later. The technician who had engineered that system, Al Simon, was brought to *I Love Lucy* as production manager and noted cinematographer, Karl Freund, was employed as director of photography.

The method of shooting pioneered by Ball, Arnaz, Simon, Freund, and various *I Love Lucy* directors quickly established the specific look and sound of the multicam sitcom that I detailed earlier in terms of mise-en-scene, cinematography, editing, and audio (especially the laugh track). Moreover, it established a unique comedic style in which a recorded performance *appears* to be a live transmission and comes equipped with its own audience response, which, obviously, is not part of the experience of a humorous film in a theater. The laughter of studio audiences became so essential to the sitcom experience that even shows recorded without live audiences came to employ them. The first such wholly fake laughter accompanied the short-lived and now-forgotten *Hank McCune Show* (1950), which was only on network television for three months in fall 1950. The humble beginnings of the fabricated laugh track deserve little more than a footnote in American TV history, but it's important to recognize that this key component of the sitcom form was established soon after the transition to television. Thus, by the early 1950s, the sitcom's mode of production had bifurcated into two dominant strains: (1) live-broadcast and live-on-film multicam productions *with audiences* and (2) single-camera productions *without audiences*, but with manufactured laugh tracks. Live broadcasts of sitcoms would essentially become extinct by the 1960s and multicam productions nearly did the same during the following decade, which was dominated by single-camera productions with fake laugh tracks; but multicam production and its live-audience response track resurrected in the late 1960s and are still with us in the 21st century.

I Love Lucy's enormous ratings success and its innovative mode of production certainly distinguish it, but it was also important in terms of confirming that television comedy would follow radio comedy in its privileging of the American family as the site of humor. Other notable family sitcoms of the decade included *The Goldbergs*, *Mama*, *The Adventures of Ozzie and Harriet* (1952–1966), *Make Room for Daddy* (1953–1965), *Father Knows Best* (1954–1960), *The Real McCoys* (1957–1963), *Leave It to Beaver* (1957–1963), and *The Donna Reed Show* (1958–1966). Later, in the chapters on family and gender, I will consider whether or not these programs were patriarchal propaganda, but it's worth noting here that there was a wealth of family sitcoms to choose from in the 1950s—although *Mama*, *I Love Lucy*, *The Real McCoys*, and *Father Knows Best* were the only four sitcoms to crack the Nielsen top 20. As significant as the family sitcom was to the 1950s, it was rivaled by comedies set in workplaces, which paid only brief attention to home life. Workplace comedies included *Amos 'n' Andy*, *Our Miss Brooks* (1952–1956), *Private Secretary* (1953–1957), *The Bob Cummings Show* (1955–1959), *The Phil Silvers Show* (1955–1959), and *The Jack Benny Show* (1950–1965). There was some variation in the comedies of the first decade of television—e.g., *Topper* (1953–1955) and a cast that includes ghosts—but sitcoms of this time did not stray far from the home and the office.

The domestic and workplace sitcoms of the 1950s shared significant demographic characteristics. They were largely populated by white characters of the middle and upper-middle classes. Radio sitcoms had more race/ethnic and class diversity, despite their reliance upon demeaning stereotypes. Early in the '50s, television sitcoms seemed like they might follow suit. *Amos 'n' Andy* and *The Goldbergs* each came to television after success on radio, bringing with them African Americans and working-class Jews, respectively. And the initially highly rated *Mama* focused on a Norwegian immigrant family. However, *Amos 'n' Andy* was called to task for its history of racist portrayals of blacks and *The Goldbergs* ran afoul of the Communist blacklist of one of its key actors, Philip Loeb. *Mama* was a strong presence in the early 1950s, but by the middle of the decade its ratings had declined. With the demise of these and similar shows, the sitcom was given over to a whitewashed view of American society, with rare exceptions such as Desi Arnaz, a Latino originally from Cuba.

By 1955, the television sitcom had all but vanquished its antecedents on the radio. Some radio programs made fairly successful transitions to the new medium, but most did not. The sitcom had become a mature genre once its basic premises from the radio days were adapted for a visual medium. The sitcom painted an idealized portrait of white, middle-class life in America during a decade of prosperity, Cold War political conservatism, and seemingly calcified gender roles. There were significant developments in the African-American Civil Rights Movement during the mid-1950s, but the sitcom avoided engaging this and most other controversial topics and chose to effectively erase minority identities from its programs. As the 1960s began, the sitcom was firmly established as a TV genre, even if only two or three of its shows had been ratings successes. The 1960s would then see the genre grow exponentially, coming eventually to dominate prime-time programming.

1960s Sitcoms: The Genre Comes of Age

The 1960s were, of course, a turbulent time. A counterculture challenged conventional beliefs regarding race, gender, social class, popular music, the Vietnam War, and recreational drugs. However, the sitcom was slow to address any of these issues head-on. Instead, the decade's first sitcom successes were distinctly rural in their setting and small-town in their discourse. *The Andy Griffith Show*, *The Beverly Hillbillies* (1962–1971), *Petticoat Junction* (1963–1970), and *Gomer Pyle, U.S.M.C.* (1964–1969) all focused on Southern small-town characters and chronicled their encounters with urban values that perplexed them. Two are set in small towns (*The Andy Griffith Show* and *Petticoat Junction*) while two track journeys of backwoods innocents through modern life in Beverly Hills and the US Marine Corps.

The Beverly Hillbillies was typical of these rural sitcoms in that its narrative problematic—what might serve as the show's logline—is: unsophisticated "hillbillies" and their folk customs disrupt life in modern, "civilized" Beverly Hills.[6] It thus relies on the familiar "fish out of water" character mix, as Evan Smith and others would put it. The title characters are the Clampetts, who come into a large amount of money when oil is discovered on their property somewhere in a never-specified area of the rural South. Jed Clampett (Buddy Ebsen), the widowed head of the family, is then persuaded to move to a mansion in Beverly Hills. Humor arises from the incongruity between their folk lifestyle and their new surroundings. They think of their swimming pool as a "cement pond." And they turn their billiard table into a "fancy eatin' table," using cue sticks as "pot passers." Pronouncing billiard as "billyard," they assume the animal (a rhinoceros) mounted on the wall must be the exotic billiard. And Granny (Irene Ryan), Jed's mother-in-law, remains devoted to hill-country traditions such as making moonshine and practicing folk medicine. In contrast, California modern culture is epitomized by a greedy banker, who thinks of nothing but money, and his wife, who boasts of her aristocratic ancestry and is obsessed with status symbols and proper etiquette. The modern characters are invariably shown to be fools. Various other gold-diggers and big-city charlatans try to take advantage of the naive Clampetts, but their schemes typically blow up in their faces. Thus, it would be wrong or at least incomplete to assume that rural sitcoms such as *The Beverly Hillbillies* relied on the viewer feeling superior to the naive rubes and hillbillies. In most instances, the hillbillies were portrayed much more sympathetically than the representatives of modern life and lifestyles of privilege and thus were morally superior to urban characters.

Although immensely popular at the time, rural sitcoms had their detractors. Critics excoriated them and Emmy Awards seldom came their way. Probably the most lauded sitcom from the first half of the 1960s was *The Dick Van Dyke Show* (1961–1966), which also managed to frequently land in the Nielsen top 20. *The Dick Van Dyke Show* inherited the white, upper-middle-class home in the suburbs from 1950s shows such as *Leave It to Beaver* and *Father Knows Best*, but its protagonist, Rob Petrie (Dick Van Dyke), also works as a TV-comedy writer in Manhattan and many of its storylines are based there—where his boss is played by the show's actual creator, Carl Reiner. Thus, *The Dick Van Dyke Show* is distinctly suburban-urban instead of entirely rural and it's also a hybrid sitcom in that it fairly evenly balances the home and the workplace. Although the Petries have a son, the narrative problematic of the show is less frequently concerned with his upbringing than with the humorous situations encountered by Rob and his wife, Laura (Mary Tyler Moore), their neighbors, and Rob's work friends. Although a television writer, Rob is not a sophisticated character. Rather, he's positioned as a 1960s everyman trying to make sense out of the urban and suburban worlds he commutes between.

In the 1960s, the genre took a turn toward fantasy and the frankly bizarre, which was established early on by the 1961 debut of *Mister Ed* (1961–1966). Centering on the misadventures of a talking horse that could only be heard by one human, this show's premise somehow managed to support 143 episodes. In its wake, sitcoms would be based on a talking car (*My Mother, the Car* [1965–1966]), a Martian visiting Earth (*My Favorite Martian* [1963–1966]), a witch married to a mortal (*Bewitched* [1964–1972]), a genie married to an astronaut (*I Dream of Jeannie* [1965–1970]), astronauts who travel back in time (*It's About Time* [1966–1967]), a nun whose habit gave her the gift of flight (*The Flying Nun* [1967–1970]), a man training a robot that perfectly resembled a woman (*My Living Doll* [1964–1965]), a cottage haunted by a sea-captain's ghost (*The Ghost and Mrs. Muir* [1968–1971]), and families of suburban monsters (*The Munsters* [1964–1966]) and odd ghouls with sado-masochistic tendencies and a butler who resembles

Frankenstein's monster (*The Addams Family* [1964–1966]). Further, during this time there was one sitcom placed in a Nazi prisoner-of-war camp (*Hogan's Heroes* [1965–1971]) and animated sitcoms set in the far past (*The Flintstones* [1960–1966]) and the far future (*The Jetsons* [1962–1963]).

The diversity of these narrative premises signals the maturation of the sitcom genre as a format. Radio and 1950s-TV sitcoms had established a mode of production and a method for generating humor that could now support any number of outlandish tropes and characters. And all of the programs listed earlier adhered to the single-camera mode of production, with a fabricated laugh track. With the exception of *Bewitched*, none of them were sustained ratings hits and their fanciful nature illustrates just how disengaged the genre and American television were from 1960s social issues: civil rights for African Americans, the rise of the second-wave women's movement, opposition to the Vietnam War and the military draft, the "war on poverty" initiated by President Lyndon Johnson, drug culture and its suppression, and so on. This would all change in the 1970s sitcom.

1970s Sitcoms: The Genre Becomes "Relevant"

In the 1970s, the sitcom began to engage many of the controversies that had pervaded American culture in the previous decade. Leading the way in these new, "relevant" sitcoms were two influential and very dissimilar programs: *The Mary Tyler Moore Show* (1970–1977) and *All in the Family* (1971–1979).

The Mary Tyler Moore Show brought back to American television the actor who had played Laura Petrie, the wife on *The Dick Van Dyke Show*: Mary Tyler Moore. Much like Lucille Ball, Moore was a savvy businesswoman and she and her husband, Grant Tinker, created MTM Enterprises in order to sell CBS on the idea of a program centered on an independent woman trying to make her way in a world in which gender roles were changing. This character, Mary Richards, seemed to capture the spirit of the times. As James L. Brooks, one of its producers/writers, said,

> We dealt with problems, the day-to-day stuff that ordinary people go through as opposed to big themes. Our timing was very fortunate, the way the women's movement started to evolve. ... [W]e did not espouse women's rights, we sought to show a woman from Mary Richards' background being in a world where women's rights were being talked about.[7]

In other words, Mary does not identify as a feminist, but her situation is still informed by second-wave feminism. She is a 30-year-old single woman living independently in a large city (Minneapolis) who takes a traditionally male job as an associate news producer at a television station. The irony is, though, that the conventional secretarial position she could have taken had a higher salary—a subtle criticism of income inequality between genders. The show's often-parodied opening credits show Mary in a stylish pants suit enjoying urban life as the peppy theme song, "Love Is All Around," concludes "You're gonna make it after all!" Mary does make it, of course, but love is not "all around" her. Although she dates men, she remains unattached for the show's entire seven seasons. *The Mary Tyler Moore Show* was both a ratings and critical success, setting a record by winning 19 Emmy Awards over the course of its run.

Compared to what MTM Enterprises did in *The Mary Tyler Moore Show*, influential producer Norman Lear was much more aggressive in foregrounding contemporary social issues in *All in the Family* and other 1970s shows he produced: *Sanford and Son* (1972–1977), *Maude* (1972–1978), *Good Times* (1974–1979), *The Jeffersons*, and *Diff'rent Strokes* (1978–1986). He himself cataloged the taboo-for-the-sitcom topics his shows highlighted:

> Our stories dealt with death, infidelity, black family life, homosexuality, abortion, criticism of the economic and foreign policy, racial prejudice, problems of the elderly,

alcoholism, drug abuse, menopause, the male mid-life crisis. Such health issues as heart disease, hypertension, breast cancer, lung cancer, mental retardation, depression, manic depression, plastic surgery and more.[8]

All in the Family, in particular, set up its narrative problematic for conflict by bringing together a family in which the father is an arch-conservative and his daughter and son-in-law are arch-liberals. This intra-familial, generational conflict mirrored a perceived societal conflict between the "over-30" and the "under-30" generations, between the "establishment" and the youth- or counter-culture of the time. In most episodes, the narrative is triggered by the father, Archie Bunker (Carroll O'Connor), being angered by a situation involving sexual "liberation," "commies," feminists, or racial/ethnic/religious minorities that he unrepentantly refers to as "Chinks," "Polacks," "wops," "dagos," "spicks," "spades," "hebes," and "fags." CBS's "Program Practices" Department (its censorship office) normally prohibited such derisive words, but Lear argued for their necessity to give bite to the show's social satire. CBS eventually relented, but so that there would be no doubt about the program's intent, a disclaimer ran during the credits of its first six episodes: "[*All in the Family*] seeks to throw a humorous spotlight on our frailties, prejudices and concerns. By making them a source of laughter we hope to show—in a mature fashion—just how absurd they are."

All in the Family was the first successful US sitcom to so pointedly offer itself as contemporary social satire. And so it was the first to so pointedly raise the question, "What if some audience members miss the satiric aspect?" Debates rage to the present day about whether a bigot such as Archie Bunker encourages bigotry or combats it. It's an argument that can also be applied to subsequent sitcoms' characters—such as bad parents like Fred Sanford (from another Lear comedy, *Sanford and Son*) and Homer Simpson. We know from publicly available statements that *All in the Family*'s showrunner had a liberal agenda and each episode systematically counters Archie's prejudiced rants, but the program also illustrates how television's polysemy functions.

All in the Family offers a variety of meanings and reading positions. Despite Lear's intentions, many viewers had their prejudices validated by Archie's pronouncements, as was confirmed by at least one empirical study.[9] Moreover, *All in the Family* illustrates the slippery nature of humor and its reception. Will its effect be progressive or regressive? Often, it's impossible to say for certain.

All in the Family and *The Mary Tyler Moore Show* thus illustrate two very different ways that 1970s sitcoms engaged with the contemporaneous zeitgeist. They also share the distinction of reintroducing multicam production to the genre. During the 1960s, the sitcom had come to rely on single-camera production and a laugh track was added in post-production. Virtually all of the 1960s' top-rated sitcoms were produced in this fashion, with the notable exception of the multicam production, *The Dick Van Dyke Show*. When it came time to pitch her first sitcom to a network, it's not surprising that one of its alums, Mary Tyler Moore, felt most comfortable with that mode of production. The only real difference between the production of the earlier show and *The Mary Tyler Moore Show* was that the latter was shot with color film stock instead of black-and-white. Lear also preferred multicam production before a studio audience, reportedly for the energy it provided the cast; but he chose the cheaper option of recording on (color) videotape instead of film. For the next three decades, multicam production—on film or tape—with a studio audience would be the sitcom's dominant mode of production. To this day, it defines the term "sitcom" to many. A significant exception to this rule of thumb was *M*A*S*H* (1972–1983), but then it was rather singular in several ways.

There had been military-themed sitcoms before *M*A*S*H*—notably, *Sergeant Bilko* (a.k.a., *The Phil Silvers Show*) (1955–1959) in the 1950s and *Gomer Pyle U.S.M.C.* and *McHale's Navy* (1962–1966) in the 1960s—but none of those shows had been as assertively antiwar as *M*A*S*H* was. Those antecedent shows also avoided engaging with the horrors of war and its human cost. Rather, they told stories of military hijinks during peacetime or, in the case of *McHale's Navy*, at a World War II location far from the front. By setting itself at a Mobile

Army Surgical Hospital (MASH) embedded in a Korean War combat zone, *M*A*S*H* directly confronted the carnage of war and provided a thinly veiled critique of the Vietnam War, in which the USA was militarily involved until just after *M*A*S*H*'s third season ended in 1975. *M*A*S*H* originated in a darkly comic novel (1968) that was turned into a boisterously satiric film (1970) by New American Cinema director Robert Altman. The TV show seems relatively tame and toned down when contrasted with the source material, but within the context of the sitcom genre, it broke many rules.

First, its creators, Larry Gelbart and Gene Reynolds, argued vociferously against a laugh track being added to this single-camera show, as was the standard of the day. CBS executives demanded they include one, but compromised to the extent that during operating-room scenes the laugh track went silent. The unnecessary nature of the laugh track is illustrated by DVD releases that give the viewer the option of turning it off entirely! Second, *M*A*S*H* experimented with narrative form in ways that had never before been seen in the genre or series television, in general. Most episodes worked within a conventional narrative problematic that established a military or romantic predicament for one or more of its ensemble of surgeons, nurses, and support staff and worked through it in two sitcom acts, but the program was occasionally adventurous during its 11 seasons. "Dear Dad" (May 20, 1973), for example, was the first of several episodes based on letters written home. In this instance, Captain "Hawkeye" Pierce (Alan Alda) writes his father, and the episode presents a series of vignettes tied together by Hawkeye's voice-over narration instead of a standard exposition-conflict-resolution format. More unconventionally, "Point of View" (November 20, 1978) was filmed literally from the point-of-view of a wounded soldier. Charles Dubin directed the episode entirely with a subjective camera so that the viewer sees through the soldier's eyes.

Perhaps the greatest departure from sitcom form, however, is found in "The Interview" episode from February 24, 1976. Eschewing both color film and a laugh track, the black-and-white episode features war correspondent Clete Roberts playing himself and interviewing members of the MASH unit. As the characters talk about the war and their lives, a microphone is visible in the frame. Gelbart developed the script by having an assistant interview the actors in character and molding their improvised answers into a basic framework. Then, he directed the episode by having Roberts ask the questions to the actors on-camera—telling him to add some of his own questions to the mix. The resulting footage was assembled to create a faux documentary, anticipating the documentary-style form that would become integral to the genre decades later. "The Interview" has humorous moments, of course, but it also aspires to pathos and tragedy. The overall message is that war is absurd and tragic. By mixing black humor with satire, antiwar outrage, and moments of melancholy, *M*A*S*H* established a new tone for the sitcom and opened genre possibilities that would have been unthinkable just a few years before.

One other development of the 1970s sitcom was the reintroduction of shows with predominantly African-American casts. Not since the controversial *Amos 'n' Andy Show* was canceled in 1953 had there been a sitcom with a mostly black cast that had met with much success. White producer Norman Lear was largely responsible for this new wave of black shows, as he created or developed *Sanford and Son*, *Good Times*, and *The Jeffersons* (an *All in the Family* spin-off)—all of which achieved ratings success, if not critical praise or Emmy Awards. In some respects, these black sitcoms were a step forward in the representation of race in the genre. Their highly visible black protagonists were certainly an improvement over the general erasure of African-American characters in television of the 1950s and 1960s. However, many of the characters in these programs were strongly rooted in comic stereotypes dating back to 19th-century minstrel shows. Black character Fred G. Sanford (Redd Foxx), for instance, is untrustworthy, lazy, and conniving.

A black bigot meant, by Lear, to mirror the bigotry of Archie Bunker, Fred is not far removed from the world of Amos and Andy. Nonetheless, casting raunchy nightclub comic Redd Foxx as Fred guaranteed that the character would not hew to the liberal principle of integration, of all the races blending together. Fred/Foxx brought a heightened sensitivity to and anger about race in America. Just as with *All in the Family*, the ability to interpret Fred's behavior in a number of ways—the polysemy of *Sanford and Son*—contributed to the ratings success of the show, which ranked second and third for its first three seasons. Later black-cast sitcoms would appeal to a much narrower demographic and a smaller audience. (The history of minority representation in the sitcom is considered in more depth in Chapter 5.)

The 1980s Sitcom: Content Innovations, Format Calcification

As the 1970s came to a close, the sitcom genre utterly dominated prime-time television's ratings. Aside from the news-magazine program *60 Minutes* (1968–), every one of the top-ten rated programs during the 1978–1979 season was a sitcom. The genre had reached a peak, but the sitcom form was also becoming quite rigid. It had calcified into an effective and efficient mode of production, privileging multicam shows. Stylistically conventional juggernauts *Happy Days* (1974–1984) and its spin-off *Laverne & Shirley* (1976–1983) were both created by influential producer Garry Marshall. They, along with the blandly vulgar *Three's Company* (1976–1984), were often at the top of the ratings. The 1980s continued in this tradition, with the most-popular and longest-running shows invariably shooting before a live audience and using a multicam set-up: for example, *Family Ties* (1982–1989), *The Cosby Show* (1984–1992), *Cheers* (1982–1993), *Who's the Boss?* (1984–1992), *Roseanne* (1988–1997, 2018), *Murphy Brown* (1988–1998, 2018–2019), *Full House* (1987–1995), and *Coach* (1989–1997). There were significant changes in the genre during this decade, but they came more in terms of content than form and often revolved around the representation of race, class, and gender. In particular, both the family sitcom and the workplace sitcom were marked by noteworthy developments during the 1980s.

The family sitcom was largely defined by two programs created by Marcy Carsey and Tom Werner: *The Cosby Show* and *Roseanne*.

The Cosby Show centers on an upper-middle-class, African-American family with a doctor father and a lawyer mother. Starring Bill Cosby as Cliff Huxtable, *The Cosby Show* was both lauded for breaking stereotypes of race and class and critiqued for failing to confront issues of race and class in sufficient depth. As such, it epitomizes the strengths and weaknesses of sitcoms being used to present positive "role models" for its viewers. *The Cosby Show*'s narrative problematic is built on intimate conflicts within the family and not America's greater social ills. In some ways it resembles a 1980s version of *Father Knows Best*. For example, in one episode the youngest daughter, Rudy (Keshia Knight Pulliam), becomes sick and the parents must juggle caring for her and their job responsibilities. In another, the son, Theo (Malcolm-Jamal Warner), is having issues with his grades. The latter episode illustrates how the African-American experience still managed to infuse the show, because it centers on Theo writing a history paper about the 1963 March on Washington, at which Martin Luther King delivered his "I Have a Dream" speech. His research becomes a lesson in African-American history for the viewer as Cliff, his wife, and his parents describe how attending the March had a personal impact on them. Cliff's image as a positive role model for African Americans has become severely tarnished in recent years as the sexual misconduct of Bill Cosby came to light. It's hard to see Cliff as a positive role model now that we know the crimes against women that Cosby was perpetrating off screen.

Roseanne, a showcase for stand-up comedian Roseanne Barr, was widely perceived as the anti-*Cosby Show*, because its central family is decidedly working-class and dysfunctional. *Roseanne* took much of its tone and themes from Barr's stand-up act, in which she declared herself a "domestic goddess" and challenged stereotypical norms of motherhood, female sexuality, and social class. Roseanne Conner (Barr) frequently makes caustic remarks about her husband, Dan (John Goodman), and her children. In one episode, her teenaged daughter Darlene (Sara Gilbert) asks her what she is working on. She replies, "Invoices. I'm ordering new children." Darlene follows up: "Yeah? Well, why don't we trade Becky [Lecy Goranson; her other daughter] in for a partially tattooed Latin boy of sixteen?" Roseanne rejoins, "Because that's my Christmas present to myself." Moreover, her mothering techniques are often unconventional. In one episode, when Becky and Darlene are quarreling, she tells them her solution: "There's only one way to solve this problem. ... [T]urn around and face each other here. [The girls face each other.] Now I want you two to fight to the death."

On-screen and in her publicly available private life, Roseanne incarnated the unruly woman—a sitcom standard since Lucy Ricardo disrupted Ricky's nightclub act. Superficially, Roseanne is more dangerous and unconventional than Lucy because she refuses to sacrifice her own needs for her husband and family, but that refusal is undermined by her fiercely protective nature toward her children and the sitcom form's demand for partial closure at the end of each episode. That is, most episodes end with Roseanne solving her family's problems, despite her cutting remarks. Although she is caustic and sarcastic, her parenting usually works. Thus, in most regards, she functions like a conventional sitcom mother, even though she may not sound like she is one. *Roseanne* originally ran for nine seasons and continued well into the 1990s. The later years became increasingly strange, resulting in a final episode in which it is revealed that the entire series was Roseanne Conner's fabrication and that much of what had been previously presented was false. By then, *Roseanne*'s ratings had declined precipitously and it was no longer the touchstone series it had been. When it was revived in 2018, it once again tapped into the social issues of the day—rooted in actor Barr's and the character Roseanne's adamant support of controversial president Donald Trump. It garnered large ratings, but when Barr tweeted an offensive, racist remark that referred to an African-American political advisor (Valerie Jarrett) as an ape, ABC promptly canceled the program. It returned as *The Conners* (2018–), without Barr's participation.

The workplace comedy reached critical and popular peaks in the 1980s. Emmy Awards went to *Taxi* (1978–1983), *Barney Miller* (1975–1982), and *Cheers*, which are set in a taxi company's dispatch garage, a police precinct, and a neighborhood bar, respectively.

Additionally, there were numerous workplace comedies turning up in the top-ten rated programs: *Night Court* (1984–1992), *Murphy Brown* (1988–1998, 2018–2019), *Designing Women* (1986–1993), and *Coach* (1989–1997). In most respects, these workplace shows did not cover much new comedy ground, but two of them—*Designing Women* and *Murphy Brown*—took up the mantle of liberal discourse that Norman Lear had first assumed in the 1970s. (They appealed to a similar demographic and were scheduled together as a block by CBS.)

As with *All in the Family*, *Designing Women* was created and produced by an outspoken liberal advocate, Linda Bloodworth-Thomason. *Designing Women* is set at an interior design firm launched by two sisters and run by a small group of women and one man. The program takes on a variety of topical, 1980s social issues: the AIDS epidemic, racism, violence against women and gays, and so on. In "The Strange Case of Clarence and Anita," an episode written by Bloodworth-Thomason herself, the show analyzes the confirmation hearings of Supreme Court justice Clarence Thomas and the allegations of sexual harassment made against him by his former assistant, Anita Hill. The episode could hardly have been more topical. Justice Thomas was confirmed October 15, 1991 and the episode ran three weeks later (November 4, 1991). In fact, the episode even includes video footage from the hearings themselves. As is common in *Designing Women* episodes on topical issues, the women of the design firm are split in their opinions about "Clarence and Anita," but the most eloquent, convincing dialogue is given to the women attacking Thomas and defending Hill. And their arguments revolve around women's rights and the oppressively patriarchal US government, particularly the US Senate. As is fitting with sitcom conventions, the immediate issue is resolved by the end of the episode: specifically, Thomas is confirmed and the matter is thus finalized. But this breaks with sitcom convention in that the protagonists are defeated. The ending is an unhappy resolution for those criticizing Thomas. Like many of the "relevant" sitcoms of the 1970s onward, *Designing Women* sometimes had to defeat sitcom expectations to recognize that many contemporary problems are unsolvable.

The workplace sitcom's profusion in the 1980s illustrates, perhaps, the sitcom's weakening reliance upon the family as the central source of humor. And it permitted the intermingling of a greater diversity of individuals than the family sitcom ever could. The numerous workplace sitcoms opened the door to the defining shows of the 1990s, which eschewed the bonds of family for those of friendship: *Seinfeld* (1989–1998) and *Friends* (1994–2004). However, these two sitcoms existed in a rapidly changing television industry and the sitcom genre played a key role in those changes.

1990s Sitcoms: Broadcasting Becomes Narrowcasting

The 1980s marked the beginning of the end of the so-called "network era," that time period during which NBC, CBS, and ABC (accompanied by their public-TV cousin, PBS) utterly dominated the television airwaves. *Broad*casting was inexorably becoming *narrow*casting. The seeds were sown in the 1980s with the rise of the cable-TV industry and the videocassette, both of which provided new alternatives to programming by the Big Three. Initially, cable-TV systems were modest operations that shared TV stations with small towns that were beyond the reach of transmitters located in the major metropolitan areas. But then national satellite-based networks were born and began to locally distribute their signal via cable-TV systems. The pay channel, HBO, was the first such network to deliver a continuous signal via satellite, beginning in 1975, and it was soon joined by other premium services such as Showtime, The Movie Channel, and The Playboy Channel. In the 1980s, smaller programming interests were served when channels such as ESPN (Entertainment and Sports Programming Network), MTV (Music Television), CBN (Christian Broadcasting Network), The Weather Channel, and CNN (Cable News Network) joined the satellite club—all of which were added to "basic" cable services. Also in the new mix challenging the Big Three were so-called "superstations"—powerful big-city stations that bounced their local signal off the satellite. The Big Three were further threatened by new networks of terrestrial (i.e., land-based) stations. The most successful of these networks was and is Fox, which launched in 1986 and was later joined by The WB, UPN, The CW, and Spanish-language network, Univision (which had operated previously as the Spanish International Network [SIN]).

The TV-industry tumult of the 1980s had negligible impact upon the sitcom genre at the time. The new channels/networks' voracious need for programming provided fresh outlets for sitcoms in syndication, but, initially, they themselves did not do much by way of original comedy production. However, this changed radically in the following decade. Leading the charge were Fox's productions of *Married... with Children* (1987–1997) and *The Simpsons*. Fox had been struggling to establish a brand that would distinguish it from NBC, CBS, and ABC and it found its identity with these two groundbreaking sitcoms.

Married... began with the family dysfunction of *Roseanne* and the bigotry of Archie Bunker and blended in sexual innuendo, references to various bodily functions, misogyny, and misanthropy. For example, when Al Bundy (Ed O'Neill) tells his wife, Peggy (Katy Sagal), that their ATM card doesn't work, she replies suggestively, "Sound familiar? How many times have I told you, Al? You gotta stick it in the right way. And you know, pressing the right buttons wouldn't hurt either." Unlike *Roseanne*, the parents in *Married...* have a fundamental dislike for each other and their parenting skills do not function to undermine their sarcasm to nurture the children by an episode's end. And unlike *All in the Family*, anti-hero Al doesn't have a liberal counterpart balancing his sexist commentary. *Married...* is peopled with unrepentantly ill-behaved characters who were perceived as offensive by a significant portion of the viewing public, but the program was what Fox needed to distance itself from the Big Three networks, whose programming was increasingly seen as bland, safe, and predictable. Fox was able to claim that it had an edgy quality not to be found on older broadcast networks.

However, the impact of *Married...* is a bit hard to quantify despite its 11 seasons on the air. Its ratings were never that high, due largely to the fact that Fox's network of affiliate stations was much smaller than those of the Big Three. Consequently, *Married...* was not even available in some major markets when it debuted in 1987. *The Simpsons*, in contrast, has had a television and popular culture impact that cannot be disputed. It has won innumerable awards over a run that, since April 29, 2018, is the longest of any scripted, prime-time American program—comedy or drama. It has aired more than 636 episodes (*Gunsmoke*'s [1955–1975] old record) over 29 seasons. It has spawned a movie, video games, and a massively successful merchandise campaign; and catchphrases such as Homer's "D'oh!" have entered common parlance. It was Fox's first true hit and helped establish it as a legitimate competitor to ABC, CBS, and NBC, which was further confirmed when Fox landed an NFL contract in the mid-1990s.

In the early years of *The Simpsons*, it was as edgy and more fundamentally unconventional than *Married...*. It was the first network animated prime-time series since *The Flintstones* went off the air 23 years earlier. Its success led to a wave of cartoons for adults that likely would not have existed otherwise: for example, *King of the Hill* (1997–2010), *South Park* (1997–), *Family Guy* (1999–), and *Bob's Burgers* (2011–). At first glance, *The Simpsons* follows the conventions of a live-action family sitcom, with its bumbling father, nurturing mother, and three kids—one a troublemaker, one perfectly behaved, and one a baby. However, *The Simpsons* has actively parodied and critiqued those conventions more often than not. And its animated format allows it the freedom to create outrageous storylines where the characters might interact with aliens or enter different dimensions or age 30 years or have adventures that would strain credulity in a live-action show. The annual "Treehouse of Horror" episodes regularly kill central characters and yet they return the following week. In terms of family-sitcom conventions, then, *The Simpsons* seldom follows and often makes fun of the well-worn narrative problematic of a disruption of the family's stasis that is resolved by the end of an episode. The flexibility of its central premise opens it up to wide-ranging social satire—more so than virtually any sitcom that came before it. Its satiric targets have included: politics and politicians; the nuclear industry; the failures of American education; the war on drugs; racial, ethnic, and LGBTQ prejudice; gun rights; contemporary journalism; advertising and product branding; and, perhaps most controversially, organized religion and Christian evangelists. (We consider *The Simpsons* in more detail in Chapter 6.)

Married... with Children and *The Simpsons* succeeded by appealing to a narrow, young demographic, in contrast to the wide net that ABC, CBS, and NBC cast in their programming. After their success, Fox realized that it could develop other programs for under-served segments of the American population. In particular, it targeted African Americans that might have found *The Cosby Show* to be too middle-class and removed from their own life experiences. Consequently, Fox developed several sitcoms with predominantly black casts and African-American characters living in less idealized circumstances: *Roc* (1991–1994), *Martin* (1992–1997), *Living Single* (1993–1998), and the short–lived *The Sinbad Show* (1993–1994) and *South Central* (1994). Additionally, the sketch-comedy show, *In Living Color*, ran on Fox from 1990 to 1994. Fox was not alone in using comedy to pursue the African-American viewer. The newly created United Paramount Network (UPN)—which essentially operated for just eleven years, beginning in 1995—also relied heavily on black-cast shows: *Moesha* (1996–2001), *The Parkers* (1999–2004), and, slightly later, *Girlfriends* (2000–2008). Similarly, The CW network launched the same year as UPN with the black-cast sitcom *The Wayans Bros.* (1995–1999) and followed it with two other sitcoms seeking black audiences: *The Parent 'Hood* (1995–1999) and *Sister, Sister* (1994–1999). Thus, African Americans were no longer invisible on American television and in the sitcom genre, but they were largely segregated into programs on networks that didn't even cover the entire US. And, at the same time, the shows with the highest ratings with general audiences and those that were the most critically lauded were including fewer and fewer black characters—as could be seen in the decade's most popular, influential, and innovative shows: *Cheers*, continuing from the 1980s and spinning off long-running *Frasier* in 1993; *Seinfeld*; and *Friends*.

For the most part, *Cheers* and *Frasier* had been conventional multicam, workplace sitcoms whose format was honed for maximum efficiency by veteran producer/director James Burrows. *Seinfeld* and *Friends* continued that sitcom tradition, but with one key difference: they were not set in a workplace. Like the workplace comedy, *Seinfeld* and *Friends* chronicle the interactions of characters who are not tied by family bonds, but, unlike the workplace comedy, they are brought together by friendship and not work obligations. Perhaps surprisingly, there are very few precedents in the sitcom genre for groups of characters gathered together by neither family nor work, but, rather, solely by friendship. Even *Friends* is not a pure example of this as Ross (David Schwimmer) and Monica (Courteney Cox) are brother and sister and two pairs of the "friends" marry and start families by the series' conclusion. However, *Friends*' over-arching narrative problematic, as with *Seinfeld*'s, is still informed by the lack of familial or work connections, which allows both shows to develop a greater variety of plotlines than is available to the workplace or the family sitcom. Moreover, because the characters are not employed at a common workplace, many of the narrative predicaments can be about them searching for employment or having difficulties at a variety of jobs. And because the characters are not wed to one another, romantic predicaments with a variety of partners are possible.

Connecting the friends in each show are communal locations: eating establishments (*Seinfeld*'s Monk's Café and *Friends*' Central Perk) and apartments with doors that are seldom locked, even though both take place in New York City. These recurring settings serve the narrative function of bouncing characters off one another—just as job sites and family homes provide in the workplace sitcom and the family sitcom, respectively. By opening up the sitcom to human interactions beyond those of work and family, *Seinfeld*, *Friends*, and their ilk made a space where later in the decade *Will & Grace* (1998–2006, 2017–2020) could bring together a group of roommates and friends, some of whom were gay and some of whom were straight. *Will & Grace* was not the first TV series with LGBTQ characters, but it was certainly the most popular, longest-running one in which one of the title characters was gay and it consequently had an enormous impact on LGBTQ representation on American broadcast TV. (The history of LGBTQ sitcom characters is chronicled in Chapter 4.)

In addition to its workplace/home innovations, it would not be hyperbole to say that *Seinfeld* reinvented the genre—introducing thematic, narrative, and tonal innovations that would continue to reverberate into the 21st century. Consider first its central theme: a show about "nothing." In its fourth season, *Seinfeld* aired a series of episodes in which Jerry (Jerry Seinfeld) and George (Jason Alexander) pitch a sitcom to NBC based on their own lives. Written by Larry David (who actually did pitch the show with Seinfeld to the real NBC and who is the real-life model for George), the episode titled "The Pitch" (September 16, 1992) is not subtle in its self-reflexivity. Jerry and George brainstorm the premise of the show-within-the-show while at Monk's Café:

Jerry: So, we go into NBC, we tell them we've got an idea for a show about nothing.
George: Exactly.
Jerry: They say, 'What's your show about?' I say, 'Nothing.'
George: There you go.

[Pause]

Jerry: I think you may have something there.

David's script is facetious and played for laughs, but its characterization of *Seinfeld*'s logline is quite accurate. It is a show about "nothing," if one understands that to mean that it is not about the conventional "somethings" over which the sitcom genre obsesses: family, work, romance, financial success, etc. By finding humor in nothing specific, *Seinfeld* generates humor from *everything*, including the most petty and mundane challenges of everyday life: losing your car in a parking garage, waiting interminably for a table at a restaurant, riding the subway. This, unsurprisingly, is also the premise of Jerry Seinfeld's stand-up act and its observational humor. He observes small aspects of the human condition and builds a routine around them, usually prefaced with "What's the deal about ... ?" One can even see this low-key approach operating in his current Web series, whose simple premise is spelled out in its title: *Comedians in Cars Getting Coffee* (2012–).

Of course, it would be an exaggeration to say that every *Seinfeld* episode is about nothing. In fact, most episodes have specific story arcs about the characters' desires for romance, gainful employment, and financial success. And yet, it is quite remarkable how many episodes turn on the smallest detail—such as a Pez candy dispenser on Elaine's (Julia Louis-Dreyfus) lap.

Over the course of its run, *Seinfeld*'s story structure became increasingly convoluted, inspiring new narrative structures for subsequent sitcoms. At the time of its debut, the standard sitcom narrative had calcified into a rigid two-act structure, plus teaser and tag; and acts commonly had two or three scenes within them. Thus, a typical half-hour episode had perhaps six or seven scenes. In contrast, the median number of *Seinfeld* scenes consistently increased from 10 in the first season to a peak of 26 in the eighth season. This resulted in average scene lengths of less than 60 seconds![10] And it's not just in raw quantity of scenes that *Seinfeld* disrupted sitcom norms. It also unsettled the conventional exposition-conflict-commercials-conflict-resolution format that typically twined together "A" and "B" story lines. *Seinfeld*'s four central characters—Jerry, George, Elaine, and Kramer (Michael Richards)—often embark on divergent adventures that ingeniously intersect at the conclusion. This led, according to *Seinfeld* production designer, Tom Azzari, to shows that went into "'double letter' scenes"; that is, after labeling 25 scenes A through Z, they'd start over with AA, BB, CC, etc. Perhaps the most extreme example of this is "The Subway" episode (January 8, 1992). The exposition in Monk's Café quickly establishes that each character has a separate goal that requires a ride on the subway. Jerry is retrieving his stolen car from a Coney Island impound lot; George is heading to a job interview; Elaine is attending a "lesbian wedding"; and Kramer plans to pay off parking tickets. Off they go on their four separate journeys, told in 23 scenes. They have no contact with each other until the very last scene when they reconvene at Monk's and briefly allude to their adventures. For the most part, they do not achieve their goals. Thus, the ending defeats our expectation for at least partial resolution of a sitcom predicament. Instead of solving the predicament(s) posed at the start, "The Subway" takes us on four different digressions rendered in very short scenes, averaging about 60 seconds each. In terms of *Seinfeld*'s mode of production, it was still a multicam sitcom with a conventional laugh track, but in terms of its narrative pace and structure, it threatened to shatter the mold of the sitcom.

Seinfeld exemplifies one final aspect of 1990s sitcom narrative form. It helped break down the distinction between "series" and "serial" American television. The sitcom series format, as it had evolved in the 1950s and 1960s, favored a narrative that posed a specific situation and then resolved it, while also allowing a program's narrative problematic, its basic premise, to recur each week. Serial shows, in contrast, continued the story from one episode to the next, as exemplified most commonly in the soap opera. The sitcom worked best as a series, because, among other mode-of-production reasons, this enabled the episodes to be shown in syndication without strict regard for the order of the episodes. One could watch daily broadcasts of *I Love Lucy* in so-called "stripped syndication," for instance, and experience the episodes in virtually any order—although the birth of little Ricky sometimes confuses matters some. In contrast, *Seinfeld*, *Friends*, and other 1990s shows often continue a story arc over several episodes, counting on viewers' knowledge of what had aired previously and requiring them to tune in the following week to see it resolved. Nonetheless, *Seinfeld* and *Friends* have had immense success in syndication, despite any narrative inconsistencies that might arise. By the turn of the century, the division between series and serial, in both comedies and dramas, had blurred significantly.

Seinfeld's distinctive theme and its ambitious narrative structure (especially for a multicam show) underpin a significant shift in tone. The show brought a new level of humiliation and discomfort to the genre by dwelling on characters prone to pretense, in the sense discussed in Chapter 1 that draws on Evan Smith's "character mixes." In short, *Seinfeld* pioneered what has come to be known colloquially as "cringe-worthy" comedy. Of course, what is meant by this is that viewers cringe while they watch these sitcom characters make utter fools of themselves. George is likely the *Seinfeld* character who elicits the most cringes as he often overestimates his intelligence/skills, makes impolitic comments, and suffers through numerous debasing incidents—such as his mother discovering him masturbating. But virtually all the *Seinfeld* characters contain some amount of pretense, are somewhat unlikable, and are prone to doing/saying things that are embarrassing. They are, at the least, all unpleasant narcissists who, in the series finale, wind up in jail for "criminal indifference." The judge, while sentencing them, declares,

> [Y]our callous indifference and utter disregard for everything that is good and decent has rocked the very foundation upon which our society is built. I can think of nothing more fitting than for the four of you to spend a year removed from society so that you can contemplate the manner in which you have conducted yourselves.

The comedy of disreputable, borderline immoral characters has flourished since *Seinfeld*. It became a common feature of HBO's comedies in particular—beginning with *The Larry Sanders Show* (1992–1998), which overlapped with *Seinfeld*. And the comedy of cringe may well have peaked in the 2000s with a show produced by and starring *Seinfeld* creator, Larry David: *Curb Your Enthusiasm* (nine seasons between 2000 and 2017).

The decade of the 1990s included several conventional and popular sitcoms, but *Seinfeld* and *The Simpsons* tested the genre's fundamental assumptions about mode of production, sound/image style, narrative structure, theme, and tone. They're largely responsible for paving the way toward a radically different half-hour comedy that emerged as television moved into the 21st century.

The 2000s Sitcom: The Fall of the Sitcom, the Rise of the Sitcom

The 1990s was the last decade that sitcoms would have a strong presence in the TV ratings' top ten. In fact, in the 2000s, only two sitcoms regularly received such high ratings: *Two and a Half Men* (2003–2015) and *The Big Bang Theory* (2007–2019). Audiences had turned away from comedies and toward reality-TV shows, which was exacerbated during the 2007–2008 season when a writers' strike meant no new scripts were being created. Even worse than the threat of reality TV, a dangerous new competitor for network television was luring audiences away. Online video had arrived. YouTube, in specific, first started streaming video files in 2005. Moreover, Netflix's streaming service lurked just around the corner as the century began. That company began as a DVD delivery service in 1997, but its streaming, video-on-demand platform gained ground throughout the 2000s until, by 2010, it came to supplant DVD delivery as Netflix's core revenue maker. Fortunes were so poor for network sitcoms in the 2000s that *M*A*S*H* creator, Larry Gelbart, announced, "It is just over" in 1999 and numerous articles appeared in trade and general publications proclaiming the "death of the sitcom."[11]

In the sense of being able to command massive audience shares like *I Love Lucy* and *M*A*S*H* did, it is true that the sitcom died in the early 1990s and will never be fully resurrected; but the 21st-century sitcom has also seen a blossoming of new half-hour comedy formats that have expanded the sense of what a sitcom can be and appealed to new, more narrowly defined audience niches. This is largely evident in programs that prefer the single-camera mode of production and fully exploit its potential. As we have seen, the sitcom's peak years of the 1970s through the 1990s were dominated by multicam production with its "zero-degree style," heightened sense of liveness, and emphasis on capturing actors' comic performances (discussed in Chapter 1). Even the single-camera shows from the 1960s (e.g., *The Andy Griffith Show*) were quite conservative in their shooting and editing style. (See Table 1.2 to review the differences between multicam and single-camera productions.) We can see very rare departures from this zero-degree of style—of shows offering some "visual exhibitionism"[12]—in individual instances such as the *M*A*S*H* episode described earlier where a fake documentary is presented in black-and-white and thereby draws our attention to its "documentary-ness." But it would be difficult to find many pre-1990 sitcoms that employ a televisual approach on a consistent basis (see discussion of John Caldwell's term, "televisual", in Chapter 1).

In the 1990s, this began to change. Three notable televisual examples threatened to turn the genre inside out. First and most extreme, *The Simpsons* exemplifies televisuality through its animation format, which constantly reminds you of its televisual status. Further, many of its gags rely on the viewer enjoying its visual gymnastics, intertextuality, and self-reflexivity. (Discussed fully in Chapter 6.) The first live-action sitcom to embrace televisuality fully might be *Parker Lewis Can't Lose* (1990–1993), which arrived the year after *The Simpsons'* debut. It makes frequent use of unconventional camera angles (Dutch angles, extreme high and low angles), special effects, sound effects and odd music cues, abrupt cuts, speeded-up action, and unusual camera movement. For example, in one shot the camera is attached to a guitar flying over people's heads. In short, the video medium itself is a constant source of its humor. A third notable 1990s televisual sitcom was *The Larry Sanders Show*, which relied on a strict televisual conceit. A series about a talk show and its host, *The Larry Sanders Show* shot the show-within-a-show segments on videotape and the behind-the-scenes segments on film. Viewers with a keen eye could discern the difference in resolution and other visual qualities between the two shooting modes. Thus, *The Larry Sanders Show* invited the viewer to consider its televisuality through rather subtle visual cues.

When the 2000s arrived, the sitcom may have seemed moribund, but a crop of new single-camera shows revived critical interest in the genre and ushered the genre into the 21st century. Several of these shows took the televisual innovations of the 1990s and augmented them with their own particular and sometimes peculiar brands of intertextuality and self-reflexivity. *Scrubs* (2001–2010), *Arrested Development* (2003–2006, 2013, 2018), *30 Rock* (2006–2013), and *Community* (2009–2015) are densely filled with allusions to other cultural texts, previous sitcoms, their own status as sitcoms, and the apparatus of television production. The 2000s and 2010s also saw a rash of "mockumentaries." The mockumentary or "comedy *vérité*" mocks the conventions of the documentary by, among other techniques, including character interviews and having characters acknowledge and look at the camera, which is often handheld and shaky.[13]

These parodies are considered televisual when they draw attention to themselves as using a specific television form, the documentary. *M*A*S*H*'s "The Interview" episode also employs the documentary form, but does not parody it. Rather, in that instance, the form provides a patina of authenticity to the fictional narrative, marking it as "serious" and "significant." The 21st-century mockumentaries took a different tack—mining the form for humor. This trend was popularized by *The Office*, which originated in the UK in 2001 and was adopted for American television in 2005, where it had a successful nine-year run. When *Arrested Development*, *The Office* and, later, *Parks and Recreation* (2009–2015) shot in a documentary style, they used it in an ironic way—undercutting its seriousness. And *Modern Family* (2009–2020) uses the style without any pretext of a documentary film being made, as was crucial to *The Office*.

A single-camera show need not necessarily engage with radical, self-reflexive televisuality in order to distinguish itself from multicam production's zero-degree style. As discussed in Chapter 1 with regard to *The Goldbergs*, many contemporary single-camera shows make expressive use of television technique to enhance the humor of scenes. There had been limited efforts in this regard in the late 1980s, in rare single-camera sitcoms such as *Frank's Place* (1987–1988), *The Days and Nights of Molly Dodd* (1987–1991), and, most influentially, *The Wonder Years*; but the 2000s saw a more sustained interest in programs that generated humor through style. Leading the way were *Sex and the City* (1998–2004) and *Curb Your Enthusiasm* on premium cable (HBO) and *Malcolm in the Middle* (2000–2006) on a terrestrial network (Fox), followed by *The Bernie Mac Show* (2001–2006), and *My Name Is Earl* (2005–2009), among others. All of these single-camera shows—both the televisual ones and the stylistically expressive ones—share what some think of as a defining characteristic. Unlike single-camera shows of the 1950s and 1960s, they have no laugh track. This lack of a laugh track has become a marker for prestige or quality sitcom production. In fact, between 2004 and 2018, each Emmy Award for "Outstanding Comedy Series" has gone to a single-camera show, with the sole exception of *Everybody Loves Raymond* (1996–2005) in 2005.

Despite the critical acclaim, none of these single-camera series have been ratings successes insofar as earning big numbers. However, several of them have found favor with a key, younger demographic: viewers between the ages of 18 and 34, with considerable disposable income. This is what has been largely responsible for them earning long runs on broadcast television despite their modest overall ratings. The most recent development in the production of half-hour sitcoms has been the rise in comedy production by subscription video-on-demand (SVOD) services that include Netflix and Amazon Studios, which have produced award-winning shows such as *Unbreakable Kimmy Schmidt* (2015–2019) and *Transparent* (2014–2019), respectively. *Unbreakable Kimmy Schmidt* is particularly interesting because it was originally developed by Tina Fey for NBC, but then sold to Netflix—illustrating how 21st-century comedies can find life outside of network television. Similarly, *Arrested Development* had its first run on Fox, but several years after it was canceled, Netflix produced additional seasons. Furthermore, more and more production companies are developing comedies that are not intended for broadcast on the Big Three or premium cable networks. For instance, Darren Starr, who had created *Sex and the City* for HBO, developed *Younger* (2015–) for TV Land, the cable channel.

Thus, the current state of the sitcom within the television industry and American culture can be described as "the best of times and the worst of times." There are many more venues for sitcoms to be distributed now than there were during the genre's golden era, but individual sitcoms no longer attract the mammoth audiences they once did. The network-television industry as a whole is embroiled in a period of disruption and change, and the sitcom genre was one of its mainstays. If we are indeed in a post-network era, as some analysts contend, will the sitcom fall with the Big Three, or will it flourish in new distribution channels with their smaller, but devoted, audiences? No one has a crystal ball that can accurately predict where the sitcom will be in five or ten years, but it seems unlikely to me that such a long-lived and beloved genre will perish entirely. In Chapter 6, I examine the sitcom's current status in more depth.

Notes

1. "CBS Peddles New Lucille-Desi Show," *The Billboard* (April 28, 1951), 11.
2. Charles J. Correll and Freeman F. Gosden, *All About Amos 'N' Andy And Their Creators Correll And Gosden* (New York: Rand McNally, 1929), 51. Emphasis added.
3. According to tables reproduced in Christopher H. Sterling and John M. Kittross, *Stay Tuned: A Concise History of American Broadcasting*, 2nd ed. (Belmont, CA: Wadsworth, 1990), 73,120.
4. R. W. Stewart, "McGee Spends a Week Here: Fibber and Molly Talk About Their Comedy," *New York Times*, July 14, 1940, p. 110.
5. Mary Kay and Johnny Stearns, interviewed by Michael Rosen, *The Archive of American Television*, August 25, 1999.
6. David Marc further discusses this clash between folk culture and modern culture in "The Situation Comedy of Paul Henning: Modernity and the American Folk Myth in *The Beverly Hillbillies*," in *Demographic Vistas: Television in American Culture*, Revised Edition (Philadelphia, PA: University of Pennsylvania Press, 1996), 39–64.
7. Gerard Jones, *Honey, I'm Home!: Sitcoms: Selling the American Dream* (New York: Grove Weidenfeld, 1992), 194.
8. Quoted in Mick Eaton, "Television Situation Comedy," *Screen* 19, no. 4 (Winter 1978/79): 80. Lear originally made these remarks in a lecture at the Edinburgh International Television Festival, on August 28, 1978. His use of the phrase, "mental retardation," was in keeping with the terminology of the day, but is recognized now as demeaning persons with disabilities.
9. Neil Vidmar and Milton Rokeach, "Archie Bunker's Bigotry: A Study in Selective Perception and Exposure," *Journal of Communication*, 24, no. 1 (Winter 1974): 36–47.
10. Ben Blatt, "The Evolution of *Seinfeld*," *Slate*, July 12, 2015, http://www.slate.com/articles/arts/culturebox/2015/07/seinfeld_on_hulu_how_jerry_kramer_george_and_elaine_evolved_over_the_sitcom.html, accessed June 12, 2019.
11. Quoted in Steve Lopez, "Death of The Sitcom": "It's not the first time sitcoms have fallen on hard times. But with more networks and fewer wits and sages, this is anything but the golden age of comedy. Is there still hope, or are we squeezing the last laughs out of TV's ailing genre?," *Entertainment Weekly* 481 (April 16, 1999): 26(1), *Academic OneFile*. Gale, accessed 18 June 2008.
12. John Thornton Caldwell, *Televisuality: Style, Crisis, and Authority in American Television* (New Brunswick, NJ: Rutgers University Press, 1995), 352.
13. Brett Mills, "Comedy *Vérité*: Contemporary Sitcom Form," *Screen* 45, no. 1 (Spring 2004): 63–78; Ethan Thompson, "Comedy *Vérité*? The Observational Documentary Meets the Televisual Sitcom," *Velvet Light Trap* no. 60 (Fall 2007), 63–72.

3

COMEDY, FAMILY, AND SMALL TOWNS

For dozens of situation comedies, the core "situation" is built upon the relationship among parents and children. The domestic arena is particularly well-suited to TV comedy. Families provide a constant, relatively fixed cast of characters that can be mined for humor individually or together. They have a readily available narrative problematic: will the harmony of the family be disrupted? Or, perhaps more commonly, that problematic could be expressed as: *how* will the harmony of the family be disrupted and how will it be (temporarily) restored by the end of the episode? Further, as early television broadcasters discovered and exploited, the mise-en-scene of the family is inexpensive to assemble. Build a living room set and a dining room set, and you're prepared for a variety of family interaction. It was not a coincidence, therefore, that the first TV sitcom, *Mary Kay and Johnny* (1947–1950), and the phenomenally successful and influential *I Love Lucy* (1951–1957) were about couples who began on-screen families. (Both programs incorporated real-life pregnancies into their plotlines.) Moreover, several current series—*Modern Family* (2009–2020), *The Middle* (2009–2018), *Bob's Burgers* (2011–), *Mom* (2013–), *Black-ish* (2014–), and *Fresh Off the Boat* (2015–)—illustrate that family sitcoms continue to find innovative ways to extract humor from family dynamics in the 21st century.

In the sitcom, family is often the lens through which societal values may be viewed. And, certainly, over the decades since network-television's inception after World War II, those values have seen some significant shifts, but, in many cases, ideas about family have remained remarkably resistant to change. This chapter will highlight the crucial American discourses that have intersected with the family: gender roles in traditional and nontraditional families, parent–child relations (generation gaps), socioeconomic class, and suburban lifestyle. To see how these discourses are played out in the sitcom, I will examine recurring character types, common narrative structures, and aspects of sound and image style. I will not exactly provide a history of the American family, but it is impossible to talk about sitcom families without discussing social history. Statistically, the American family is significantly different today than it was at the end of World War II in 1945. People are marrying later; more families have two working parents; gay marriage and adoptions by gay parents are legal; single parenting and divorce are more common; and so on. However, many of the same ideals about parenting and familial bonding persist. The aptly named series, *Modern Family*, reflects this blend of the modern and the traditional. Of the three families on the program, one has two gay men as parents, which would have been illegal in post-War America; and another is a blended family of two previously divorced parents, which was atypical 70 years ago; but the third family could have been transplanted from a 1950s sitcom with a bumbling dad, a reliable mom, and three children. Thus, many of the meanings associated with the family on network television still pertain in the 2010s, even as the network system is being radically disrupted.

After this chapter has charted the characteristics of the family sitcom, I will use *The Andy Griffith Show* (1960–1968) as a case study to examine in more detail how family dynamics play out in a single series. This program was the most consistently highly rated sitcom of a group of rural and small-town shows that dominated the genre in the late 1950s and early 1960s—including *The Real McCoys* (1957–1963), *Petticoat Junction* (1963–1970), *Green Acres* (1965–1971), and *The Beverly Hillbillies* (1962–1971). These shows were regarded as confirming traditional American values and ignoring the social upheavals of the 1960s, such as civil rights activity and the women's movement. *The Andy Griffith Show* centers on a single-parent family and it's set in the sleepy, fictitious Southern town of Mayberry, where few African Americans are ever seen and women are expected to fulfill conventional roles of wife and mother. One would anticipate that a show such as this from this particular time frame would confirm traditional, patriarchal values and be far removed from today's "modern families." To a large extent this is certainly true, but television's polysemy and the often surprising functioning of humor allow *The Andy Griffith Show* to work through these values in sometimes unexpected ways.

The Traditional Family of the Second Half of the 20th Century

During the post-World War II era, an image of the family solidified within the American imagination as being ideally comprised of a father, a mother, and two or more children. This quickly became the taken-for-granted family structure, with other types of families viewed as aberrations or abnormal. Perhaps inspired by the "nuclear age" that the world irretrievably entered after the nuclear bombings of Hiroshima and Nagasaki at the conclusion of the War, this family structure came to be called the "nuclear family," with its heterosexual parents forming a nucleus around which orbited their biological children. The notion of the American nuclear family had been disrupted during the War years while men served overseas, but it returned after the War ended and the family's primacy was foundational to the "baby boom" of 1946 to 1964. During this time, one function that TV served was to confirm the legitimacy of the nuclear family, although it sometimes did so in conflicted ways. Still, it cannot be disputed that some sitcom episodes of this time served as little more than fables that provided blunt morals extolling the virtues of the conventional nuclear family.

Critical to the nuclear-family structure are rather rigid gender roles relying on narrow definitions of masculinity and femininity. Masculinity in this era was associated with aggression, sexual assertiveness and experience, self-confidence, strength, lack of emotion, leadership, work outside the home (bringing home a paycheck), logical thought, financial acumen, and worldliness, among other qualities. Correspondingly, femininity connoted passivity, sexual submissiveness, empathy, dependence on others, physical inferiority to men, emotional unpredictability, work within the home (cooking, caring for children), screwball or illogical thinking, sexual innocence, and so on. Fathers had the task of working outside the home and financially supporting the family, which, in 1950s sitcoms, typically had just one working parent. Mothers stayed at home, caring for children and serving as the family's emotional core. The power dynamic between father and mother in nuclear-family sitcoms relies on the notion of paternal authority, of the father being in control. In shows such as *Father Knows Best* (1954–1960) and *Leave It to Beaver* (1957–1963), the mother and father do share governance of the household, but it is the father who holds ultimate authority. Thus, the mother often defers to the father when it comes time to discipline or advise the children. *My Three Sons* (1960–1972) carries this paternal authority to its ultimate conclusion by making the father a single parent (a widower) with no wife to contest his opinions and decisions. Cooking and housekeeping in this show are performed by a "housewife" surrogate—a crusty old male curmudgeon.

It would be inaccurate and incomplete to suggest that the nuclear-family sitcom has always been founded on paternal authority. Indeed, the nuclear-family sitcom is populated with numerous instances of fathers who are incompetent dolts married to strong, reasonable matriarchs. According to Mary Desjardins, even the producers of *Father Knows Best* were unsure whether father always *did* know best and considered appending a question mark to the program's title, as in *Father Knows Best?*[1] And in a 1955 episode titled, "Father Is a Dope," the program directly parodies earlier family sitcoms with oafish fathers—such as *The Honeymooners* (1955–1956) and *The Life of Riley* (1949–1958). Further, it's easy to track fathers who are ineffectually clueless parents, at best, or those who are boorish louts, at worst, across many nuclear-family shows right up to the present day: Ozzie in *The Adventures of Ozzie and Harriet* (1952–1966), Fred in *The Flintstones* (1960–1966), Al in *Married… with Children* (1987–1997), Homer in

The Simpsons (1989–), Tim in *Home Improvement* (1991–1999), Doug in *The King of Queens* (1998–2007), Jim in *The World According to Jim* (2001–2009), and Peter on *Family Guy* (1998–). In many respects, these men behave like large infants and their wives are forced to take care of them as if they were children.

The model for the intrepid, formidable mother who holds the family together through tough times and dispenses wisdom to her children was established early on in one of the first radio sitcoms, *The Goldbergs* (1929–1946), which starred and was created and written by Gertrude Berg and went on to be a success in television, beginning in 1949 and running until 1957 (and not connected to the currently running *Goldbergs* program [2013–]). Molly Goldberg fits the ethnically defined gender role of the "Jewish mother" from the Bronx who speaks in dialect, is strong and nurturing, but can also be meddlesome. There is no doubt that she and her concerns are central to the storylines. Similarly, another early television series, *Mama* (1949–1956), revolves around a strong, ethnically identified matriarch—of a Norwegian immigrant family. Arguably the most notable matriarch in sitcom history, however, is the title character of *Roseanne* (1988–1997, 2018). Drawn from the 1980s stand-up comedy of Roseanne Barr, the character of Roseanne Conner takes an acerbic attitude toward motherhood and housework. She clearly rules her household, from her husband to her three children.

Barr produced and controlled the program and imbued it with the qualities of her stand-up act. In a particularly self-reflexive, two-part episode titled, "All About Rosey" (March 1, 1995), actors who had played mothers in previous sitcoms appear and are referred to as the "Sitcom Moms Welcome Wagon." The episode is structured as a "clip" show, with the Sitcom Moms discussing excerpts of *Roseanne* episodes (see Figure 3.1). After seeing the outrageous, un-motherly things that Roseanne does, one sitcom mom incredulously asks her, "You mean you're the boss in your own family?" She self-reflexively replies, "Yep, and I get all the good jokes too." Later, she continues, "The important thing is, on my show, I'm the boss, and father knows squat." When *Roseanne* was rebooted in 2018, it re-asserted the power

Figure 3.1 Actresses who played mothers on sitcoms appear in a self-reflexive episode of *Roseanne*: from left, June Lockhart, Isabel Sanford, Roseanne Barr, Barbara Billingsley, Pat Crowley, and Alley Mills.

of its matriarch and was once again closely associated with the off-screen persona of Roseanne Barr. Thus, when she tweeted a racist post that referred to an African-American political advisor (Valerie Jarrett) as the "baby" of *Planet of the Apes* (1968) and the Muslim Brotherhood, ABC promptly canceled the show. For better and worse, there have been few mothers who dominated their sitcom families as completely as Roseanne did hers. Still, it's important to recognize an element of dominating maternal authority that runs counter to the father-knows-best, paternal authority found in several sitcoms in the time between World War II and the social upheavals of the 1960s.

As far as gender roles go, a core "lesson" the nuclear-family sitcom teaches is that such roles are "natural" and necessary to the proper functioning of human society. Consider a familiar story premise of a wife or husband rebelling against their conventional gender role and how the story's conclusion reveals assumptions about the taken-for-granted nature of gender roles. These role-reversal episodes might have the wife try a job outside the home or the husband assume cooking and house-cleaning duties. Of course, they fail miserably at their attempts to assume a different gender role and happily return to "their place" at the episode's conclusion. Gender roles are thereby re-confirmed and normalized as if they were innate and always biologically determined. Viewed through the lens of the family sitcom's narrative problematic, we can see that the stability and security of the nuclear family are (repeatedly) threatened through this rejection of gender roles, but that threat is defused when the gender roles are reconfirmed at the end. Because of the nuclear-family sitcom's reliance on paternal authority, these role-reversal stories are particularly potent when the woman challenges patriarchal conventions and seeks work outside the home—often resuming a career that she had surrendered when they started a family—only to prove her incompetence and surrender her "foolish" career aspirations.

In the sitcom, in specific, and in American popular culture, in general, women are often forced to choose between a career and motherhood. The nuclear-family sitcom is predicated on a woman accepting the mother and housewife roles and thus these shows as they developed in the 1950s cannot endorse a woman choosing a career path. However, the wealth of storylines in which women reject housework and attempt to enter the workforce—as when Lucy tries to break into Ricky's nightclub act—suggests that there is an on-going ideological tension around this issue. When Ricky proclaims, "Lucy, you've got some explaining to do," he's typically upset with her rejecting her conventional gender roles as wife and mother and attempting to become a performer.

These role-reversal episodes lend themselves to against-the-grain readings and could be said to have a heightened sense of polysemy. That is, it might be supposed that some viewers relish the stories of female rebellion and are disappointed by the woman's subjugation at the conclusion. The meaning such viewers take away from these episodes is the pleasure and possibility of female rebellion, despite the evident lesson at the end. Over the course of the 1960s and beyond, the binary opposition of "career woman" vs. "housewife" began to erode. During the late 1960s and 1970s, more and more sitcom women were both raising children and working outside the home. This can manifest itself as women in white-collar jobs, such as lawyer Clair Huxtable (Phylicia Rashad) in *The Cosby Show* (1984–1992) and real estate agent Jules Cobb (Courteney Cox) in *Cougar Town* (2009–2015), or it can be represented as working-class women such as Frankie (Patricia Heaton) in *The Middle* and Linda (voiced by John Roberts) on *Bob's Burgers*. And, of course, since *The Mary Tyler Moore Show*'s debut in 1970, we've also seen career women who are relatively satisfied to be husband-less and childless, although the desire to obtain a husband and/or children seldom evaporates entirely (it ran from 1970 to 1977). The satisfaction, or lack thereof, that these women experience with their work life and home life commonly aligns with social-class divisions. The women in high-paying jobs have a much easier time balancing work and home and are represented as feeling rewarded in both private and public spheres. In contrast, working-class women are often trapped in dead-end jobs that they did not choose, but, rather, were taken out of financial desperation.

Parent–Child Relations (Generation Gaps)

The children in nuclear-family sitcoms are small engines of chaos who must be contained and trained to be productive members of society by their parents. Bart Simpson (*The Simpsons*) and the aptly named title character from *Dennis the Menace* (1959–1963) are two extreme examples of young troublemakers who disrupt the calm of sitcom households, but most of the children in nuclear-family sitcoms are far less anarchic than these two repeat offenders. The majority of nuclear-family sitcoms contain children that commit mischief that leads to "teachable moments." Many of sitcom children's indiscretions revolve around mastering aspects of gender roles. Girls are taught lessons about femininity: flirting and coquetry, homemaking skills, shopping and consumerism, compassion toward others, and so on. And boys are taught parallel lessons about masculinity: proper date behavior, competing fairly in sports, earning a living, acting ethically toward others (the "golden rule"), and so on. The specific lessons that are taught have evolved over the decades, but even in 21st-century sitcoms there are nuclear families in which parents are guiding their kids to adulthood—as can be seen in *The Bernie Mac Show* (2001–2006), *Modern Family*, *The Goldbergs*, and *Fresh Off the Boat*.

One interesting narrative device that runs through several nuclear-family sitcoms is shifting the perspective to that of the children. *Leave It to Beaver*, for example, has numerous scenes in which the parents are nowhere to be seen; often the parents have to deal with the consequences of these scenes after the fact. Even more pointed in their engagement of a child's perspective are series that are narrated by one of the children. The earliest instance of a child-narrated program might be *The Many Loves of Dobie Gillis*, premiering in 1959 and running until 1963, but we can also find instances of it in the 1960s (*Gidget* [1965–1966]), 1980s (*The Wonder Years*; although it's narrated by an adult version of one of the children [1988–1993]), 1990s (*Parker Lewis Can't Lose* [1990–1993]), and 2000s (*Malcolm in the Middle* [2000–2006]). In each instance, the child-narrator directly addresses the viewer, breaking the fourth wall. Their commentary is frequently a reflection on what the story has taught them about family, gender roles, and life in general. The lessons that are learned do transform over the decades, but they often reinforce traditional notions of masculinity and femininity. Adolescents Dobie (1950s) and Malcolm (2000s) tend to be perplexed about girls and what it means to be a man in ways that are much more similar than different. Further, sitcom narrators are particularly explicit in articulating the precise lessons they've learned. At the end of Dobie's and Malcolm's episodes, we customarily hear the teenager summarize what he has learned about family and becoming an adult.

Nuclear-family sitcoms have sought humor in the generation gap between children and parents. In the 1950s, this could be found in "hip" teenagers rebelling against their "square" parents—engaging with rock 'n' roll music and youthful hairstyle and fashion trends. Perhaps most notable of these early rock 'n' rollers was Ricky Nelson, whose substantial music career was launched by his real-life parents, Ozzie and

Harriet Nelson, on a 1957 episode of their sitcom, *The Adventures of Ozzie and Harriet*. Several episodes find the Nelsons bemused by their son's musical antics, but, in the end, they come to accept its energetic charm. Moreover, the Nelson parents' approval of rock 'n' roll in the late 1950s helped to make that musical form more acceptable to many older viewers. After all, if the all-American Nelson family could tolerate rock 'n' roll, then maybe it is not so evil after all.

There have been several generation-gap sitcoms since then, such as *Family Ties* (1982–1989), which developed humor from the incongruity of conservative children with liberal parents; but the most intense sitcom clash between the generations occurred in 1971 at a time when Americans were sharply stratified into generations and young persons proclaimed that one should not trust anyone over thirty. Exploiting this zeitgeist was *All in the Family* (1971–1979), a Norman Lear production about a bigoted, working-class father (Archie) and his long-suffering wife (Edith). Verbally battling with him are his liberal, 20-something daughter (Gloria) and her outspoken husband (Mike). Its narrative problematic engages with social issues each week—civil rights, protests against the Vietnam War, women's rights, the war on poverty, affirmative action, etc.—and positions Archie and Mike at odds with one another. Lear definitely brought a liberal perspective to the writing of the show, but these issues were (and are) so thorny that easy solutions seldom occur in individual episodes. There haven't been many sitcoms that so bluntly addressed the generation gap since *All in the Family*, but *The Carmichael Show* (2015–2017) recently mined similar sources of humor; however, it did so from an African-American perspective. These shows, with their adult children, are seldom the straightforward morality tales that scholars find in 1950s nuclear-family sitcoms, but they do often raise debates about the structure of the family in contemporary society.

Socioeconomic Class and the Suburban Lifestyle

Family sitcoms seldom focus on the extravagantly wealthy or the oppressively poor. Even when a parent works in show business or is a business executive, their presumed wealth is normalized and presented as if it is unremarkable. For example, the costly California homes in *Two and a Half Men* (2003–2015), *Modern Family*, and *The Bernie Mac Show* and the spacious Seattle apartment in *Frasier* (1993–2004) are never commented on within the shows as being expensive. These characters live in distinctly high-priced surroundings, but they do not recognize them as such. On the other end of the economic spectrum, unemployed parents who are living in abject poverty are also not common protagonists in family sitcoms. Virtually every family-sitcom parent has a job of some sort—even if it's an underpaying one that they detest. Sure, Fred Sanford is working in a junkyard (*Sanford and Son* [1972–1977]) and Christy is waiting tables (*Mom*), but at least they're all working. Thus, the family sitcom positions itself in an expanded center of the American economic spectrum, eliminating the extremes of wealth and poverty. From this position, it is imbued with taken-for-granted values about money and work.

In the family sitcom, money only becomes visible when it's difficult to obtain. And thus, economic class is virtually transparent unless the characters are working class. Shows in which the characters are well off do not typically generate storylines that deal with money concerns for the parents. In series as different as *Leave It to Beaver*, *Family Ties*, *The Cosby Show*, *Frasier*, *The Bernie Mac Show*, *Everybody Loves Raymond* (1996–2005), and *Modern Family*, the parents' comfortable financial situation is taken-for-granted and thus it's invisible and unacknowledged. These shows enact a specific sense of middle-class-ness in that their families are located in between the working class and the ostentatiously wealthy. Thus, they are "middle" class, even though their parents' presumed income might be well above the national average. As Nina Leibman observes regarding 1950s family sitcoms, "the middle class is held to be the most easy-going, happy, and principled of the various social strata—a class envied by both the wealthy (whose lives are prim and proper) and the lower classes (who are tired of dirt, junk, and cheese sandwiches)."[2] In other words, the middle class is presented as the most desirable class. Many storylines on these shows deal with the children's greed or rampant consumerism and offer homilies about the value of hard work and thrift. In these stories, it's good to have money, but not too much money. Conspicuous consumption—buying fancy cars or ostentatious clothes—is frequently critiqued or satirized in sitcoms of middle-class families.

What are typically referred to as middle-class family sitcoms are strikingly different from programs about working-class families. True, working-class families also exist in society's statistical "middle," but in the world of the sitcom these families are distinguished from so-called "middle-class" families because money is *always* an issue and the parents are constantly battling to stay afloat financially. *The Honeymooners* is an obvious early example of this, but financial difficulties are a key part of the narrative problematic of later shows such as *All in the Family*, *Sanford and Son*, *Married... with Children*, *Malcolm in the Middle*, *Bob's Burgers*, *Mom*, and *The Middle*. As you might imagine, these shows take a different attitude toward work than the shows of middle-class families do. In the middle-class families, the parents are professionals: doctors, lawyers, business executives, sports reporters, entertainers, and so on. Their jobs are vocations to which they feel called. For instance, in *The Cosby Show*, the father is a doctor and the mother is a lawyer and they both get much of their self-worth and identity from their professions. Because they enjoy their occupations, their jobs seldom result in narrative conflict and thus they are infrequently the subject of an episode's storylines. In *The Middle*, in contrast, the father works at a quarry and the mother has difficulty holding down a job—having sold cars and worked as a dental assistant. The parents of *The Middle* clearly see their jobs as menial obligations that produce paychecks that are insufficient for their household expenses. The mother getting fired from one crummy job or searching for another informs several episodes. And their inability to pay for appliance repair or other household maintenance is routinely commented on.

The discourses of class in American life go beyond income to include the locations where families establish themselves. Within the American sitcom, there are essentially three types of locales: urban, rural, and suburban. The early radio and TV series, *The Goldbergs*, draws much of its atmosphere from its setting in the Bronx. And the TV sitcom's first big success, *I Love Lucy*, was a notably urban show. Lucy and Ricky live in a modest New York apartment and their best friends drop in on them via the fire escape from upstairs. *The Honeymooners* has a similarly gritty and urban atmosphere. Its protagonist drives a bus and his best pal works in the sewer. What could be more urban? However, the sitcom came to prominence at the same time that a massive post-War American migration was happening: the move from urban centers to the suburbs. By the late 1950s, the bulk of family sitcoms were set in these new suburbs, but the families in such shows as *Leave It to Beaver* and *Father Knows Best* tended to be middle-class, not working-class. And so the suburbs that were represented in this time period were upscale ones where white lawyers and doctors took their children to escape the "dangers" of city centers and their diverse racial and ethnic composition. As Jeffrey Sconce contends,

> Throughout the 1950s and into the 1960s, television developed a highly codified series of narrative conventions to represent this emerging suburban ideal, constructing a middle class utopia of labor-saving appliances, manicured lawns, and spacious architecture, all designed to showcase the white suburban housewife as the ultimate symbol of material success and domestic bliss.[3]

Around 1960, a third type of sitcom location emerged to compete with the urban vs. suburban opposition. The so-called "rural" sitcoms of the time mostly transpired in an idealized small-town America, where 19th-century ideals of community and social customs could be revived. *The Andy Griffith Show* was the most culturally significant sitcom of a trend that included *Petticoat Junction*, *Green Acres*, and two shows from the late 1950s, *Lassie* (1954–1973) and *The Real McCoys*. *The Beverly Hillbillies* is often grouped together with these rural sitcoms; even though it's set in a wealthy area of Los Angeles, its central family is transplanted from the rural Ozarks. In fact, *Petticoat Junction*,

Green Acres, and *The Beverly Hillbillies* all exist in the same television universe (on CBS, as did *The Andy Griffith Show*) and characters occasionally cross over from one show to the other. These shows' narrative problematics often pitched a representative of "modern" life against the "traditional" values of small-town America. Outsiders frequently come to town and disrupt the town's harmony and stability. These traditional values reinforce constrictive gender roles, where men are expected to enact a certain type of masculinity and women a certain type of femininity. Of course, LGBTQ individuals are invisible in these narrative worlds, or at least they are closeted and not identified as LGBTQ. The nuclear family is again the ideal against which all other families are seen to be aberrations. And "city slickers" are shown to have compromised moral systems where it's acceptable to steal, lie, and consume alcohol to excess. The world of the CBS rural shows is also notably white, Anglo-Saxon, and Christian. Very few non-white, ethnic, or non-Christian characters enter this universe. Such characters aren't disruptive of these small towns; they just do not exist.

CBS summarily canceled all its rural shows around 1970. Despite their continuing popularity, they appealed to an older demographic that wasn't valued by the network. In their stead debuted shows about urban and suburban families that were more connected to the issues of the times—sitcoms such as *All in the Family*, *Maude*, *Sanford and Son*, *The Jeffersons* (1975–1985), and so on. Hardly any family sitcoms have been set in small towns like Mayberry and Hooterville since the 1960s. Further, the meanings attached to urban and suburban lifestyles have shifted since the 1950s and templates like the urban *I Love Lucy* and the suburban *Leave It to Beaver* have evolved. First, urban settings have shown greater variety in family sitcoms of recent decades. *The Jeffersons*, *The Cosby Show*, *Mad About You* (1992–1999), *Frasier*, and the MTM Productions *Rhoda* (1974–1978) and *Phyllis* (1975–1977), which were spun off the single-girl-in-the-city show, *The Mary Tyler Moore Show*, are all set in urban environments that are less sordid and more benign than the world of *The Honeymooners*. Most of these shows center on "middle-class" families, in the sense that I have used it earlier, who are able to live comfortable, but not extravagant, lives in their respective cities.

Second, since 1970, the distinction between the urban and the suburban has blurred, and the social status associated with the suburbs has diminished. *All in the Family*, *The King of Queens*, *Roseanne*, *That 70s Show* (1998–2006), and *Mike & Molly* (2010–2016), among others, place their families in houses—not apartments—in metropolitan areas. These working-class families definitely represent an urban experience with greater diversity of races and other demographics, but their homes and neighborhoods are structured more like suburbs than the apartment lifestyle found in a city center. Further, today's suburbs—in sitcoms and in real life—are no longer exclusive enclaves of the wealthy. The original suburban planning of the 1950s eventually evolved to include modestly priced developments designed for working-class families. Twenty-first-century family sitcoms like *Malcolm in the Middle* and *The Middle* can be set in rather indeterminate neighborhoods that might be suburbs or might be small towns or might be part of general urban sprawl. The distinctive middle-class suburbs that seemed to express post-War ideals so effectively are seldom seen in today's sitcoms. In fact, one recent series, *Suburgatory* (2011–2014), specifically satirizes that utopian view of the suburbs by suggesting that suburban life is actually a purgatory of sanitized, too-perfect behavior.

To summarize the family sitcom's attitude toward social class and the suburbs, we can see that it avoids extremes in its representation of family finances—ignoring both the extraordinarily wealthy and the extraordinarily impoverished. It features families that are in the center of America's social classes. The so-called "middle class" in this context refers to financially stable parents and storylines that extol "American" values of conventional gender roles (men work outside the home; women work inside), thrift, hard work, obedient children, and ethical behavior. In contrast, the sitcom's "working class" encompasses families that have jobs, but can't seem to climb that next rung of America's social ladder to enjoy the fruits of the middle class. Instead, life for them is a constant, but humorous, financial struggle.

These two predominant sitcom classes play out their narratives in settings that are either urban, suburban, or rural. Over the history of the sitcom, these settings have served different purposes, but, in the end, the urban, suburban, and rural have blended in various ways.

The Non-Traditional Family: Single Parents, Uncles, and Aunts

To this point, I have focused on family sitcoms that rely on the traditional nuclear-family structure: wife, husband, and children. However, the genre has long included other forms of parenting. Most notably, this has centered on single parents, but there have also been comically blended families (peaking with *The Brady Bunch* [1969–1974]), husband and wives without children (e.g., *The Honeymooners*) and other non-traditional family groupings. The non-nuclear family can be traced back to at least 1941 on radio and the popular sitcom, *The Great Gildersleeve*, which was broadcast on radio from 1941 to 1957 and had a relatively short run on television in 1955. As is often the case with sitcoms of non-parents raising children, the program centers on a man taking care of a sibling's children, specifically, his niece and nephew. The same premise can be seen more recently in *The Bernie Mac Show*. Sitcoms with absent spouses have been plentiful as well. Until 1962, those absent spouses were always dead and not missing due to divorce. The follow-up to *I Love Lucy*, which was titled, *The Lucy Show*, broke new ground that year by introducing the first sitcom divorcée. The show featured two single mothers, Lucy and Viv, but only Viv is divorced. According to Lori Landay, "the creative team decided to make Lucy a widow because they feared the audience would reject the idea of a Lucy who had divorced Ricky [her spouse in real-life and on *I Love Lucy*]."[4]

We can identify many single-parent sitcoms. Single-father series include *Bachelor Father* (1957–1962), *Silver Spoons* (1982–1986), *Diff'rent Strokes* (1978–1986), *Family Affair* (1966–1971), *The Courtship of Eddie's Father* (1969–1972), *Full House* (1987–1995), *My Three Sons*, *The Nanny* (1993–1999), *One on One* (2001–2006), *Two and a Half*

Men, and *Louie* (2010–2015). And single-mother series include *The Partridge Family* (1970–1974), *One Day at a Time* (1975–1984), *Murphy Brown*, *Julia* (1968–1971), *The Ghost and Mrs. Muir* (1968–1970), *Alice* (1976–1985), *Good Times* (1974–1979), *What's Happening!!* (1976–1979), *Kate & Allie* (1984–1989), *The New Adventures of Old Christine* (2006–2010), and *Better Things* (2016–). Recently, four single parents were brought together in a single program, bluntly titled, *Single Parents* (2018–). And to create a situation of a single mother paired with a single father, *Sister, Sister* (1994–1999) presents the improbable circumstance of a single mother of one twin and the widowed father of another being brought together years after the twins had been separated and adopted.

The variety of family structures in these single-parent sitcoms indicates, on the one hand, a healthy diversity in the representation of family on television. The constrictive emphasis on the nuclear family in 1950s family sitcoms certainly could not be sustained during the 1960s and 1970s when American families looked less and less like the universes of *Leave It to Beaver* and *The Donna Reed Show* (1958–1966). Something had to change as the family changed. But, on the other hand, non-nuclear families are often the targets of superiority humor. That is, their humor is supposed to arise from what single parents lack and the ways they are inferior to conventional husband–wife families. They become cautionary tales of the supposed dangers of a single-parent lifestyle. Thus, you have episodes about single fathers trying to cope with their daughters' first menstrual period and single mothers being embarrassed when they bring home a date and have to introduce him to their children, who invariably hate them. The humor here is based on how these parents deviate from the norm of nuclear-family parents and are thus implicitly inferior to them. If these parents weren't single, the lesson seems to be, they would not get into these predicaments.

Single-parent families also disrupt aspects of the gender roles in nuclear families as they are represented in sitcoms. Unlike nuclear-family mothers, the single mother must work outside the home in order to earn a living for herself and her children. Similarly, the single father must feed and clothe his children and take care of their home in a way that nuclear-family fathers do not. Thus, mother and father must each adopt roles that are incongruous with their nuclear-family counterparts. This can bring the conflict between work and family into sharp relief as each gender struggles to fill a role for which society deems them unfit: the employed mother and the home-making father. Some sitcoms circumnavigate these incongruities by incorporating a surrogate spouse. This is particularly common in single-father sitcoms, where a character performs housewife duties: e.g., the butler in *Family Affair*, the irascible cook in *My Three Sons*, and the title character from *The Nanny*. The fathers in these shows are liberated from maintaining a home and children and can more easily work at their jobs outside the home and might even romantically pursue women. A double standard exists here, however, because single mothers in sitcoms have far fewer options for surrogate spouses—a husband substitute that, among other masculine services, disciplines the children and provides money for rent and groceries. Indeed, a mother who accepts money from a man other than her husband is represented as a prostitute. Thus, in the world of sitcoms, single mothers are forced to go to work outside the home and humor is generated from the conflict between work and home while single fathers have many more options and the work/home conflict is often moot.

Case Study: *The Andy Griffith Show*

The Andy Griffith Show arrived at the tail end of the post-World War II baby boom, just as the 1960s were beginning. It virtually spanned that turbulent decade—running for eight successful seasons, from 1960 to 1968. To many observers, the series appeared to wholly retreat from the issues of the day. For instance, despite being set in a Southern town called Mayberry, which loosely resembled star Andy Griffith's hometown of Mount Airy, North Carolina, there is a marked absence of African Americans. North Carolina was the site of significant civil-rights actions during the year that the series debuted, including protests against whites-only lunch counters, but no mention of them or other civil-rights controversies was ever made on *The Andy Griffith Show*.[5] The whiteness of Mayberry was so obvious that the NAACP brought the matter to CBS's attention in 1966. The producers' token response was the casting of its first credited black actor, Rockne Tarkington, as a football coach. Despite the series' willful disinterest in Southern race relations, it is inaccurate to contend that it was untouched by all 1960s social issues. In fact, numerous storylines deal with outsiders disrupting Mayberry's bucolic serenity with their modern-world values: feminism, upper-class greed and ostentation, an obsession with work and social climbing, sexual "liberation," alcohol abuse, and so on. It is the conflict between traditional values and modern values that makes *The Andy Griffith Show* a particularly illuminating case study for the sitcom's representation of family.

The Andy Griffith Show's Logline, Its Narrative Problematic

The logline for *The Andy Griffith Show* might have been: "a small-town sheriff solves predicaments involving his son and the town's citizens." In other words, the series' fundamental, repeatable narrative problematic involves a disruption of Mayberry's equilibrium, which must be resolved by an episode's end. At the program's core is the Taylor family: the principal protagonist, sheriff Andy Taylor, a widower; his young son, Opie (Ron Howard); and his Aunt Bee (Frances Bavier), who serves as their cook and housekeeper. The rural beauty of Mayberry and the show's focus on a father–son bond are encapsulated in a memorable opening credit sequence showing Andy and Opie ambling down a country road, fishing poles on their shoulders, toward a lake in the pines—all accompanied by a jaunty, whistled theme song titled, "The Fishin' Hole" (see Figure 3.2).

The inhabitants of Mayberry extend the Taylors' family. Most significant of these is Andy's deputy sheriff and friend, Barney Fife (Don Knotts), but recurring characters also include the barber, Floyd Lawson (Howard McNear), service station attendants, Gomer and Goober Pyle (Jim Nabors and George Lindsey, respectively), and the town drunk, Otis Campbell (Hal Smith). Out of the series' 249

COMEDY, FAMILY, AND SMALL TOWNS

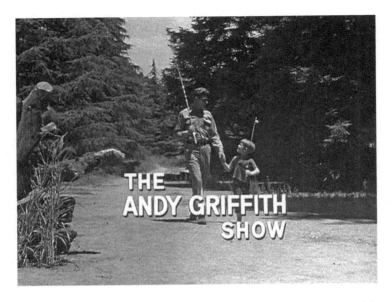

Figure 3.2 Andy and Opie Taylor stroll down a country road, while accompanied by a whistled song ("The Fishin' Hole"), during the homespun credits for *The Andy Griffith Show*.

episodes, many deal with incidents wholly contained within this small, slow-paced environment. The action was dependably mundane, as this typical dialogue illustrates:

Barney: You know what I think I'm gonna' do?
Andy: What?
Barney: I'm gonna' go home, have me a little nap, and then go over to Thelma Lou's and watch a little TV.
Andy: Mmm-hmm.
Barney: Yeah, I believe that's what I'll do. Go home ... have a nap ... and then over to Thelma Lou's for TV.
Andy: Mmm.
Barney: Yep, that's the plan. Home ... little nap ... then ...

Other narrative examples include "The Loaded Goat," in which a goat eats dynamite and Andy and Barney must neutralize it before it levels Mayberry. And in "Opie the Birdman," Opie accidentally kills a mother bird with a slingshot and Andy has him care for the orphaned baby birds. Tales of small-town life such as these define the show's enduring appeal as its fans frequently speak of how it evokes earlier, presumably simpler and less stressful times. Moreover, episodes such as "Opie the Birdman" clearly operate as homilies about responsibility and other traditional "American" values.

However, *The Andy Griffith Show*'s predicaments are not contained within Mayberry's town limits. Its inhabitants must also contend with a remarkable number of intrusions from outside their small town. These intruders often come from larger metropolises (such as Raleigh, North Carolina) and carry with them modern values that threaten Mayberry's traditional values. A variety of city slickers, as well as con artists, hoboes, and even dangerous bank robbers, find their way to the town, wreaking large and small havoc. Not all of Mayberry's intruders are more urbane than the locals, however. Its citizens are also contrasted with backwoods, "mountain" folk who are even more removed from contemporary life than Mayberry's citizens. Specifically, Andy has to contend with the Darlings, a mountain family whose bluegrass music is often featured (performed by the Dillards), and Ernest T. Bass (Howard Morris), a wild mountain man who is even more unruly and disruptive than the Darlings. The Darlings and Ernest T. have their own social conventions, many of which don't suit Mayberry propriety. Ernest T., for instance, is fond of throwing rocks through windows for simple amusement. Of course, this does not sit well with the respectable citizens of the town. As Barney exclaims, "He's a nut!" Thus, small-town Mayberry is positioned in between two cultural extremes: the modern city and the Appalachian hills.

Family Discourse: Gender Roles

Viewing *The Andy Griffith Show* through the lens of American discourses about the family and how they are represented in the sitcom, we should first address how gender roles are handled in the show. As explained earlier, in the battle of the sexes, sitcoms have hosted stories of both paternal authority and maternal authority. Does *The Andy Griffith Show* tend toward the father-controlled family of, say, *Leave It to Beaver*, or the mother-controlled family of, say, *Roseanne*? The answer initially seems simple, because Andy is in near-total control of his household. His wife is deceased at the start of the series and the one maternal figure within his family circle, Aunt Bee, is in no position to challenge his authority over his son, Opie. A matronly older woman, Aunt Bee is not literally a domestic servant, but, in terms of gender roles, she largely functions as one—cooking and cleaning for Andy and Opie. Although she occasionally offers advice regarding child-rearing, Andy is never obliged to take it. Moreover, as sheriff of Mayberry he is also in a position of authority over the town's inhabitants, who sometimes squabble like young children. He resolves arguments and passes judgment during disputes in a manner that recalls the actions of the wisest fathers of 1950s sitcoms.

Conventional family gender roles are affirmed in many episodes. The series offers two episodes that are overtly in the tradition of sitcom role-reversals (discussed earlier). "Andy and Opie, Housekeepers" (March 13, 1961) begins with Aunt Bee chiding the men of the family for living so slovenly. Father and son are soon pressed into service in the "feminine" role of housekeepers when Aunt Bee leaves town to take care of an ailing relative. They quickly fail in this role, but when Aunt Bee phones to say she'll be home early, Andy and Opie hurriedly put the place in order. As they survey the tidied-up living room, however, Andy realizes that by seeming to usurp Aunt Bee's role as housekeeper, he and Opie "are going to give Aunt Bee the feeling that she ain't needed." Consequently, they hastily mess the house up again. There are some additional complications, but eventually Aunt Bee finds Opie's disheveled room and dirty dishes in the sink and exclaims, "You're helpless, absolutely helpless. If it wasn't for me, this house wouldn't be fit to live in!" An episode from the second season, with the similar title of "Andy and Opie, Bachelors" (October 22, 1962), uses the same narrative device of Aunt Bee being called out of town and Andy and Opie being forced to assume feminine roles around the house. In this case, Andy makes a disastrous attempt at cooking and is rescued by his girlfriend, Peggy McMillan. She sees Andy's badly burned chicken and offers to cook dinner: "Now, you just go out on the porch and get the chicken smoke out of your lungs and I'll call you when supper's ready. ... You're not imposing on me, it'd be fun for me." She adds later that she "feels sorry for a couple of helpless bachelors." As with other role-reversal sitcom episodes, gender roles in the family are affirmed at the end. And women, in particular, are shown to relish stereotypical roles in which they serve helpless men. These episodes suggest that women will feel unneeded and unwanted if they are not taking care of men and that cooking and cleaning are pleasurable for them. If Andy and Opie had been successful as housekeepers or cooks, it would have disturbed the taken-for-granted gender roles of the nuclear family of this time period.

Andy's paternal authority is not without challenges, however. In fact, it is questioned during his attempts to find a romantic partner and wife. He remains single throughout the initial run of *The Andy Griffith Show*, but he is romantically linked with several women, and in the spin-off, *Mayberry R.F.D.* (1968–1971), he marries one of them, Helen Crump (Aneta Corsaut), in the first episode. Helen and an earlier girlfriend of Andy's, Ellie Walker (Elinor Donahue), are examples of how characters from outside of Mayberry can agitate the town's inhabitants and challenge their values. Neither of them is a Mayberry native. And, notably, Helen and Ellie are both women with careers—a schoolteacher and a pharmacist, respectively—and thus are seldom shown performing stereotypical "feminine" duties such as cooking, cleaning, or taking care of children. And both Helen and Ellie directly dispute Andy's paternalistic attitude. In fact, Andy meets these women through quarrels and misunderstandings after they move to town. In each of these initial disputatious encounters, Andy must recognize that his judgement is mistaken and accept Helen/Ellie's perspective.

Furthermore, Ellie is featured in an episode where she advocates for women's rights and rejects the stereotype of women solely as homemakers. In "Ellie for Council" (December 12, 1960), she is irked by Andy dismissing the idea of a woman running for political office and so she mounts a campaign for election to the town council. A Mayberry outsider who comes to town to help her uncle, she represents the women's movement that would blossom later in the decade, but is not generally evident in Mayberry. Interestingly, her disruptive, out-of-towner discourse finds some support within the episode. After Andy hears his son and other town members mouthing demeaning comments about the inferiority of women, he changes his mind, supports Ellie's candidacy, and thereby validates the (mildly) liberal value of women being worthy of public office. The episode does not specify whether or not she won, but later episodes show her serving on the town council. Thus, *The Andy Griffith Show*, as with many network-era sitcoms, could support a multiplicity of interpretations—in this case, both sexist and anti-sexist, or both patriarchal and matriarchal. In terms of family discourses, "Ellie for Council" specifically illuminates how the seemingly unassailable 1950s assumption that women could only be housewives was beginning to crack and fissure in the early 1960s. Significantly, this episode also illustrates how Andy can function as an in-between figure. As sheriff, he literally arbitrates between opposing parties. As an ideological figure, he can also exist between antithetical values and either shift from one side to the other (as in this episode) or somehow reconcile those two sides.

Family Discourse: Generation Gaps

The Andy Griffith Show is renowned for the close bond between father and son and the homespun wisdom that Andy imparts to Opie in the series' numerous one-on-one conversations. Opie—who ages from 6 to 14 over the course of the series—is not nearly as disruptive as the previously mentioned Bart Simpson and the title character of *Dennis the Menace*. In most regards, he's an obedient child, but Andy is a rather firm disciplinarian and Opie's featured storylines are still based on trouble within the family sphere. These storylines result in "teachable moments" that reinforce middle-class values of the early 1960s.

I previously discussed how "Opie the Birdman," in which his careless use of a slingshot results in a mother bird's death, provides Andy with an opportunity to instruct Opie about taking responsibility for one's actions, especially one's errors in judgment. Other episodes rather pointedly teach Opie about ideologically loaded subjects such as socioeconomic class, the Puritan work ethic, and gender roles.

Parent-child conflict is illustrated, for example, in "Opie and the Spoiled Kid" (February 18, 1963). While performing the chore of cleaning out the garage, Opie meets Arnold Winkler (Ronnie Dapo), a boy who has just arrived from the big city (Raleigh) who tells Opie he's "been around." He has a fancy bike that he rides on Mayberry's sidewalks, heedless of the danger to pedestrians. He boasts to Opie that he didn't have to save up for this luxurious $75 bike and doesn't do any chores at home, unlike Opie who only earns a 25 cent weekly allowance in exchange for a variety of tasks. Opie is fascinated by this openly rebellious boy and pays rapt attention as Arnold lists his disobedience techniques: holding his breath, crying, stamping his feet, and throwing himself on the floor in a full tantrum. Opie goes to the courthouse and requests a father–son talk, asking, "Are there rules for how a pa should treat his son if he's a kid?" Andy explains his take on child rearing and the Puritan work ethic:

> There are no rules for pa's and sons. ... Each mother or father raises his boy or girl, as the case may be, the way that he thinks is best. And I think it's best for you to get a quarter and work for it. You see, when you give something—in this instance, cleaning the garage—and you get something in return, like a quarter, that's the greatest feeling in the world.

Later, Opie demands a raise in his allowance and when Andy denies it, he works his way through each of Arnold's techniques. Andy ignores all of them and Opie finally gives up his attempts at defiance.

Soon after, Arnold gets his comeuppance. He drags his father to the courthouse where his bicycle has been impounded. It becomes evident that his father has coddled him when he refers to his son as a "sensitive child." Andy lectures him, "If we don't teach children to live in society today, what's going to happen to them when they grow up?" Andy suggests that if the father won't take responsibility for his son's actions that he might have to lock him (the father) up. This sparks a tantrum from Arnold who shouts, "Go on, Dad! Show them they can't push me around! Go on, put him in jail. He won't care!" The father looks at his son, shocked, and realizes how he's been spoiling him. He tells Andy he wants the bike back so that he can take it from Arnold and sell it. Andy tells the father there's a "woodshed" out back he can use to continue his conversation with his son. After they leave, Opie, who has witnessed the whole exchange, asks if Arnold is going to be spanked. Andy says, "Don't you think he deserves it?" Opie's answer is politic: "I don't want to say. After all, he is one of my own kind." The scene then fades to black.

The overt message of the episode is quite blunt: unruly, rebellious children must be physically punished to be brought under control. It advocates for a method of discipline that is currently discredited within most, but not all, segments of American society. However, *The Andy Griffith Show* as a whole advocates for reasoning with children over corporal punishment. In fact, Opie is never spanked on screen, although there is at least one instance where Andy tells Aunt Bee that Opie has "got to get a whipping."[6] Instead, dozens of episodes feature earnest, productive discussions between father and son about proper behavior, which Opie usually takes to heart. The episode arrives at this disciplinary method as a way to reinforce an economic principle of capitalism: there is no reward without hard work. As Andy tells Opie, earning money for work you've done is the "greatest feeling in the world." At the very end of the episode, Opie tells his father that he's going to get right back to work on his chores so that he can save up enough money for a bike. Lesson learned.

As a second instance of how the series handles issues involving children and develops them into morality plays, consider "Opie's Girlfriend" (September 12, 1966), in which the battle of the sexes takes center stage. Andy's girlfriend, Helen's niece, Cynthia (Mary Anne Durkin), is yet another out-of-towner who generates trouble for a Mayberry resident. When she visits town, 12-year-old Opie is coerced into playing with her even though he disdains girls: "If I got to play with a girl on Saturday, I'd just as soon be in school!" He quickly learns that she is athletically superior to him, and he is humiliated that a girl can run faster than him and is better at football. They get into an argument during a touch-football game and she gives him a black eye. When Opie's injury is revealed to Aunt Bee and Andy, Andy assumes that he got it "protecting a girl" and Opie doesn't correct him. Parallel to this boy–girl dispute in the A story is a B story of an incident between the grown-ups. Helen beats Andy at bowling and he is a poor loser, claiming that he was defeated because he didn't have his own personal bowling shoes. Obviously, he is also chagrined to have lost a physical contest to a woman.

In this instance, a father–son talk only makes the situation worse, because after their conversation Andy is indignant that Cynthia took advantage of Opie's supposed chivalry and violated the conventions of femininity when she punched him. The resolution of the conflict falls to Helen and an aunt–niece talk:

Cynthia:	Why do boys always think they have to be better at everything than girls?
Helen:	I don't know, they're just funny that way.
Helen (later):	It has something to do with male ego. ... Down through the centuries, man's been provider for the family, protector of women ... I guess he naturally feels he just has to be stronger and do things better than women. I was just thinking, maybe it's not a bad idea for us to help them feel that way.
Cynthia:	You mean, even when he isn't?
Helen (smiling):	Even when he isn't.

Cynthia puts the advice into action in the following scene. First, we see her skillfully roller-skating through Opie's neighborhood, where she notices him on his front lawn. Before Opie can see that she is an accomplished skater, she takes off her skates, approaches him, and, feigning inferiority, asks him to teach her to skate. Opie is happy to show his superior knowledge and explains the principles of skating to her. For him, the incident reinforces his patriarchal view that girls are inferior to boys. And the clear over-arching lesson of the episode is that girls/women must fulfill the conventional stereotype of physical inferiority to boys/men and stoke the "male ego." However, there is an opening for an against-the-grain reading here. The female figures in this episode are not just physically superior. They're also more intelligent, empathetic, and better understand "human nature." The male figures, in contrast, are deluded buffoons who do not recognize their own limitations. A feminist might negotiate a reading of the show, then, that values the women's intelligence and physical strength—which dominates 90% of the episode—and she might thus dismiss the stereotypical conclusion.

Opie's struggles with the work ethic and the opposite sex are those that 1960s television expected from a pre-teen boy and do not engage with the full-blown generation gap that was present a few years later in *All in the Family*. However, toward the end of *The Andy Griffith Show*'s run, there are some intimations of a more rebellious side of Opie. In "Opie's Group" (November 6, 1967), he joins a rock band, the Sound Committee, that practices in the Taylor family garage. Aunt Bee is appalled and Andy, who is often featured playing folk tunes on an acoustic guitar, is baffled by this strange, loud music. Of course, Opie's new musical interests lead him to neglect his studies, as well as to begin talking like a hipster. The older generation is annoyed to hear words like "groovy" and "cool" coming from young Opie, and Andy is angered by Opie's lax attitude toward his studies. Once again, *The Andy Griffith Show* resolves its conflict through a reconciliation of opposites. Much like "Ellie for Council," this episode solves the conflict between modern culture and traditional culture by positioning a character in between the two extremes. In this case, it's not Andy, but, instead, Aunt Bee's friend, Clara, who is the in-between figure. She attends a practice of the Sound Committee in the Taylor living room and, as Andy puts it, "She goes right over to the enemy." That is, she starts playing piano with the group. But then Andy finds out that she has agreed to be the group's manager and will thereby keep music in perspective for them—presumably preventing Opie from neglecting his studies again. Hearing this news, Andy admits his parenting mistake and thanks Clara for setting him straight. The episode's tag then has Opie practicing *acoustic* guitar and talking about music with Andy. Once more, their bond has been reestablished. Thus, we can see again how *The Andy Griffith Show*'s narrative problematic introduces a disruptive outside force from modern culture, but then neutralizes the threat that such a force might generate. In "Opie's Group," the equilibrium of Mayberry is momentarily disturbed by rock music and the counterculture, but at the episode's conclusion traditional values are able to accommodate that disturbance.

Family Discourse: Socioeconomic Class and the Suburban Lifestyle

The Andy Griffith Show's mise-en-scene differs markedly from the new-suburban shows that began in the 1950s and overlapped with it in the first years of the new decade, such as *Father Knows Best*, *Leave It to Beaver*, and *The Donna Reed Show*. Those latter shows are distinctly suburban, and Mayberry is distinctly "small town" as it exists in the American imaginary, but, practically speaking, both suburban and small-town lifestyles define themselves in contrast to urban life. They offer slightly differently inflected ways to escape from factory jobs, crime-related violence, drug abuse and alcoholism (although Mayberry features a cheerful, self-jailing "town drunk" and colorful moonshiners), minorities and LGBTQ individuals, and so on. Thus, *The Andy Griffith Show* is much closer to *Leave It to Beaver* than it is to *All in the Family*, which debuted three years after *The Andy Griffith Show* ended.

It is not surprising, therefore, that *The Andy Griffith Show* espouses middle-class values similar to those I discussed earlier in the 1950s family sitcoms. And it achieves its middle-class-ness in much the same way. Once again, the central family in a sitcom is neither working class nor extravagantly wealthy. By virtue of Andy's position as sheriff, the Taylors are in a social stratum above the town's working class (service-station attendants and barbers) and the semi-primitive mountain folk (the Darling family and Earnest T. Bass), but they are positioned below affluent individuals such as the Winkler family in "Opie and the Spoiled Kid" and various narcissistic snobs who blow through town, usually speeding in their too-expensive cars. Like suburban, middle-class sitcom families and unlike urban, working-class sitcom families, the Taylors are seldom in financial difficulties or, indeed, even discuss money unless it's to teach Opie the value of earning it through hard work. Moreover, Andy's middle-class status is reflected in his romantic life. In several episodes, he is aggressively pursued by mountain woman Charlene Darling (Maggie Peterson), but her infatuation makes Andy very uncomfortable, and clearly she is not a good match for him because she is socially inferior.

On the other end of the social spectrum from Charlene is Andy's short-lived girlfriend, Peggy McMillan (Joanna Moore). In an episode tellingly titled, "Andy's Rich Girlfriend" (October 8, 1962), Andy discovers that Peggy comes from a wealthy family. Barney is disgusted by the upper class and lectures Andy at length about "the rich," who, he cautions, are born with a "silver spoon in their hand," coddled by French-speaking nannies, and given bicycles of "solid chromium, with at least six or seven red reflectors" before they are sent off to "refinishing school." He's certain that "To [Peggy] you are, Joe Ordinary, just a toy to enjoy for a while." Although Barney's rant is undercut through humorous incongruities in mangled phrases such as "silver spoon in the hand" and although Andy initially refuses to accept Barney's perspective, class lines are later clearly drawn when Andy and Peggy go on a date and he shudders at the thought of eating escargot ("Snails?," he asks warily) and is intimidated by her worldly knowledge of Paris and New Orleans. Andy knows his place and begins avoiding Peggy. It appears, then, that the episode is endorsing Barney's perspective that the rich are different from common folk like him and Andy and, further, that they are effete snobs and should be shunned. The episode's conclusion, however, validates the middle class in a slightly different manner. Andy and Peggy run into each other at the lake, where she is skipping stones. She turns the tables on Andy and accuses him of being a "snob": "You certainly are. Just because my father's rich, you're snubbing me." After pointing out Andy's class prejudice, she then extols the virtues of small-town life and how superior it is to "Paris, New Orleans, wherever." Andy accepts her explanation and the scene/episode ends with them leaving the lake arm-in-arm. The moral of the episode is clear: once the wealthy experience the pleasures of middle-class, small-town life, they will recognize its moral superiority to a life of extravagances in exotic locations.

The Andy Griffith Show Case Study: Conclusion

In many respects, *The Andy Griffith Show* exemplifies the sitcom genre in its purest form: a clear narrative problematic, a segmented episode structure, middle-class characters and setting, a functional single-camera visual style, a laugh track, and humor stemming from highly conventionalized tropes. The series' conventional nature enables us to see just how the genre handles discourses surrounding American life in the middle of the 20th century. In this case study, I have focused on gender roles, the parent–child relationship, socioeconomic class, and the small-town lifestyle. In each instance, we've seen how a sitcom can function as a morality play that advocates for certain meanings surrounding ideologically loaded concepts such as masculinity, femininity, child rebellion/discipline, and money. But we've also seen how network-era sitcoms permit a certain, limited polysemy—a multiplicity of meanings. Yes, *The Andy Griffith Show* does mostly adopt a patriarchal view of family and the relationships between men and women, but it also allows for against-the-grain readings that value how unruly women disrupt that patriarchy. This polysemy was essential to the sitcom at a time when the Big Three networks cast a wide, inclusive net over all viewers all the time. In the next chapter on sex and gender, I examine many closely related discourses and, for my case study, I look at a program, *Sex and the City* (1998–2004), that aired on a premium cable channel with a much narrower audience than *The Andy Griffith Show* had on CBS.

Notes

1 Mary Desjardins, *Father Knows Best* (Detroit, MI: Wayne State University Press, 2015), 26.
2 Nina C. Liebman, *Living Room Lectures: The Fifties Family in Film and Television* (Austin, TX: University of Texas Press, 1995), 245.
3 Jeffrey Sconce, "The Outer Limits of Television," in *The Revolution Wasn't Televised: Sixties Television and Social Conflict*, Lynn Spigel and Michael Curtin, eds. (London: Routledge, 1997), 33. Quoted in Joanne Morreale, "Dreams and Disruption in the Fifties Sitcom," *Journal of e-Media Studies* 4, No. 1 (2015).
4 Lori Landay, *I Love Lucy* (Detroit, MI: Wayne State University Press, 2010), 105.
5 Non-violent protests were mounted in Greensboro, North Carolina, about 60 miles from Mount Airy, from February to July 1960.
6 In the episode, "The Keeper of the Flame" (January 8, 1962), Andy incorrectly believes Opie is responsible for setting a barn on fire. When Opie refuses to explain what happened, Andy threatens the punishment and then the scene ends.

4

COMEDY, SEX, AND GENDER IDENTITY

Sex and comedy make a potent cultural combination. Along with other bodily functions, sex is frequently a social taboo, something that just isn't talked about in polite society. Since it is hidden and stifled, it commonly escapes its repression in humor, where society's forbidden topics tend to dwell. Sex might, for example, be the subject of a smutty joke that is told in a locker room, nervously giggled about at a slumber party, or part of a nightclub comedian's adults-only routine. Grotesque sexuality—along with excrement—are key elements of psychoanalyst Sigmund Freud's theories of the subconscious and philosopher Mikhail Bakhtin's idea of carnivalesque excesses. And both theorists contend that comedy provides a way to release social tensions that build up around sexuality. Television comedy provides a fascinating window into American attitudes toward sexuality and allied notions of gender identities, because for many years the industry strictly restricted *any* references to sexual activity (especially by women) and promoted restrictive gender norms that subordinated women; but as the women's movement began to have an impact on American sexual mores in the 1960s, television had to adjust to those norms' evolution. It had to accommodate the "liberation" of women and the modification of gender roles.

This chapter remains alert to television's polysemy, to its ability to signify a multiplicity of meanings, when representing sexuality in comic situations. However, we must also recognize that network television's first two decades (and more) produced comedies that were largely informed by heterosexual, patriarchal, and cisnormative discourses. That is, women's roles in these comedies were presumed to be in pursuit of heterosexual romance, subservient to men, and free of transgender blurring of the lines between femininity and masculinity. These are the rigid gender structures of the 1950s that I discussed in the previous section on the family, which, with notable exceptions, encased women in limited gender roles as mother to her children and wife to her husband. The second wave of the American women's movement—decades after the first wave fought for women's right to vote—began to destabilize these roles in the late 1960s. This second wave pushed for women's equality with men and advocated for equal hiring and pay in the workforce, among other issues. By the late 1960s, the sitcom began to respond to these societal shifts and roles for women showed increasing variety. And, once cable-television channels like HBO came on the scene in the 1980s, we saw an increase in sexually explicit material that could define women's desires in new ways. HBO's *Sex and the City* (1998–2004) exemplified a new frankness in its stories of the adventures and misadventures of sexually active, single women in New York City at the turn of the century. For this reason and because the four main characters incarnated distinctive attitudes toward gender and sexuality, I have chosen it for this chapter's case study.

In this chapter I will principally consider how sexual politics—in Kate Millet's famous phrase—have played out between the heterosexual men and women of the sitcom, but I will also account for the rise of gay characters in the genre. Of course, American comedy culture has long exploited LGBTQ individuals with demeaning stereotypes and the sitcom certainly has its share of such characters. However, the late 1990s also saw a significant change in LGBTQ representation in sitcoms. Gay characters became increasingly common and less "exotic." This chapter will provide a brief history of the LGBTQ presence in sitcoms. Even though my case study, *Sex and the City*, focuses on four mostly heterosexual women, it is typical of the contemporary sitcom in the sense that it has recurring gay characters with no fanfare about their sexual orientation. This chapter will seek to transcend the analysis of LGBTQ stereotypes to address how LGBTQ identities function within the genre.

Understanding Gender in Cinema and TV Studies

The first analyses of gender, in general, and women, in specific, in the cinema were part of an initial growth in media studies in the 1960s, which saw the media through the lens of second-wave feminism. This approach centered on identifying negative stereotypes of women—fictional character types that put women in subservient roles or exploited their sexuality. And this approach also championed characters who were positive role models—women, for example, who fought against patriarchal expectations of women. This "image of women" approach presumes that women in media texts are direct reflections of the society of their time, which is certainly true to some degree. However, it is built on a rather narrow understanding of how media and society relate to one another. As we saw in the previous chapter on the family, television can take elements from the general, dominant culture of the time—say, the image of the perfect housewife—but is able to express resistance to dominant discourses—as when Lucy rebels against Desi's patriarchal attitudes or the authority of sitcom dads is shown to be a sham. Network-era television, in particular, enacted tricky, polysemic narratives that reflected the messiness of cultural discourse.

An approach to gender in television that is more supple and subtle than the image-of-women approach relies on the concept of gender identity. A gender identity may be thought of as a receptacle, a container, of society's ideas pertaining to femininity and masculinity—of what it means to be feminine and masculine. We all learn these ideas as we grow from girls/boys into women/men and we essentially *perform* an image of femininity or masculinity. This concept stems from the work of Judith Butler who suggests, "Consider gender … as *a corporeal style*, an 'act,' as it were, which is both intentional and performative, where '*performative*' suggests a dramatic and contingent construction of meaning."[1] Butler and those inspired by her concept of gender as a performance reject the definitions of gender that are determined by biology. In her view, masculinity and femininity owe less to one's genitals and more to social constructions of gender. How does this manifest itself in media studies, in general, and in our understanding of the sitcom genre, in particular? It leads the scholar of women's and men's images on screen to consider the processes by which sitcom characters are identified as masculine or feminine. Moreover, it is not satisfied with the binary division of gender into masculine and feminine. It considers characters that blur the distinction between those two—characters that are *both* masculine and feminine and characters that are biologically one sex, but identify with a different gender. It's easy to see how these interests lead us to LGBTQ representation where characters often do not adhere to social, cisnormative constructions of masculinity and femininity and, indeed, might even be transitioning from one to another.

Another concern of feminist media scholars that transcends the image-of-woman approach is the exploitation of the feminine body for the pleasure of the gazing, masculine viewer. A quick comment on the sitcom and the male gaze might therefore be appropriate before we continue. Based in Freudian notions of voyeurism, what came to be called "gaze theory" postulates that many media forms display women as passive objects or "spectacles" for the pleasure of active male subjects or "spectators." This use of the feminine body to satisfy masculine desire can be tracked through centuries of figurative art to salacious 19th-century photographic postcards to some of the earliest movies, which featured exotic dancers. The sitcom genre has used titillation for humor, but it hasn't proven to be central to the form.

The limitations of sexually infused humor in the genre are illustrated by the late-1970s comedy, *Three's Company* (1977–1984), which was quite controversial for its time due to its reliance on sexual innuendo. Known as "tits and ass" (T&A) television, it features a heterosexual young man (Jack) who shares an apartment with two attractive, heterosexual young women—one of whom (Chrissy) often appears braless and in tight clothing. Jack (John Ritter) pretends to be gay so that the landlord will allow the cohabitation of a man and two women, which at the time was still slightly scandalous. There is a large amount of superiority humor in jokes making fun of gays, which I'll address later, but most of the innuendoes and double entendres are incongruity humor about sexual activities that the heterosexual characters wish they were having, but are not.

In an episode aired March 24, 1977, Janet (Joyce DeWitt), Mrs. Roper (Audra Lindley), and Jack are at a restaurant where a buxom young woman in a low-cut top leans over to take his order. He stutters while he leers unabashedly at her breasts (see Figure 4.1). The audience on the laugh track begins to hoot and chuckle in anticipation of him making a sexually charged comment about the waitress' cleavage. As she walks away, he continues to ogle her and says, "She's *so* healthy." The audience laughs vigorously. Janet recognizes his lust and

Figure 4.1 Jack comments on his "healthy" waitress in *Three's Company*, a show that titillated network-era audiences before nudity and franker sexual humor became common on HBO and other premium-cable channels.

advises him to restrain himself, saying "Down, boy." The humor of Jack's line is based on the obvious incongruity of referring to the waitress as "healthy" instead of "sexually enticing." The scene also illustrates how the male gaze functions—with a woman placed on display, turned into a spectacle, for the sexual pleasure of the man's look. The woman is exploited for her physical attributes, but she is not the target of superiority humor. The audience does not feel superior to her, but, rather, it is superior to Jack, who is unable to pursue the waitress because he is pretending to be gay in front of Mrs. Roper and Janet is there to tamp down his lechery. Thus, his lust for the waitress is thwarted and the audience laughs at his predicament. He is the butt of the humor, not she. Titillating humor such as this illustrates how network television skirted around the edges of taboo behavior and language. TV wouldn't be able to show nudity and sexual activity on the screen until the rise of premium cable channels in the 1990s—resulting, eventually, in a show like *Girls* (2012–2017) where explicit nudity can be blended with humor.

The scene with the waitress in sexually alluring clothing illustrates another aspect of sexuality's function in humorous radio and TV programs: the burlesque and Vaudeville traditions of gag comedy, which I have previously distinguished from situation comedy. In gag comedy, women function as objects to be ogled at or ridiculed, as was common in Vaudeville where comedians were often interspersed with burlesque and striptease acts. Patrons of such shows would hear a comic rattle off jokes about "dumb blondes" or wives spending all of their husbands' hard-earned money, and then an act would follow where women dance suggestively and perhaps remove articles of clothing. There were exceptions, but for the most part gag comedy was the province of heterosexual male comedians. Women were either objects of derision by many such comedians or they were placed on display for men's sexual gratification. In the situation comedy, from its start in radio, this was less the case. Women were often the protagonists, the subjects of the narratives instead of the objects of gags and sexual exploitation. This was especially true in the sitcoms based on families (as chronicled in Chapter 3), but it also holds true in sitcoms about working women (see below). At the risk of over-generalizing, we can say that gag or joke comedy—comedy that is not embedded in a story—used superiority humor to ridicule and subordinate women; or, at least, that was the case until women comedians began doing stand-up comedy and speaking for themselves. Joan Rivers and Phyllis Diller were among the first to do so, and their legacy can be found in the stand-up work of Lily Tomlin, Whoopi Goldberg, Tracey Ullman, Roseanne Barr, Margaret Cho, Wanda Sykes, Amy Schumer, Ali Wong, Sarah Silverman, Tig Notaro, and others.

In contrast to gag-based comedy, situation-based humor has positioned women as subjects of the narratives, the protagonists of the stories. Of course, these protagonists could also be stereotyped and put in demeaning situations, but there has seldom been a woman protagonist of a sitcom who was presented as the object of the male gaze. Moreover, in the past 20 years, women stand-up comedians such as those listed above have been given their own sitcoms, often with creative control of the shows. This has resulted in programs that feature a woman's perspective in a variety of ways.

Take a program such as *2 Broke Girls* (2011–2017), which was created by a woman (Whitney Cummings) and a writer/director/producer who identifies as a gay man (Michael Patrick King) and who has many connections to *Sex and the City*. *2 Broke Girls* stars two conventionally attractive women: Kat Dennings as Max and Beth Behrs as Caroline. It is loaded with jokes based on sexual innuendos, but they are not at the expense of the women and the women's sexual allure does not pander to the masculine viewer. In the episode titled "And the Booth Babes," a series of circumstances results in Max working at a video-game convention as a "booth babe," a sexually enticing woman hired to passively stand next to products in a display booth to lure in heterosexual men. Max is dressed in an outfit that emphasizes her breasts—leading Caroline to call her "Boobarella"—and has the potential to be demeaning and exploitative (see Figure 4.2). However, Max refuses to be turned into a passive spectacle. Her character, "Death Bitch," she says, is a "hypersexualized, violent version of me who kills everyone who gets in my way. ... This chick is my spirit

Figure 4.2 On *2 Broke Girls*, Max uses her sexuality to dominate men, jokingly calling herself 'Death Bitch'.

animal." Max/Death Bitch resists subjugation and ridicules the male spectators that fawn over her. One gamer requests, "Can you chop my head off?" She archly alludes to fellatio in her reply: "This will be the best head you'll ever get." Thus, the androgynously named Max is clearly the protagonist of this humor, the subject who speaks the joke instead of the object or butt of the joke, which is how women were commonly used in gag comedy of the early 20th century and before.

Funny Single Women, with Jobs

In the previous chapter, I considered how women function within the sitcom family as wives and mothers. These wife/mother roles defined the vast majority of female sitcom characters for the first two decades of the genre. Unmarried women were usually relegated to secondary roles, where they might cause a narrative complication that an episode must resolve. As we saw with both Helen and Ellie in my consideration of *The Andy Griffith Show* (1960–1968) earlier, women without husbands can run for mayor or otherwise perturb the peace of a small town, but their disruption must be contained by the end of the half-hour time slot. In the years before the arrival of the second-wave women's movement, the TV industry was uninterested in a woman who wasn't defined by a man. Unless a comedy centered on a family, women would not be their central protagonists until the mid-1960s.

Two notable exceptions were *Our Miss Brooks* (1952–1956) and *Private Secretary* (1953–1957). In both shows, women are the titular characters and were played by actresses who had had significant movie careers before turning to the small screen—Eve Arden and Ann Sothern, respectively. Arden was known for portraying sharp-tongued, wise-cracking women who were sidekicks to the protagonists of feature films, such as her Oscar-nominated supporting role in the film noir, *Mildred Pierce* (1945). She originated the role of Miss Brooks on radio in 1948 and was retained when the show made the transition to television in 1952. As emphasized by the show's title, Connie is a "Miss" and not a "Mrs." However, she is no shrinking violet, waiting for a man to turn her into a wife and mother. She actively pursues a love interest (the oblivious Mr. Boynton), but has many other interests and retains a cynical attitude toward married life. In one episode, she schemes to impress Mr. Boynton (Robert Rockwell) with her domestic skills by pretending to cook him a home-cooked meal, which is actually prepared by her elderly neighbor, Mrs. Davis (Jane Morgan). While Mr. Boynton is out and the women are working in the kitchen, they have this exchange:

Mrs. Davis:	I think it was smart of you to get rid of the bashful goon [Mr. Boynton] so that I could sneak over and cook his dinner. 'Course, after you get married, you'll have to tell him you're not much of a cook.
Miss Brooks:	By then, who cares?
Mrs. Davis:	You're right, dear. After marriage, all a girl needs is a lipstick and a good can opener.
Miss Brooks:	And if she has the right lipstick, she doesn't even need a can opener.

Sothern's character in *Private Secretary* has a similarly jaundiced attitude toward men. Although Susie MacNamara works in a secretarial position for a theatrical agent, she does not pursue him as a husband

and is positioned as his equal in their business. Thus, the lead characters of *Private Secretary* and *Our Miss Brooks* break from the dominant gender role (wife/mother) that was constructed for women in the 1950s and anticipate the single working women that would arrive in the 1960s and 1970s.

At the forefront of these new working women was TV-news producer, Mary Richards, a virtual poster child for second-wave feminism and the central figure of *The Mary Tyler Moore Show* (1970–1977)—a program both starring Moore and produced by her production company, MTM Enterprises. Launched in 1970, the program assays the life of a woman in her workplace, much like *Private Secretary* and *Our Miss Brooks*, but, unlike Miss Brooks and Susie MacNamara, Mary is less interested in finding a husband than in excelling at her job. Consequently, the program is able to incorporate topics that were central concerns of the second-wave women's movement—including equal pay and job opportunity for women—although it does so gently and without propounding a specific message the way that Norman Lear's issue-oriented sitcoms attempted more bluntly. Mary remains cheerful and relentlessly spunky despite her on-again, off-again dating experiences—including one failed prospect who turns out to be gay, a somewhat daring plot twist for 1973. Over the run of the show, she comes to terms with being a working woman. In the final episode (March 18, 1977), she explains her attitude about being single:

> Sometimes I get concerned about being a career woman. I get to thinking my job is too important to me. And I tell myself that the people I work with are just the people I work with, and not my family. And last night I thought, 'What is a family, anyway?' They're just people who make you feel less alone and really loved. And that's what you've done for me. Thank you for being my family.

The Mary Tyler Moore Show's success opened the door for sitcoms in which women and men were not confined to their roles within a traditional family or wholly defined by a desire to obtain a spouse and create a nuclear family—including, in the 1970s, *Alice* (1976–1985), *Taxi* (1978–1983), and *WKRP in Cincinnati* (1978–1982); and in the 1980s, *Cheers* (1982–1993), *Kate & Allie* (1984–1989), *Designing Women* (1986–1993), and *Murphy Brown* (1988–1998; 2018–2019). And, as discussed in the chapter on the family, the formerly taboo character type of the divorced woman became increasingly common in sitcoms of this time. The unspoken network ban on divorcées had been broken in 1962's *The Lucy Show* (1962–1968), but there were few noteworthy sitcom divorcées until several ground-breaking characters arrived in the 1970s and 1980s: the once-widowed and twice-divorced Maude (Beatrice Arthur) of the show of the same name (1972–1978) divorces her husband in a 1975 episode; divorced mother Ann Romano (Bonnie Franklin) raises her daughters as a single parent on *One Day at a Time* (1975–1984, 2017–2019); and Dorothy Zbornak's (Beatrice Arthur, again) divorce leads her to move in with three widows on *The Golden Girls* (1985–1992). Whether never married or formerly married, sitcom women of the 1970s and 1980s were no longer cloistered within the family scene.

The decade of the 1980s ended with the premiere of the extremely influential *Seinfeld* (1989–1998), a show that was the most successful and highly rated of a slew of 1990s workplace and/or friend-centered comedies: *The Larry Sanders Show* (1992–1998), *Ellen* (1994–1998), *Friends* (1994–2004), *Caroline in the City* (1995–1999), *NewsRadio* (1995–1999), *The Drew Carey Show* (1995–2004), *Suddenly Susan* (1996–2000), *The Jamie Foxx Show* (1996–2001), *The Steve Harvey Show* (1996–2002), *Veronica's Closet* (1997–2000), *Becker* (1998–2004), *Sex and the City*, *Sports Night* (1998–2000), and *Will & Grace* (1998–2006; 2017–). Women in workplace sitcoms from this time period benefitted from the gains the women's movement had achieved, but they still struggled with balancing their personal and professional lives. This struggle is at the heart of the comedy-drama, *Ally McBeal* (1997–2002), which was featured in the *Time* magazine issue (1998) that pondered, "Is Feminism Dead?" As has become evident in the two decades since that issue, feminism is not dead, but it has evolved into a third wave that engages with media, in general, and comedy, in specific, in different ways than second-wave feminism. The third wave has sought to address certain lacks of the second wave—including a greater attention to race as it intersects with gender and a "playful embrace of popular culture, exuberant expression of sexual identity and desire, rejection of a feminist/feminine binary, and an individualistic understanding of choice."[2]

Around the same time that *Time* was mulling over the death of feminism, the sitcom genre was also in a quiet phase and many industry pundits declared that it was over for this hardy genre. But the new millennium has ushered in a host of comedies. Many of them star and/or are produced by women, and, moreover, a raft of these new shows present unmarried women as their protagonists—releasing them from the often-confining roles of wife and mother. Shows with women creators that centered on women who are single included (creators in parentheses) *Girlfriends* (Mara Brock Akil, 2000–2008), *Reba* (Allison M. Gibson, 2001–2007), *Weeds* (Jenji Kohan, 2005–2012), *The Comeback* (Lisa Kudrow and Michael Patrick King, 2005, 2014), *30 Rock* (Tina Fey, 2006–2013), *The New Adventures of Old Christine* (Kari Lizer, 2006–2010), *The Mindy Project* (Mindy Kaling, 2012–2017), and *Broad City* (Ilana Glazer and Abbi Jacobson, 2014–2019). Contemporary single-women shows often engage with third-wave feminism in meaningful ways. The most notable and notorious third-wave comedy—although some dispute its comedy classification—of the past twenty years is *Girls*.[3] The HBO production was created by Lena Dunham and starred her as Hannah, one of four young, white, self-absorbed, sexually adventurous, young women seeking their own identities within Manhattan's art/literary/music scene. *Girls* embraces third-wave feminism's "exuberant expression of sexual identity and desire." Hannah's and the other women's sexual experiences are grounded in their desires and not dependent upon men's initiatives. Because it was produced by HBO, *Girls* was not restricted by broadcast-television standards, which permitted it to present nudity and profanity. Dunham took advantage of that freedom to showcase her own body, which is not conventionally slender and was not shot in a way to satisfy the male gaze. The show's sex scenes are often messy, awkward, and embarrassing. They can be both satisfying and unsatisfying to their participants, but they showcase the complexity of feminine desire, of what women want. *Girls* confronts difficult elements of the human sexual/emotional experience and, unlike mainstream heterosexual pornography, does so largely from a woman's point of view. Dunham thus challenged patriarchal attitudes toward women's bodies in a way that aligns with the tenets of third-wave feminism.

Girls also taps into the third-wave women's movement's enthusiasm for the diversity of feminine forms. The other three titular women are all white and all feminine, but in different ways. Marnie (Allison Williams) derives the least amount of pleasure from sex and is portrayed as using it to advance her singing career. Of the four, she may be the most "masculine" in her callous attitude toward intimacy. Ironically, it is she that shows unanticipated tenderness and steps up to assist Hannah with her unexpected baby when it becomes obvious that she (Hannah) is ill-prepared for motherhood. Jessa (Jemima Kirke) stands out as the most impulsive and narcissistic of the four women— one whose bohemian appearance, affair with Hannah's former love interest (Adam [Adam Driver]), and addiction to drugs signal an utter lack of discipline. The final "girl" is Shoshanna (Zosia Mamet), whose fashion sense is that of a girly girl and who begins the series as a nervous, unfulfilled virgin. Over the course of the program's six seasons, she comes into her own and recognizes that the selfishness of the other three women is weighing her down. Third-wave feminism is, perhaps, more accepting of different gender forms and could endorse the various feminine-identity constructions of Hannah, Marnie, Jessa, and Shoshanna. However, there are other 21st-century comedies that do a better job of exploring third-wave feminism's commitment to racial and ethnic diversity (see *Jane the Virgin* [2014–] and *Insecure* [2016–]) and its affection for playful and satiric collages of popular culture (see *Broad City* and *30 Rock*).

A Brief History of LGBTQ Representation in the Sitcom

To this point, I have considered sexuality and gender from a heteronormative perspective that presumes clear-cut distinctions between male and female, between masculine and feminine. But gay men and lesbians depart from that perspective and blur those distinctions. In the intolerant years when many states criminalized homosexuality, teachers could lose their jobs if they identified as gay, and LGBTQ couples could not marry, television did not take a leadership role in breaking long-standing prejudices and biases. For the first three decades of television as a mass medium, networks' Standards and Practices departments restricted direct references to homosexuality—making LGBTQ individuals virtually invisible except in documentaries and news programs. There were, of course, effeminate male characters and masculine female characters that were the targets of derisive, superiority humor and there was the occasional figure who was coded as "gay" (if you knew what to look for), but they were not specifically labeled as LGBTQ. Stephen Tropiano, in a history of gays and lesbians on television, includes Uncle Arthur on *Bewitched* (1964–1972), Felix Unger on *The Odd Couple* (1970–1975), and Sally Rogers on *The Dick Van Dyke Show* (1961–1966), among several others, on a list of "gay-straight" characters who "for all purposes *should* be gay or lesbian." He suggests, "There's certainly something different about the way these characters walk, talk, dress, and crack a joke."[4] It wasn't until the 1970s, however, that TV series/serials finally began featuring LGBTQ characters that were not in the closet; and the sitcom proved to be an important genre for including them in television narratives.

The sitcom, in fact, would be the first television genre to feature a recurring gay character in a prime-time show. That beginning was not an auspicious one, however, as it was in a limited-run, summer show titled *The Corner Bar*, which ran just eight episodes during each of the summers of 1972 and 1973 and dropped the gay character after its 1972 episodes ran. It never developed much of an audience and is today remembered only, if at all, for this LGBTQ milestone. More significant to LGBTQ representation was the "Judging Books by Covers" episode of the massively popular show, *All in the Family* (1971–1979), that aired February 9, 1971, the year before *The Corner Bar*. This Norman Lear-produced sitcom addressed many controversies of the day from a liberal perspective, using a central conservative character named Archie Bunker (Carroll O'Connor) to satirize a militaristic attitude toward the Vietnam War and prejudices against minorities, immigrants, and the poor. In this episode, Archie disdains one of his daughter's male friends, because his flamboyant, affected behavior convinces him he must be homosexual—referring to him as "Roger, the fairy" (Anthony Geary). Archie is not shy about using other derogatory terms for gays, such as "fruit," "fag," and "queer," and he much prefers the company of his hyper-masculine, rough-and-tough, former football player friend, Steve (Philip Carey). The twist to this episode's plot is that Steve is gay and Roger is not, which is revealed through a series of machinations that result in Archie and Steve intimately arm wrestling when Steve comes out to him. Archie is disbelieving and Steve says, "Have it your own way, Arch. The truth's in the eye of the beholder anyway." Then, Steve gives him a robust punch in the arm as he leaves. The last line of the scene is Archie saying, "If that's the punch of a fruit" followed by the camera zooming in on his baffled and concerned expression. The episode ends with a coda in which Archie mistakes his daughter's female friend, Jerry (Linn Patrick), for a man. He has the episode's final line: "Nowadays you can't bet on nothin'." He has once again judged a book by its cover and been shocked to find it does not match its contents.

The moral of the episode fits into a discourse of assimilation—holding that LGBTQ people are "just like everyone else" and should assimilate into heteronormative society. It's okay for them to do what they do, as long as they don't "flaunt" their differences from heterosexuals. A similar discourse surrounds racial and ethnic groups and will be considered in more depth in the following chapter. It also aligns with second-wave feminism's advocacy for equal rights for women and equal job opportunities. As the parallel arguments go, women should be treated the same as men and gays should be treated the same as straights. This does not necessarily mean that women should *act* the same as men or that gays should *act* the same as straights, but that is how it is often misconstrued. Moreover, it is easier for gays to perform heterosexuality than it is for women to perform masculinity, because of the lack of obvious physical differences between gays and straights. At the time of the *All in the Family* episode—two years after the Stonewall riots of 1969 marked the beginning of the modern gay rights movement—assimilation was a sign of progress from the years of gay persecution.

Steve appeared on just this one *All in the Family* episode, and the show never had a recurring LGTBQ character.[5] The first notable TV character who identified as gay and appeared on a recurring basis in a regular-season show was Jodie Dallas, portrayed by Billy Crystal in the comedy, *Soap*. Created by Susan Harris in 1977 for ABC, *Soap* (1977–1981) took a rather ambivalent attitude toward its gay character. Jodie has several heteronormative experiences. He has sexual contact with one woman that results in a child and he eventually proposes marriage to another. However, he does identify as gay throughout the series' run and thus *Soap* does not fall into the trap of "conversion therapy." Gay rights groups expressed approval about Jodie not being converted to straight, but they took exception to *Soap*'s blurring of the distinctions among a gay man's identity, transvestitism, and sex reassignment surgery—all of which were included in Jodie's storylines. After gay representatives contacted *Soap*'s producers about these concerns, there were changes made to Jodie's character—dropping, for example, his desire for sexual-reassignment surgery. All in all, *Soap* was a step forward for LGBTQ representation on television, because Jodie was a smart, quick-witted character and a responsible gay parent, who did not engage in stereotypically "flamboyant" behavior. In sum, for the most part, he wasn't subject to derisive humor where the audience was positioned as superior to him.

As groundbreaking as Jodie was, he did not open the floodgates for LGBTQ characters in the years that immediately followed. After *Soap* went off the air in 1981, there was a dearth of LGBTQ characters in the sitcom for about 14 years, although there were several aborted attempts at incorporating gays into the genre. *Love, Sidney* (1981–1983) premiered the year *Soap* went off the air and was technically the first prime-time sitcom with a lead, titular character who is gay, but the producers effectively erased Sydney's sexual orientation during the show's run. He is specifically identified as gay in the TV movie, *Sidney Shorr: A Girl's Best Friend*, that introduced the series; but in the show itself, his sexual orientation is never mentioned and his Platonic relationship with a young woman and her daughter is emphasized. LGBTQ representation continued to be limited to occasional one-episode characters and small roles throughout the 1980s.

When the 1990s arrived, more and more LGBTQ characters found their way into significant story arcs. In 1991, *Roc*'s (1991–1994) main character has a gay uncle and one episode features a party for him and his partner (1991). The phenomenally popular *Roseanne* arrived in 1988 and started regularly featuring LGBTQ characters in the 1990s—including Roseanne's friend Nancy coming out (1992), a gay wedding between another friend and his partner (1995), and, during a final season containing many oddly contradictory plot lines, Roseanne's mother's identification as a lesbian, but then, in the last episode, it's said that she's not gay but rather that Roseanne's sister is. A kiss between straight-identifying Roseanne and a lesbian friend of Nancy's generated more controversy than any of these other LGBTQ storylines. So much so that ABC almost did not air the 1994 episode, only relenting after *Roseanne*'s producers went public about the cancellation and public pressure convinced ABC to let it run. Other 1990s LGBTQ characters were also featured on *Friends* (the first prime-time lesbian wedding) and *Mad About You* (1992–1999).

Despite all the LGBTQ characters popping up in sitcoms in the 1990s, there still were no shows with gay protagonists until the latter part of the decade when *Ellen* and *Will & Grace* arrived. *Will & Grace* would have a longer run than *Ellen*, but the latter attracted more media attention when its star, Ellen DeGeneres, and her character, Ellen Morgan, came out as lesbian during its fourth season—the first time in the history of television that a prime-time star and the character she played came out simultaneously. Rumors had long circulated about DeGeneres's sexual identity. The rumors spiked when it became known that she had negotiated with ABC to have her character come out during the fourth season. In the early episodes of that season, there were jokes hinting at her imminent coming out—as when she made a point of walking into a closet and then literally "coming out" of it. Two weeks before the coming-out episode, DeGeneres's announcement was made officially public with a *Time* magazine cover story headlined, "Yep, I'm gay" (April 14, 1997). A subsequent interview on *The Oprah Winfrey Show* was broadcast on the same day as the airing of "The Puppy Episode" (April 30, 1997), as it had been covertly titled during production. And Winfrey appeared in the episode itself, playing a therapist to whom Ellen Morgan confides her sexual confusion. DeGeneres's and Morgan's coming out was not without controversy—including at least one ABC affiliate that refused to air it and ABC marking the show with a parental advisory before each episode. And once the glare of media attention to her coming out had subsided, the program struggled to hold an audience. It was renewed for a final season, but went off the air in the spring of 1998. The following fall, *Will & Grace* debuted.

Will & Grace benefitted from the path-clearing work of DeGeneres and *Ellen*. Will (Eric McCormack) is a gay man living with a straight woman, Grace (Debra Messing), and one of their closest friends is the flamboyantly gay Jack (Sean Hayes). The program showcases the different ways in which men can be gay—although ironically it received criticism from some quarters for making Jack too stereotypically gay and Will not gay enough. Nonetheless, *Will & Grace* was the first network-TV program to be centered on gay characters from its inception. It quickly found an audience and had an initial run of eight seasons, from 1998 to 2006. In fact, it was so popular that it was revived eleven years later, featuring the same cast. However, *Will & Grace* does illustrate the hazards of actors identifying as LGBTQ. The title character of Will is played by a straight-identifying actor, Eric McCormack. And Will's gay friend, Jack, is played by Sean Hayes, who many assumed was gay, but he himself was evasive about his sexuality during the program's initial incarnation. He came out publicly four years after the first run ended—leading an *Us Magazine* article to echo DeGeneres's *Time* cover, stating "Yup, he's gay in real life, too."[6] Reportedly the media attention paid to Jack and criticisms of him being "too gay" overwhelmed the young actor. In a 2013 interview, he stated, "It made me go back in the closet [with the media] because I was so overwhelmed at 26 or 27. I didn't want the responsibility, I didn't know how to handle the responsibility of speaking for the gay community. I always felt like I owed them a huge apology for coming out too late."[7] Thus, even though DeGeneres had paved the way for LGBTQ actors to play LGBTQ characters, *Will & Grace* had no main actors who were publicly out of the closet at the time of its initial seasons.

By the 2010s, LGBTQ characters had become commonplace in network and cable sitcoms, but gay-parenting storylines remained rare, even though the first gay father had appeared in 1977 (Jodie in *Soap*). The lack of LGBTQ parents reflected US social mores where most states did not permit same-sex marriages and many locations restricted gay men and lesbians from adopting children. American acceptance of gay couples was anticipated in the popular, award-winning comedy, *Modern Family*, which premiered on ABC in 2009 and, as of this writing, is in its eleventh and final season. The show features a gay couple, Mitchell (Jesse Tyler Ferguson) and Cameron (Eric Stonestreet), as one of its three core "families" of its title and it highlights their adoption of a girl in the pilot episode. They were married over two episodes in May 2014. Set in California, where same-sex marriage was legalized in 2004, Mitchell and Cameron's wedding occurred the year before the US Supreme Court made same-sex marriage possible throughout America. Another landmark program in terms of the representation of LGBTQ parenting is *Transparent* (2014–2019), the title of which alludes to its central character, Maura (Jeffrey Tambor), a transgender woman who is the parent of two children. This Amazon Studios' production contains the only transgender woman in TV-comedy history, although Netflix's *Orange Is the New Black* (2013–2019)—which some describe as a comedy-drama—also features a key figure who is a transgender woman.

This brief history of LGBTQ characters in the sitcom is not meant to be exhaustive, but it should illustrate how such characters have evolved from being targets for derision or simply being ignored to assimilation into popular, critically acclaimed programs. For decades, LGBTQ actors have had to perform heterosexuality, as Judith

Butler might put it, in order to find work. Today, that is much less the case, but the large number of gay characters that are played by cisgender men and women—including the actor who plays *Modern Family*'s Cameron—suggests there are still cultural barriers to casting gay actors as gay characters. It may well be that some LGBTQ actors reasonably fear that playing such roles will limit their choices in the future and that casting directors will not consider them for cisgender roles if they're typecast as an LGBTQ performer. Thus, in many instances, straight-identifying actors perform homosexuality in TV programs. The performance of gender identity in television sitcoms remains complicated, but the variety of LGBTQ roles has never been greater. Now, the question will be whether such characters will be totally assimilated into the sitcom's fabric as "just the same as" cisgender characters (a new type of invisibility) or if the diversity of gender expression will find representation on television.

Case Study: *Sex and The City*

Sex and the City offered an intriguing look at the state of gender identity and female sexuality across the millennium divide, airing from 1998 to 2004. It was followed by two feature films in 2008 and 2010 and a prequel TV show—titled *The Carrie Diaries*—from 2013 to 2014. The show centers on four women who are emblematic of the contemporary (affluent, white) female experience. Charlotte (Kristin Davis) is the most conventional—dressing femininely and determined to find a husband and have children. Miranda (Cynthia Nixon) hues closely to second-wave feminist principles of equal rights for women. Samantha (Kim Cattrall) is a libertine with a "masculine" approach to sexual adventures. And Carrie (Sarah Jessica Parker) exists somewhere among the other three—incarnating the program's perspective with a voiceover explanation of the theme for each week's episode. Carrie's voiceover stems from the program's original source material, which was a mid-1990s newspaper column written by Candace Bushnell and titled, "Sex and the City." She turned those columns into a best-selling book of the same name, which was then developed into the HBO program by producer Darren Star. The TV show became one of the most talked-about and argued-about programs of its time—overlapping with *The Sopranos* (1999–2007) and helping establish HBO's reputation as producer of prestigious productions. Central to discussions about the program are the ways that it represents women and their sexual lives and desires. Additionally, it incorporates lesbian, gay, and bisexual storylines that allow for a panoply of sexual experiences. Exploring how it builds these storylines can illuminate discourses surrounding gender identity.

Sex and the City's Logline, Its Narrative Problematic

Sex and the City's narrative problematic is no mystery. It stems from Bushnell's original newspaper column, which told the stories of her and her friends' amorous activities. One can imagine a pitch session in which a logline was offered—something like, "Four attractive, high-fashion, single, 30-something women navigate Manhattan's sexual scene." But in terms of a repeatable narrative problematic, something that could recur every week for what turned out to be 94 episodes, something more concrete is required. The problematic is posed by Carrie and Charlotte in the pilot episode in response to this pronouncement by Samantha: "This is the first time in the history of Manhattan that women have had as much money and power as men. Plus, the equal luxury of treating men as sex objects."[8] Charlotte reacts in shock and asks, "Are you going to just give up on love?" And Carrie, the show's literal voice as she narrates the episodes, poses a closely related question, "What about romance?" These questions are at the heart of *Sex and the City*'s recurring problematic. Each episode, in one form or another, chronicles an impediment to true love and lasting romance. As with all successful sitcoms, the show inventively delays answering its central question, which could be reduced to: "Will Carrie and her friends find satisfaction in love?" Or, as Bushnell herself says in the introduction to the collection of her columns, "*Sex and the City* sets out to answer one burning question—why are we still single?"[9]

Sex and the City's episodes are even more bluntly structured than those of *The Andy Griffith Show* discussed in the previous chapter. *Sex and the City* borrows Bushnell's technique of exploring a particular question in individual columns. Similarly, each TV episode has Carrie, a "sexual anthropologist" (as she calls herself), ponder a specific issue related to sex, love, and/or romance. At some point in most of the episodes, she types that issue into a word processor as a question or as something she "wonders" about—whereupon the camera cuts to text on the computer screen for us to read along with her narration. These "think-and-type" scenes, as the crew and fans referred to them, quickly became the show's signature element.[10] Some samples include:

- Are the men of today less threatened by a woman's power, or are they just acting?
- Are men just women with balls?
- How can two people, mired in the mess, ever figure it out. Do we need distance to get close?
- Is there a secret cold war between marrieds and singles?
- In a city like New York, with its infinite possibilities, has monogamy become too much to expect?

When Carrie types these questions and/or verbalizes them via voiceover, she summarizes the narrative enigma of that specific episode—one that fits within the program's over-arching narrative problematic, "Will Carrie and her friends find satisfaction in love?" However, she seldom actually answers these questions. Often, the question is posed at the very end of the episode, leaving no time for resolutions. This allows it to be posed again, perhaps in slightly different forms, in subsequent episodes. And it also allows story arcs to continue over several episodes—more like a serial (like daytime soap opera) than a series (like *The Andy Griffith Show*). If the four women were to find satisfaction in love, then the program's narrative engine would run out of fuel. There would be no more questions to be posed. *Sex and the City*'s narrative problematic did not end with the series finale in 2004, however, because the program spawned two movie sequels starting four years afterward—continuing the TV show's storylines in movie theaters with *Sex and the City* (2008) and *Sex and the City 2* (2010). The latter film resolved many of the questions that had threaded through six television seasons: Carrie and Mr. Big become engaged; Miranda figures out how to balance raising a child and work; Charlotte is happily married; and Samantha is happily unmarried, continuing to pursue sexual adventures. As is characteristic of the genre, the characters' happy endings did not occur within the confines of the TV episodes. Rather, they required a feature film and the possibility of a more closed ending to the story.

According to Amanda D. Lotz, the emphasis on first-person narration here and in other women-centered shows such as *The Days and Nights of Molly Dodd* (1987–1991) and *Ally McBeal* (1997–2002) enables protagonists to have self-questioning conversations with themselves—allowing insights into the characters that more commonplace storytelling techniques struggle to express. She contends, "These techniques exhibit the inner lives of the characters and effectively strip a layer of surface to reveal their uncertainties and flaws to a degree that is less evident in other dramatic narrative types."[11] *Sex and the City*'s first-person narration thus becomes an essential component of its narrative problematic as it lays bare the feelings about love, sex, and romance that Carrie and company are negotiating. It's less a program about acts of sex and romance, but, rather, it's about the women's emotions regarding those acts. These emotions are extensively discussed in *Sex and the City*'s other signature element: "chat-and-chew" scenes, in which the four women experience a Manhattan eatery and talk about topics from Carrie's think-and-type sessions.[12] Taken together, the think-and-type scenes and chat-and-chew scenes enable *Sex and the City* to probe the inner emotional lives of the characters to an extent that is rare on television. Moreover, the chat-and-chew scenes allow the program to transcend a single perspective in its examination of contemporary attitudes toward sex, love, and romance. Carrie's think-and-type frames the instigating question, but then Miranda, Samantha, Charlotte, and Carrie herself offer varying answers to that question. As we shall see in the following section, this is what prevents *Sex and the City* from being a didactic morality lesson from a single point-of-view.

Discourses of Sex, Love, and Romance:
Second- and Third-Wave Feminism

Sex and the City's narrative structure showcases discourses about sex, love, and romance that are associated with patriarchal ideology, second-wave feminism, and third-wave feminism. Each of these three discursive positions has a champion in the show's characters—although I am simplifying the characters' ideological functions for the sake of clarity. Charlotte is the most conventional of the group, accepting many of values promulgated by a male-dominated society. She has a career as an art dealer, but would give it up to marry a man and have children. She is also the biggest believer of conventional romantic mythology in the quartet and often expresses shock at the other women's cynical attitudes. Miranda, in contrast, clearly espouses the values of second-wave feminism and the need for women to define themselves without relying on a man to do so. In the pilot, she is identified as a "corporate lawyer," a job that in previous decades would have been the sole province of male attorneys. Her longest plotline chronicles her struggle to find a balance between work and her baby. She is positioned as a woman who has benefitted from second-wave feminism's advocacy for equal job opportunity in the late 1960s, but must now figure out how exactly to "have it all"—a career and a family. Samantha is the most sexually "liberated" of all the women. Discursively, she fits within the ideology of third-wave feminism. Second-wave feminism is often accused of being anti-sex—perhaps unfairly so. Samantha is irrepressibly lusty, a societal rule-breaker, and an unrepentant "unruly woman," in Kathleen Rowe's evocative term.[13] She responds to third-wave feminism's call for women to choose their own sexual attitudes, which may well reject the masculine–feminine binary to find their own gender identities.

The discursive identities of the three women and Carrie's position as an intermediary among them are crystalized in a discussion the four women have about anal sex. Charlotte's boyfriend has requested they perform a sexual act that until only recently was strictly taboo and was associated with the equally taboo sex between gay men. Even in the 21st century, heterosexual anal sex is not uncontroversial, and feminists are divided about its implications for the power relationship between men and women. I quote at length the conversation the women have about Charlotte's situation in a taxi cab ride. It begins with just Carrie and Charlotte in the car and they then pick up the other two.

Miranda: It's all about control. If he goes up there, there's going to be a shift in power. Either he'll have the upper hand or you will. Now, there's a certain camp that believes whoever holds the dick holds the power, but ... the question is, if he goes up your butt will he respect you more or respect you less? That's the issue.

Samantha: Fuck that! Oh, who cares?! A hole is a hole.

Miranda: Can I quote you?

Samantha: Oh, don't be so judgmental. You could use a little backdoor.

Charlotte: I'm not a hole.

Carrie: Honey, we know.

Samantha: Look, all I'm saying is, this is a physical expression that the body was designed to experience. And PS it's fabulous.

Charlotte: What are you talking about? I went to Smith [College]!

Samantha: I'm just saying, with the right guy and the right lubricant ...

Second-wave feminist Miranda is the first to chime in. She sees the anal-sex issue through the lens of sexual politics, of questions of the power relationship between men and women: "whoever holds the dick holds the power." Samantha's riposte to Miranda encapsulates the third-wave response to the ostensibly anti-sex second wave: "don't be so judgmental. You could use a little backdoor." Third-wave feminists defend many sexual practices that second-wave feminists argue exploit women's bodies. Third-wave feminists counter that women should be free to choose any sexual experiences that give them pleasure. As Samantha says, "with the right guy and the right lubricant ... ."

Charlotte is clearly appalled by the prospect of anal sex and is not persuaded by either Miranda's or Samantha's arguments or the second- and third-wave, respectively, perspectives behind them. "I'm not a hole!" she exclaims with alarm and then alludes to a presumably conservative education at Smith College, a women-only institution. Carrie does not explicitly endorse any of these discourses: patriarchal (Charlotte), second-wave feminism (Miranda), or third-wave feminism (Samantha). Her main contribution to this discussion—"Honey, we know"—shows her empathy toward Charlotte and her acceptance of her conservative values, without directly contesting Miranda's or Samantha's. Carrie exists as an in-between character, an interlocutor much like Andy in *The Andy Griffith Show*, who can shift from one side to another or magically reconcile conflicting values. She's a modern, "new" woman, but she can see the value of Charlotte's conventional mores. The episode as a whole entertains a plurality of opinions on heterosexual anal sex. Second- and third-wave perspectives are aired, but, at the conclusion, Charlotte does not accept them. She avoids becoming a transgressive woman willing to have sex that does not lead to babies. She tells her boyfriend that she wants children and says, "I don't want to be the up-the-butt girl." In voiceover, Carrie adds, "They made love the Charlotte way: polite and respectful, on 300-count Egyptian sheets." Thus, the episode and the program as a whole are able to confirm patriarchal discourse while gently mocking it— alluding here to the extravagance of expensive linen. And they're able to present a polysemy of discourses about the polymorphous nature of contemporary sexuality.[14]

Discourses of Sex, Love, and Romance: The Female Gaze

Many of *Sex and the City*'s episodes focus on debates about the differences between (heterosexual) women and men. Often this is framed within the question: can women behave like men do? As Samantha suggests in the pilot: "just say 'screw it' and go out and have sex like a man. ... I mean, without feeling." Setting aside the program's overgeneralizations about gender characteristics (some men presumably have sex "with feeling") and its emphasis on heterosexual relations and cisgender characters, Carrie and her friends are most consistently unruly when they indulge in the "luxury of treating men as sex objects" (Samantha, as previously quoted). In so doing, they invert the conventions of the male gaze where the woman is a *passive* spectacle to be *actively* looked at by the man. The man derives sexual pleasure from this act of looking, which, in psychoanalytic terms, is called "scopophilia." In a ground-breaking and frequently cited essay, Laura Mulvey introduced the Freudian concept of scopophilia to film studies over 30 years ago, finding it fundamental to the act of film viewing.[15] In her view, scopophilia and the closely related Freudian phenomenon of voyeurism indicate an imbalance of power between men and women. Men are in a position of power. They control the gaze and where they choose to direct it for their pleasurable looking. Women are subordinate in this scenario—placed on display and turned into passive objects. Crucially, in voyeurism, women are not permitted to express their own desires and thus do not have access to their own "visual pleasure" (Mulvey's phrase). They exist instead to satisfy the desires of men. Mulvey's emphasis on the importance of the act of looking and the male gaze led subsequent work in this area to be labeled "gaze theory." As I have argued earlier in regard to *2 Broke Girls*, situation-based comedy does not blend male scopophilia with humor in the way that gag-based comedy often does—where sexually alluring women are turned into the targets of superiority humor. Rather, sitcom narrative often positions women as the protagonists and humor arises from the incongruity of situations they experience. CBS's *2 Broke Girls* and HBO's *Sex and the City* both center on unruly women, but HBO's freedom from broadcast standards meant that *Sex and the City* could make explicit many things that *2 Broke Girls* had to keep euphemistic. The latter alludes to fellatio in coded fashion as "getting head" while the former was known for breaking language taboos, including the liberal use of "fuck" (even in an episode title: "The Fuck Buddy") and possibly being the first US prime-time series to have a character utter "cunt" (in a surprisingly non-sexual context).

Sex and the City's characters are obsessed with the fulfilment of their every desire—from sexual experiences to sumptuous meals to luxurious clothing. Certainly, the four women are attractive and elicit the gazes of men, but they themselves gaze as much, or more so, than they are gazed at. As Deborah Jermyn argues, this leads them to disrupt the conventions of the male gaze. She refers to their active, pleasurable gazing as "transgressive scopophilia" and describes one specific instance of it in which Samantha's gaze becomes quite hyperbolic.[16] In the "Lights, Camera, Relationship!" episode, Samantha is dating a handsome young actor, Jerry, who is in a play in Brooklyn, far away from Broadway. To be supportive of his work, she reluctantly agrees to see the play, but she gets an enjoyable jolt of scopophilia when he performs a soliloquy naked (see Figures 4.3–4.4). She then takes on his career as a PR project, which includes getting him on an Absolut Vodka ad in Times Square, with a bottle functioning as a surrogate penis (see Figure 4.5). She also convinces Carrie, Charlotte, their gay friend, Stanford, and others from New York's social elite to attend the play. Director Michael Engler stages Jerry's naked soliloquy so that each character is shot in close-up, emphasizing the visual pleasure they're experiencing as they gaze at Jerry's body. Jermyn concludes that Carrie's and her friends' shared gazes at men "invite not just each other but also the heterosexual female (and indeed gay male) [television] spectator to join them in their transgressive scopophilia."[17] In this instance, Engler encourages viewers to derive pleasure from Jerry's naked body by lingering on shots of his bare chest and a close-up of his posterior. Jermyn contends, citing Kathleen Rowe's "unruly woman," "In laying claim to the (masculine) territory of sexually explicit language and active sexual desire, Samantha co-opts laughter for her own ends, brandishing it as 'a weapon of transgression and liberation' ([Rowe] 1995, 46)."[18]

By exchanging feminine "territory" for masculine, *Sex and the City* risks exploiting men in the same way that women have been exploited

COMEDY, SEX, AND GENDER IDENTITY

Figure 4.3 Jerry, an actor that Samantha is dating on *Sex and the City*, performs in the nude. The next shot ...

in the past. However, any charges of "reverse sexism" should be seen in the context of third-wave feminism's eagerness to explore multiple forms of female desire. Samantha's superficial and appearance-driven perspective on men is tempered by Charlotte's desire to find a companion that connects with her on a deeper, more conventionally romantic level—which turns out to be a short, bald, excessively hairy divorce lawyer (in the program's final season). And in second-wave feminist fashion, Miranda advocates for parity between women and men, including both genders being allowed to derive visual pleasure from looking. Carrie exists in a middle ground—enjoying the display of Jerry's body in this episode, but pursuing a relationship with an average-looking writer. Thus, the overall gender perspective of *Sex and the City* cannot be reduced to "women acting like men." Its storylines permit women to pursue pleasure by acting masculine in some situations, but then they might also behave in very "girly" ways in the

COMEDY, SEX, AND GENDER IDENTITY

Figure 4.4 ... shows her gazing lustfully at him. The conventional voyeuristic structure of a man gazing at a woman is reversed.

same episode. Due to the diverse variety of female desire chronicled in the program, the case could be made for the program conforming to the perspective of the third-wave women's movement, but without the very significant component of racial or ethnic diversity. Carrie et al., exist in a rarified slice of a rarified New York borough.

A Note about LGBTQ Discourse in *Sex and the City*

After all the episodes and the films were done, three of the four *Sex and the City* women wound up in conventional heterosexual pairs. Samantha remained on the loose, but it would have been difficult to construct a denouement for her that could contain her lusty licentiousness. She is the only one truly open to bisexual experiences, entering into a brief lesbian affair in season four before returning to sex with men. The other women identify consistently as heterosexual. Thus,

COMEDY, SEX, AND GENDER IDENTITY

Figure 4.5 Jerry becomes a public spectacle when Samantha, as his publicist, gets him a vodka Times Square billboard in which a bottle serves clearly phallic symbolism.

Sex and the City relegated most LGBTQ storylines to minor recurring characters, such as Carrie's friend, Stanford (Willie Garson), and Charlotte's friend, Anthony (Mario Cantone). Behind the camera, however, there was a strong gay presence. *Sex and the City* writer and producer, Michael Patrick King, mentioned earlier as the producer of *2 Broke Girls*, is publicly out as a gay man. He wrote the "Lights, Camera, Relationship!" episode and 30 others and was one of *Sex and the City*'s main producers. One of the cast's core actors is also LGBTQ. Cynthia Nixon, who played Miranda, identified publicly as bisexual in 2012, although she was married to a man during the production of *Sex and the City*.[19] Moreover, in terms of the reception of *Sex and the City*, a large gay fan base was quickly constructed, and straight actors Sarah Jessica Parker and Kim Cattrell have become gay icons within LGBTQ culture.

Thus, despite the lack of gay characters in the show's central group, it is clearly informed by a gay sensibility. Jermyn argues that *Sex and the City* can be "read as playfully queer."[20] This expresses itself, first, in the show's invitation to take sexual pleasure from looking at men—regardless of whether the person looking is male or female—as was discussed earlier. Second, it has fun with popular culture in ways that often gesture toward the gay aesthetic of camp, of appropriating and toying with the unvalued and disregarded elements of film, television, fashion, and celebrity culture. Jermyn provides the example of ironic references to *The Wizard of Oz* (1939) in several episodes.[21] Third, the show's characters use language associated with gay culture of the time—such as the word "fabulous."[22] Even more significant than these three elements of queer culture, contends Jermyn, are the ways in which *Sex and the City* "destabilized traditional binaries and gendered roles."[23] Here she refers to the blurring of the lines between masculine and feminine, which underpinned *Sex and the City* from the very beginning. As discussed earlier, its pilot episode immediately began the program's questioning of whether women should act like men—thereby disrupting the distinction between masculine and feminine. Of course, lesbian, gay, bisexual, transsexual, and queer gender identities also trouble the conventional masculine/feminine binary and thus *Sex and the City*'s destabilization of that binary might be its most notable LGBTQ aspect.

Sex and the City Case Study: Conclusion

Unlike the previous chapter's case study, *The Andy Griffith Show*, *Sex and the City* was not initially aired on an FCC-regulated broadcast network. This granted it the freedom to cover FCC-prohibited topics such as fellatio and anal sex, to include nudity, and to liberally use taboo-for-broadcast words such as "fuck" and "cunt." This was certainly a large part of its allure and was why it and similar taboo-breaker *The Sopranos* were greatly responsible for the growth of premium cable channel HBO as a powerful, prestigious network at the turn of the century. In this context, *Sex and the City* was a notable component of the demise of network television and the rise of cable/satellite, followed by the disruption that is the rise of streaming media. This permitted *Sex and the City* to modify the format of the sitcom in certain ways, making it more of a serial and more of a drama than in traditional shows such as *The Andy Griffith Show*. And, yet, it still held on to some genre conventions, such as a narrative problematic that was repeated each week and a cast of four protagonists among whom the A story circulated.

Viewed more narrowly through the lenses of sex and gender, *Sex and the City* is interesting for the gender identities it portrays and its sometimes schematic incarnation of specific ideological positions. Carrie, Charlotte, Miranda, and Samantha individually embody many of the traits of second- and third-wave feminism. Several episodes bring these "waves" into conflict with one another, leaving central figure and narrator Carrie to navigate among them—much as Andy Griffith was positioned as an in-between character, an intermediary between small-town life and big-city values. In *Sex and the City*, all of the values are part of urban culture (for which it was famous), but there are critical differences among the characters' associations with certain gender positions. Miranda doggedly espouses second-wave principles while Samantha's licentious behavior qualifies her as a third-wave feminist. Charlotte seems in many respects to be "pre-feminist" and to pursue a conventional, patriarchal lifestyle. *Sex and the City* positions Carrie as our surrogate and through her we can experience these differing discourses of femininity.

During its time on HBO and then in subsequent movies, *Sex and the City* attracted much discussion about what femininity is and whether women should act more like (heterosexual) men. One way to address this gender difference is in terms of women's appropriation of the right to gaze—for them to take active sexual pleasure from gazing at men who have been turned into passive sex objects. I discussed above how this might qualify as "transgressive scopophilia," thereby disrupting the power structure between heterosexual men and women. And this also led me to assay briefly a gay sensibility that might be found in the show, because its visual design encourages the gay gaze at these male sex objects and because, more generally, the show unsettles the traditional masculine/feminine binary and makes room for alternative gender identities—lesbian, gay male, bisexual, transsexual, and queer.

Notes

1 Judith Butler, *Gender Trouble: Feminism and the Subversion of Identity* (New York: Routledge, 2006), 190. Originally published in 1990.
2 A. Susan Owen, Sarah R. Stein, and Leah R. Vande Berg, *Bad Girls: Cultural Politics and Media Representations of Transgressive Women* (New York: Peter Lang, 2007), 123.
3 Defending the comedy categorization of *Girls*, A.O. Scott writes, "*Girls*, fundamentally, is a comedy—of the body, of relationships, of working, of entitlement, of generational funk. At its best, it's a satire of a lot of those things, too. But for any number of reasons—it's also a chillingly good drama, it's a show by and about women, and we're still (still) weirded out by funny women—we might overlook the strength of its humor." "Voice. Vice. Veracity," *The New York Times*, 4 February 2017, AR1.
4 Stephen Tropiano, *The Prime Time Closet: A History of Gays and Lesbians on TV* (New York: Applause Theatre & Cinema, 2002), 186–187.
5 *All in the Family* returned to the issue of LGBTQ rights six years later in an episode about Edith's cousin, who, at her funeral, is revealed to have been a lesbian.
6 "Will and Grace Star Confirms He's Gay," *Us Magazine*, March 8, 2010, https://www.usmagazine.com/celebrity-news/news/will-and-grace-star-confirms-hes-gay-201083/, accessed July 17, 2018.
7 Irene Lacher, "Sean Hayes is on top of 'the World,'" *Los Angeles Times*, October 26, 2013, http://www.latimes.com/entertainment/tv/showtracker/la-et-st-ca-sean-hayes-conversation-20131027-story.html, accessed July 17, 2018.
8 Quoted in Deborah Jermyn, *Sex and the City* (Detroit, MI: Wayne State University Press, 2009), 2.
9 Candace Bushnell, *Sex and the City* (New York: Grand Central Publishing, 1996), viii.
10 Amy Sohn, *Sex and the City: Kiss and Tell*, revised edition text by Sarah Wildman, introduction by Sarah Jessica Parker (New York: Pocket Books, 2002, 2004), 103.
11 Amanda D. Lotz, "Sex, Careers, and Mr. Right in Comedic Dramas: The 'New' New Woman of *Ally McBeal* and *Sex and the City*," in *Redesigning Women: Television After the Network Era*, (Urbana, IL: University of Illinois Press, 2006), 90–91.
12 Sohn, 102.
13 Kathleen Rowe, *The Unruly Woman: Gender and the Genres of Laughter* (Austin, TX: The University of Texas Press, 1995).
14 Emily Nussbaum, in *The New Yorker*, agrees with the idea that the women represent differing ideological positions, but she assigns the positions differently than I have: "Miranda and Carrie were second-wave feminists, who believed in egalitarianism; Charlotte and Samantha were third-wave feminists, focused on exploiting the power

of femininity, from opposing angles." "Difficult Women," *The New Yorker*, July 29, 2013, https://www.newyorker.com/magazine/2013/07/29/difficult-women.
15 Laura Mulvey, "Visual Pleasure and Narrative Cinema," *Screen* 16, no. 3 (October 1975): 6–18.
16 Jermyn, 49–50.
17 Jermyn, 49.
18 Jermyn, 47.
19 Lucas Grindley, "Cynthia Nixon: Being Bisexual 'Is Not a Choice,'" *The Advocate*, January 30, 2012, https://www.advocate.com/news/daily-news/2012/01/30/cynthia-nixon-being-bisexual-not-choice, accessed August 3, 2018.
20 Jermyn, 64.
21 Ibid.
22 Ibid.
23 Ibid.

5

COMEDY, RACE, ETHNICITY, AND RELIGION

Comedy can be a rebellious force. It can satirize the powers-that-be and challenge the status quo. However, during the network era of radio and television, comedy more often than not contributed to the suppression of groups of Americans who were not white, English-speaking Protestants of northern-European descent. Broadcasting networks during the 1930s through the 1960s, in line with the dominant culture of the time, used superiority humor to marginalize subcultures of persons of African and Asian descent, Spanish-speaking Latinxs, non-Protestant religions (principally, Jews and Catholics), and persons with disabilities, among others. And there were times when television entirely excluded such subcultures from its comedies. Whether through ridicule or neglect, the sitcom helped build representations of such subcultures as the "Other," as something different from "us." And not only were these subcultures different, they were also viewed as inferior—thus encouraging superiority humor.

Humor targeting racial, ethnic, national-descent, and religious subcultures is the foundation on which the sitcom genre was built in the radio era, as I stressed in the sitcom history chapter. In the late 1920s, *Amos 'n' Andy* (radio, 1928–1960; TV, 1951–1953) and *The Goldbergs* (radio, 1929–1946; TV, 1949–1957) attracted enormous radio audiences by exploiting stereotypes of African Americans and Jews, respectively. If listeners chuckled at these programs, they were clearly placing themselves above the programs' characters, deriving

Hobbesian amusement based on superiority—as I have discussed in the Introduction using the example of the Latina character, Gloria, in *Modern Family* (2009–2020). These radio shows debuted over 90 years ago and in the intervening time, the situation comedy has veered from exploitation to near total erasure of minority faces and voices to a more diverse representation of American cultures.

I approach race and ethnicity from a position that recognizes that race is more "performative" than it is "biological," which parallels Judith Butler's approach to gender (discussed in the previous chapter). Scholars of racial identity stress that people *perform* race and ethnicity, which, to a large extent, are *not* determined by biology. In this view, race is less a function of skin colors or facial features than it is defined by social conventions of what those colors/features mean in our culture. Thus, race and ethnicity are principally socially *constructed*. As sociologists Michael Omi and Howard Winant contend in their "racial formation" approach, we should examine how certain physical signifiers (e.g., brown skin) become anchored in specific racial meanings (e.g., African descent).[1] Crucially, this approach spurns the concept that holds that races have essential, fixed biological determinants—a perspective deemed racial "essentialism."[2]

For example, an essentialist would insist that if your skin is a certain color then you are unchangeably categorized as "white," if it's another, then you are unchangeably categorized "black." However, skin colors signify very different things in dissimilar social contexts. For example, a woman of Greek descent, whose skin could be as dark a shade as many African Americans', might be viewed as "black" in US society despite her European heritage. This hypothetical Greek is positioned as black because she is not-white; she is Other to the dominant US race of whiteness. However, in Greece, among others of a similar skin shade, she would be considered to be "white," to be European. Her race would change based on the context. It is not eternally fixed by the particular color of her skin. Moreover, other signifiers of race, especially certain styles of dress and hair, are not forever limited to the persons of that race and *only* those persons. Subcultural fashion is frequently coopted by the dominant culture.

For example, corn rows are a hair style associated with persons of African descent, but a person of Italian descent could style their hair in that fashion. Signifiers like hair style can shift across persons who identify as one race or another, but even though they are not part of one's biological racial essence, they are still not wholly arbitrary. Similarly, the highly controversial use of the n-word by persons other than African Americans illustrates how language, though not based in physical attributes of race, is firmly delimited by cultural norms and customs.

In this chapter, I will explore various comedy strategies incorporated in TV shows that present characters who are viewed as Other, who belong to America's racial and ethnic subcultures. African-American characters and their situations will provide the bulk of my examples, but it's important to remain alert to the ways that the experiences of other subcultures diverge from the black experience. The chapter begins by assaying the different racial/ethnic discourses that the sitcom has engaged. I will also provide a brief historical overview of race in the sitcom. Finally, our case study, *Black-ish*, will illuminate how these discourses function in a specific program.

Understanding Race in Cinema and TV Studies

Early work on race in the cinema and television concentrated on identifying pernicious stereotypes and rooting them out. *Amos 'n' Andy* was a particularly notorious case, because it drew heavily on 19th-century minstrel routines that ridiculed African Americans during the days of slavery and because it was written and performed by two white men, Freeman F. Gosden and Charles J. Correll, who were essentially performing in "blackvoice." As with blackface, blackvoice trades heavily on African-American stereotypes. For instance, one common stereotype was that blacks were abnormally superstitious and fearful of ghosts or "hants." The stereotype comes to life in an *Amos 'n' Andy* episode where Andy (Correll) is offered a job as a night watchman in a funeral parlor, but when he and Amos (Gosden) realize the location of the job, they are scared witless. The script for the episode spells out the dialogue in dialect:

Andy: I ruther git a job paintin' flag poles dan I would bein' a night watchman in a undertaker's place. ... It's mo' hants in a undertaker's place dan anyplace in de world.

Amos: I'se scared o' hants too—I ain't goin' mess 'round none of 'em. I'se still scared—I dont guess I goin' be able to go to sleep tonight.[3]

Reading in the 21st-century, we cringe at the obviously degrading attitude the white writers took toward black characters. When the target of the ridicule is a group of persons in a vulnerable subculture, such as blacks, Latinxs, gays, Jews, and other minorities, then the humor is being used as a weapon to keep them powerless. It limits their representation to stereotypes and subverts the development of fully rounded characters. Another archetypal radio sitcom, *The Goldbergs*, also had a distinct ethnic slant, centering on the matriarch of a stereotypical Jewish family who was played by the show's creator and writer, Gertrude Berg. It and *Amos 'n' Andy* established the viability of the genre, but they did little to break out of stereotypes that held Jews and African Americans back.

Identifying stereotypes and discussing the effects of negative images propagated by them are on-going elements of the analysis of subcultural figures in sitcoms, but a more nuanced approach explores the ideological values associated with these images. Such values have been bundled together by scholars into what may be termed a "discourse," and when they inform the representation of a subculture they are termed "discursive strategies." In *Watching Race: Television and the Struggle for "Blackness"*, Herman Gray identifies television's discursive strategies for handling race.[4] Programs use these strategies, in his words, to "construct, frame, stage, and narrate general issues of race."[5] In practical terms, such strategies determine storylines given to subcultural characters and shape how they will be presented on screen—including very basic narrative-building elements such as their costume design, hair and make-up styles, and what they say and which dialects they use to say it. Gray has found that there are three principal ways that television tells stories about African Americans—discursive strategies that guide the representation of African-American characters and their narrative constructs. He labels them "assimilationist," "pluralist," and "multiculturalist."[6]

Gray's 1995 study offers helpful lenses through which to view subculture characters in sitcoms, but I would argue that recent shifts in the TV industry have affected how these strategies function. Consequently, I will use Gray's comments on sitcoms as a springboard for my discussion of race in the genre, but the careful reader may note my departure from his conclusions—especially in his distinction between pluralist and multiculturalist discourses.[7] The following list includes Gray's examples of his discursive categories, to which I have added a few programs released after his book's publication:

1. Assimilationist (invisibility): *The Golden Girls* (1985–1992), *Designing Women* (1986–1993), *Parks and Recreation* (2009–2015), *The Mindy Project* (2012–2017)
2. Pluralist (separate but equal): *The Jeffersons* (1975–1985), *Sanford & Son* (1972–1977), *The Fresh Prince of Bel-Air* (1990–1996), *Girlfriends* (2000–2008), *The Carmichael Show* (2015–2017)
3. Multiculturalist (diversity): *Frank's Place* (1987–1988), *Roc* (1991–1994), *The Bernie Mac Show* (2001–2006), *Black-ish* (2014–)

Comedy and the Assimilationist Discourse

Sitcoms that incarnate an assimilationist discourse downplay the "otherness" of subculture groups—implying that those groups ought to fit in, to assimilate, into the broader culture. Assimilationist sitcoms minimize the differences among cultures and argue for the similarities among all humans. The narrative conflicts in such shows do not stem from a subculture's distinct struggles within the greater culture.

Rather, the minority character in such shows is put in situations that could occur to anyone—sitcom tropes, such as Evan Smith's "predicaments" and "character mixes" listed in Table 1.1. An African American or a Latinx could be caught in a "big lie" or "surefire scheme" predicament that would be the same if a white character were in it. As Gray says, assimilationism "celebrate[s] invisibility and color blindness."[8] Racially charged physical signifiers of a subculture are de-emphasized in favor of stories about the "universal" human condition and the situations that individuals experience that do not connect to the specifics of their race, ethnicity, national origin, or religion.

The assimilationist discourse can be observed in *Julia* (1968–1971), a ground-breaking sitcom that was the first prime-time program showcasing an African-American woman who wasn't a maid or a servant. Julia (Diahann Carroll) works in a white-collar, professional job as a nurse. And she is a widow with a young son, Corey (Marc Copage). The program mostly followed sitcom conventions with plots centered on the protagonist's work, family, and romantic life; and it was accused by some critics of being out of touch with African-American realities—especially during the tumultuous year in which Martin Luther King, Jr. was assassinated, just five months before *Julia* premiered.

However, the program did devote several episodes to issues of race. In one, Corey argues with a white friend about whether Santa Claus is white or black and Julia sighs in exasperation, "It's times like this that I wish everybody was beige ... or plaid ... Especially Santa Claus." And in another, the plot centers on the issue of "open housing" (i.e., equal-opportunity housing) when a white neighbor makes prejudiced remarks about Julia and her son and tries to convince the white landlord to evict them. The conflict is resolved when Julia saves the neighbor's granddaughter from choking and the neighbor comes to see the error of her bigoted ways. In both cases, the program clearly assumes a liberal, assimilationist perspective. That is, the differences between the races are minimized, emphasizing the similarities among all peoples. By suggesting that blacks should be assimilated into American culture, however, this perspective can erase the unique qualities of black culture—making everybody "beige."

In *Julia*, according to African-American activists, a black actor played a part that did not celebrate her blackness or sufficiently engage it for the episode's storylines (with those exceptions noted earlier of black-themed stories). This aspect of assimilationism is closely allied with the concept of color-blind casting—the premise of which is that actors should be placed in roles regardless of their race, ethnicity, national descent, or religion. On the surface, this sounds like a much-needed advance for minority actors, opening a wider range of roles to them. After all, the lack of race-specific roles between 1953 and 1968 caused the erasure of subculture characters from the sitcom. However, as Kristen J. Warner argues, color-blind casting has backfired in that it elides cultural differences and characters wind up being written as white English-speakers of Northern European descent. She contends, "the practice, while certainly beneficial to people of color in terms of gaining employment, ultimately produces normatively white characters who happen to be of color."[9]

Sitcom roles can be identified that were cast with what appears to be little concern for the actors' race or ethnicity. Consider, for example, producers Greg Daniels and Michael Schur's casting of *Parks and Recreation*, a workplace sitcom set in the fictitious town of Pawnee, in the American Midwest. Reportedly, the first two actors cast were both persons of color: African-American Rashida Jones and Indian-American Aziz Ansari.[10] The remainder of the initial cast was white, but African-American actress, Retta, was a recurring cast member whose role increased as the show went on. Jones, Ansari, and Retta played Ann Perkins, Tom Haverford, and Donna Meagle, respectively.

Ann, Tom, and Donna are characters whose race and national origin have little impact on their storylines. Moreover, Ann's appearance does not carry any markers of blackness. She is a character that reads as white. During much of her career, Jones has played characters of indeterminate, white, or mixed race. A mixed-race person herself, she played a character with a black father and a white mother in *Boston Public* (2000–2004) and won a National Association for the Advancement of Colored People (NAACP) Image Award for the portrayal. She's also incarnated white characters, particularly those of Italian descent—as in her roles as Karen Filippelli on *The Office* (2005–2013) and Karen Scarfolli on *Freaks and Geeks* (1999–2000). In contrast, Retta's race is clearly not indeterminate, but her character, Donna, is a quirky, unique character who does not embody black stereotypes and whose storylines don't rely on race. She is known, among other things, for her skill at real estate (Regal Meagle Realty).

Tom is an interesting character in terms of race and ethnicity, because he himself has consciously decided to erase his national origin and religion—to assimilate fully into American culture. As he explains in the pilot episode, speaking directly to the camera: "When I was 18 I changed my name from Aziz Abdul Al'Rahman to Tom Haverford. The cold hard fact is that dark-skinned people with funny-sounding Muslim names just don't make it very far in politics." He pauses and then continues, "Yes, okay, fine, Barack Obama. Why does everyone always bring up Barack Obama? That's *one* counter-example!" The pilot makes one other joke based on Tom's ethnic appearance. Leslie Nope (Amy Poehler) speaks to the camera: "Tom and I work great together. We're both outsiders—me as a woman, him as … whatever he is. I wanna say … Libyan? … *Plus*, he worships the prophet Mahomet." The camera then cuts to Tom, as if he's replying to Leslie: "*Tom Haverford*—c'mon, I'm Episcopalian. Three years now." Tom is also obsessed with mainstream American fashion and music and tries to run a nightclub. He plainly exemplifies the experience of immigrants who aspire to full assimilation. Interestingly, Ansari went on to create his own half-hour comedy for Netflix with *Parks and Recreation* writer, Alan Yang. The result, *Master of None* (2015–2017), centers on an Indian-American comic who struggles against the pull to assimilate into the American mainstream—quite the opposite of Tom Haverford.

The sitcom is a genre that has a checkered history when it comes to race. On the one hand, the genre can fall prey to stereotypes and minstrel-style superiority humor that degrades its subcultures. On the other hand, the genre can erase the markers that make subcultures distinctive, as we see in assimilationist programs. A role that reads as no particular race, ethnicity, or national origin winds up appearing to be white. Color-blind casting, which opens the doors for actors of color to play a greater variety of roles, can also have the unintended consequence of discouraging writers from building characters with distinct markers of race, ethnicity, and national origin. One solution to the paucity of roles for African Americans was the rise in the 1990s of the black-cast sitcom, as is outlined in Chapter 2, as well as below. These shows existed in a parallel universe to the white-cast sitcoms of the time, such as *Friends* (1994–2004) and *Seinfeld* (1989–1998). They exemplify the pluralist discursive strategy of "separate but equal."

Comedy and the Pluralist Discourse

"Separate but equal" was a legal doctrine that underpinned the culture of segregation in the post-Civil War South. It arose in the late 19th century as a justification for keeping the races socially divided. By law, blacks and whites were not allowed to marry or to mix in schools or in municipal facilities like swimming pools, and they did not share public bathrooms or drinking fountains. Further, white business owners were permitted to limit the patronage of movie theaters, hotels, funeral parlors and cemeteries, and barber shops and beauty salons, among other services, to their white customers. Of course, the ugly truth of "separate but equal" was that these facilities and services were seldom "equal." Blacks were channeled to separate, *but inferior*, schools, theaters, hotels, and so on. The court case of *Brown v. Board of Education*, in 1954, was the beginning of the end of this doctrine, but it took many years for all public services in the South to integrate and even today there has been a re-segregation of schools in many American communities. Perhaps the only positive consequence of segregation is that African Americans were forced to develop their own vigorous cultural traditions in music, language and literature, art, fashion, and cuisine—quite separate from dominant white culture. And they built traditions such as soul-food restaurants, historically black colleges and universities (HBCU), barber shops, and hair salons where their community bonds could be reestablished. The

African-American subculture was separate from mainstream culture for decades and in many ways it was as robust, if not more so, than that culture.

It is fitting to think of the black-cast sitcoms of the 1990s and 2000s as "separate but equal" to contemporary white-cast sitcoms, because black-cast and white-cast sitcoms did indeed live in separate worlds, but they were *not* equal in their size of audience, economic clout, or the reach of their TV networks. White-cast programs such as *Friends*, *Seinfeld*, and *Frasier* (1993–2004) were on NBC when network television was still predominant. There were some black-cast shows on the Big Three networks (e.g., *Sanford and Son* on NBC, 1972–1977), but many of the later black-cast shows were on fledgling networks that were trying to establish themselves by reaching out to an under-served niche audience (black viewers). When Fox, the WB, and UPN began developing black-cast shows in the early 1990s, they weren't even carried in all major markets in the USA. And cable-network Black Entertainment Television (BET) had to fight to be added to the line-ups of cable television giants. Thus, "separate but *not* equal" would be a more honest description of both predominantly black schools and black-cast programs. Many black-cast programs were as entertaining and humorous as white-cast ones, but the former were severely curtailed in their access to a national audience and their impact on mainstream culture.

Pluralist sitcoms, thus, are programs where most of the characters belong to a social subculture and the stories largely take place within that culture. There are three ways that pluralism may play out.

First, the subculture may be exploited for superiority humor. Superiority humor is marketed to the mainstream viewers who are amused by the ridiculing, demeaning, and dehumanizing of persons they consider inferior, positioning them as the subordinate Other. In the case of the *Amos 'n' Andy* radio show, its enormous success was mostly due to white viewers' demeaning attitude toward its black characters—made particularly obvious by its producers'/actors' use of blackvoice. When *Amos 'n' Andy* attempted a television adaptation in 1951, it was clear that white performers as black characters would no longer be acceptable to the viewing public or networks' standards and practices. Gosden and Correll hired black actors Alvin Childress and Spencer Williams to play Amos and Andy, respectively; but the characters were only slightly less offensively stereotyped than their radio counterparts. Once again, the characters were lazy buffoons who avoided work and spoke in a thick "negro" dialect. The NAACP and other organizations took exception to the show and pressured CBS and the show's main advertiser (Blatz Brewing Company) to remove it from the air. Nonetheless, *Amos 'n' Andy* aired for two seasons on television until Blatz withdrew its support and CBS canceled it. (It did continue to run in syndication for years afterward.)

Second, the conventions of the genre may take precedence over the subculture's characteristics (e.g., *Family Matters* [1989–1998]). When conventions of the genre are more important than racial/ethnic markers, programs may appeal to both mainstream audiences and those of the subculture itself, because race/ethnicity is irrelevant. In such cases, superiority humor may appear but the target of the humor is not inferior due to racial characteristics. That is, characters are poked fun of for traits that are not race-specific—being clumsy or dim-witted, for example. Additionally, such shows may downplay superiority humor in favor of more generalized incongruity humor. Programs such as these are essentially a variation on the assimilationist discourse—the difference being that instead of the subcultural character (e.g., Julia, discussed earlier) seamlessly fitting into the mainstream world and their race/ethnicity becoming invisible, the story takes place within the subcultural world itself, where the stories turn out to be the same ones told within mainstream sitcoms. A show might have a predominantly black cast, for example, and yet it might still follow many of the same conventions and deploy many of the same tropes as shows with predominantly white casts. As Gray maintains, in these programs "black people live out simple and largely one-dimensional lives in segregated universes where they encounter the usual televisual challenges in the domestic sphere—social relations, child rearing, awkward situations, personal embarrassment, and romance."[11]

In *Family Matters*, for instance, the black Winslow family faces the same sorts of domestic disturbances that, say, the white Anderson family of *Father Knows Best* did in the 1950s. An episode from *Family Matters'* first season, titled "The Big Fix" (February 9, 1990), is exemplary of the show's narrative problematic. Closely following the conventions of the family sitcom that I articulated in Chapter 3, *Family Matters* raises an issue within the family each week and each week that issue is resolved. Story arcs generally do not persist across episodes, which is part of the sitcom format established early on in the genre's history. In "The Big Fix," the A story is based on a predicament involving the teenaged daughter, Laura (Kellie Shanygne Williams), being inveigled into a date with the annoyingly nerdy Steve Urkel (Jaleel White). Urkel, as most of the characters call him, tutors Laura's brother, Eddie (Darius McCrary), in exchange for the date and Laura agrees out of loyalty to Eddie. Brothers making deals for dates with their sisters is a long-standing sitcom trope. Naturally, the date is disastrous. The particular romantic effort of this week is concluded, but the on-going enigma surrounding the kids' romantic incidents remains open for future episodes. The episode's B story falls into the well-worn sitcom category of bumbling dads as it tracks the father, Carl (Reginald VelJohnson), in his vain attempt to repair the wobbly legs of a kitchen chair. By the episode's end, the chair is in worse shape than it was at the start and his family members all enjoy his humiliating failure. During this *Family Matters* episode, the characters' race is never mentioned and plainly the storylines are not specific to African Americans' experience. However, the characters are not trying to fit in or assimilate into mainstream white society, as on *Julia*. That society is simply irrelevant to the characters' lives.

The third type of pluralist sitcom also creates a world separated from white society, but, in contrast to shows like *Family Matters*, the pluralism of the characters' race is acknowledged in the storylines and character construction. That is, black culture is a core element of narrative structure and characterizations. Programs that are designed primarily for the enjoyment of members of the subculture itself and not mainstream viewers use language and other cultural signifiers (fashion, hair style, etc.) that may be unfamiliar to the mainstream viewer. These programs adhere to a code that is shared by its producers and its viewers, but possibly not the mainstream viewer. Unlike *Family Matters*, which aired on established broadcast networks with broad appeal across demographics—ABC for eight seasons and then CBS for one—sitcoms on smaller networks and streamed on SVOD services can create stories that depend on viewers' knowledge of a subculture.

Girlfriends (2000–2008), for example, spent six seasons on a fledgling network that no longer exists: United Paramount Network or UPN. When UPN failed in 2006, *Girlfriends* moved to another new network, The CW, for two more seasons. In terms of simple quantity, *Girlfriends* did not have a massive audience, but its ratings numbers for the demographic of African Americans, aged 18–34, were very high. It played to its culturally "separate" audience by centering the stories on four single African-American women who represent different aspects of the black experience. Joan Clayton (Tracee Ellis Ross) is a lawyer and thus a black urban professional, a type that has earned the slang term, "buppie" (as a black equivalent to a yuppie). Joan's legal assistant is Maya Wilkes (Golden Brooks), who is more streetwise than Joan and is close to becoming the stereotype of the "angry black woman" from the 'hood. Joan speaks in a white dialect while Maya's speech is more conventionally "ghetto." The backstory of the other two friends—Toni Childs-Garrett (Jill Marie Jones) and Lynn Searcy (Persia White)—is that they were Joan's roommates while they all attended UCLA. Toni is presented as a black woman who is shrewd and sometimes selfish and calculating. At times she falls into the "angry black woman" or "sapphire" stereotype—an irritable character who is outspoken and has an aggressive attitude toward men. Lynn, a mixed-race character, is the most avant-garde, politically active, and sexually adventurous of the group. She breaks stereotypes of how black women are "supposed" to behave, but she also is representative of a strain in African-American culture that rejects mainstream values of middle-class culture, whether black or white. She is a musician and an artist and storylines emphasize her unconventional attitudes.

The *Girlfriends* episode titled "Hip-Ocracy" (October 2, 2000) illuminates how the show engages with black issues and uses touchstones from black culture to advance the narrative. The plot centers on Joan's blind date with Marcus (Rodney Van Johnson), a man with extraordinarily wide hips. When she visits his apartment, she examines various objects in his bedroom that have significance within black culture and which tell her what sort of African-American character he is. First, she finds CDs for jazz musician John Coltrane and R&B singer Macy Gray and then a novel by noted African-American author Walter Mosley. With each object, she expresses her approval. These objects are racially coded signifiers for, as Joan says, "good taste" within black culture. For the viewer that shares this cultural code, the objects distinctively connote Marcus as a particular type of black person. For the viewer who is removed from black culture, Joan's checklist of cultural objects will have no meaning. Other coded remarks in the episode allude to South African leader Nelson Mandela, rap musician Notorious B.I.G., actor Wesley Snipes, activist Jesse Jackson and his "Rainbow Coalition," and the Tuskegee syphilis experiment (in which poor black men in Tuskegee, Alabama went untreated for syphilis as part of a science experiment, without their consent).

The reliance upon black cultural touchstones in this episode extends beyond allusions such as these. Its narrative enigma is based on the issue of skin-tone discrimination as it manifests itself within the black community. Colorism is the discrimination against persons with a darker skin tone. It can be found in dominant culture in situations where darker-colored individuals run into biases against them when, for example, they're applying for jobs. It can also be found within black communities and that is the issue that forms the main storyline in this *Girlfriends* episode. After Joan's favorable reaction to Marcus's CDs and book, she then is surprised to find a girdle and to learn that he wears it to slim his large hips. This causes Joan to run from his apartment, screaming in voiceover. Later, her friends accuse her of being superficial and judging Marcus on his looks. This catalyzes a discussion among the friends about colorism, which the friends say parallels Joan's bias against Marcus's appearance.

The show's cast exemplifies a variety of African-American skin tones—ranging from the light, mixed-race coloring of Persia White to the significantly darker skin of Jill Marie Jones (see Figures 5.1 & 5.2). Jones's character, Toni, expresses a colorist attitude toward her own blind date, telling her friends that she rejected him because "he's too black." Her friends are appalled at her colorist attitude and defend the diversity of African-American skin tones. Maya exclaims, "Did the whole 'Black is beautiful' movement skip your ass?" And Lynn adds, "Say it loud: black and proud" and she jokes, "It's our different skin tones that keeps the white man perplexed." Toward the episode's end, Toni has a heart-to-heart conversation with Joan and describes how colorism has negatively affected her life. She says that she didn't want to have children with a dark-skinned man, because of the effect it'd have on her daughter: "I don't want her going through life hearing, 'Oh, you're cute for a dark-skinned girl.' Or, 'tar baby'

Figure 5.1 An episode of *Girlfriends* raises the issue of colorism within the black community when darker-skinned Toni ...

Figure 5.2 ... accuses lighter-skinned, mixed-race Maya of not being able to understand the struggles of African Americans with darker skin tones.

or 'skillet.'" As is common in the sitcom, this episode does not resolve Toni's issues or the larger controversy surrounding colorism and the men that she and Joan date are not recurring characters. The show's narrative problematic relies on race-related stories *not* being fully resolved so that they may be returned to again and again.

The reliance upon race for the subjects of its stories, in conjunction with the racially coded allusions to black culture, mark *Girlfriends* as a pluralist black-cast show that existed in a parallel universe to white-cast shows. A colorism-related plotline never occurred in *The Andy Griffith Show*, and the *Girlfriends* characters never went skipping down a country lane with fishing poles on their shoulders. The two shows were "separate but equal" in terms of their use of the sitcom form and their appeal to their respective demographics. However, measured in terms of budgets or audience sizes, *Girlfriends* was a relatively modest program. It remained a show for a niche audience and its impact on the broader television audience was consequently limited. Pluralist sitcoms thus tend to ghettoize its characters. Yes, they do engage with race and its issues, but they remain walled off from the general TV audience—hiding their stories. And assimilationist shows enact a different type of hiding. They erase racial difference in the name of "universal" stories, which inevitably are white stories. Gray envisions a form of discourse where the distinct characteristics of race are maintained, but they are not relegated to a separate world or defined as the Other. He argues that a multicultural discourse can achieve this while "interrogating and engaging African American cultural traditions, perspectives, and experiences."[12]

Comedy and the Multiculturalist Discourse

The multiculturalist discourse shares with pluralism the recognition of cultural diversity among whites, blacks, Latinx, and persons of Asian descent and diverging religions. Unlike assimilationist tenets, multiculturalism does not advocate the suppression of that diversity into the supposed universality of the human condition—as in *Julia*. However, multiculturalism also does not agree with the pluralist separation of cultures—as in black-cast shows such as *Girlfriends* running parallel to white-cast shows such as *Seinfeld*. In an ideal multiculturalist world, the distinctive aspects of both the dominant culture and a society's subcultures would be valued and appreciated. And because subcultures are not exploited or suppressed, the multiculturalist sitcom avoids superiority humor that relies on stereotyping and comes at the expense of subcultures. In short, the multiculturalist sitcom favors incongruity humor over superiority humor.

Of course, there are still characters in multiculturalist shows to whom the viewer feels superior, but that superiority is not built on racial or ethnic chauvinism. If, for instance, a Latinx character is ridiculed because of their poor English skills, then that would be superiority humor from a dominant perspective. If, instead, that Latinx character is made fun of because, say, they have foolishly boasted that they are able to fix a chair leg (see *Family Matters* earlier), then humor can be drawn from incongruity when they sit in the repaired chair and it breaks. As is often the case in humor, the cultural politics of superiority humor is not always clear-cut in the sitcom. Humor can theoretically be built out of the specific attributes of a race or ethnic group without stereotyping and exploiting that group, but the potential for victimization always exists because one cannot always predict the response of viewers to a narrative situation.

The potential for exploitation is illuminated by an incident involving African-American comic Dave Chappelle and his popular sketch-comedy program, *Chappelle's Show* (2003–2006). The program featured a series of "stereotype pixie" sketches, with Chappelle performing in stereotypical costume and make-up as a small imp who encourages people to behave according to racial and ethnic stereotypes. In different sketches, he appears as white, Latino, and Asian pixies. The black pixie, which Chappelle later termed the "visual personification of the n-word," wears minstrel garb and performs in blackface make-up.[13] In the sketch, the pixie appears to Chappelle while he is traveling on an airplane and the attendant offers him fish or chicken to eat. The pixie plays into black stereotypes by exclaiming excitedly, "Oo-wee! I just heard the magic word. Chicken! Go on and order a big bucket, n----r, and take a bite, you black motherfucker!" The pixie then begins dancing. Chappelle resists the pixie's demand and orders fish, which angers the pixie and he continues to castigate Chappelle, demanding he fulfill the stereotype of black people loving to eat fried chicken. By having Chappelle calmly resist the pixie's insistence to conform to a stereotype, the sketch is patently critiquing the racism behind the pixie's goading, but Chappelle began to wonder if the sketch was, in his words, "socially irresponsible." And during its taping, as Chappelle describes the incident, "somebody on the set [who] was white laughed in such a way—I know the difference of people laughing with me and people laughing at me—and it was the first time I had ever gotten a laugh that I was uncomfortable with. Not just uncomfortable, but like, should I fire this person?"[14] The occurrence so rattled Chappelle that he hastily quit the show in the middle of production and retreated to South Africa.

The dilemma that Chappelle faced can be explained in terms of the theory of humor. Chappelle's stated intention is that the sketch invokes incongruity humor. The stereotype pixie is incongruous with Chappelle's image on *Chappelle Show*, in general, and his performance in the sketch as a calm African-American passenger. The pixie also plays off of a common cinematic special effect where a small devil and angel appear on a character's shoulders and implore them to behave badly or well, respectively. Except, in this case, the devil sprite is a minstrel performer—incongruously so. Plus, having the pixie use the n-word and profanity does not fit with its diminutive appearance. These are not the words you expect a small fairy to use. Thus, the incongruities of the stereotype pixie might generate humor where the viewer is laughing *with* Chappelle and his situation. However, the pixie also relies on a very long tradition of African-American minstrel performers wearing blackface and ridiculing themselves for the amusement of white audiences, which is clearly depending on superiority humor. In these terms, we can say that Chappelle was aiming for incongruity humor, but, when the white crew member laughed too hard and too long, he feared that (white) viewers might indulge in superiority humor while watching the sketch. For him, at that time, the dilemma was unresolvable, and he chose to virtually remove himself from public performances for several years.

Multiculturalist Discourse and the Sitcom Form

Short comedy sketches are more vulnerable than half-hour comedies to the dilemmas Chappelle suffered, because the characters must be established rapidly and it's difficult to create much backstory or context for them. Multiculturalist discourse is not simple to achieve in the situation comedy either, which is why relatively few programs have attempted it. But by examining how the sitcom form accommodates this discourse, we can see certain advantages to the genre's conventions when it comes to the representation of multiculturalism.

Multiculturalist shows' loglines, their narrative problematics, feature elements of subcultures' experiences and struggles. Consider a show such as *The Neighborhood* (2018–), whose logline is: "The nicest guy in the Midwest moves his family into a tough neighborhood in L.A. where not everyone appreciates his extreme neighborliness."[15] Unspoken in its official logline is that the "nicest guy" is white and the "tough neighborhood" is historically black. Moreover, the arrival of Midwesterner Dave Johnson (Max Greenfield) rankles Calvin Butler (Cedric the Entertainer), who views him as an unwelcome intruder into his neighborhood. The show's title gestures toward the white racist fear that black neighbors will lower a neighborhood's property values, which, in this case, is reversed when whites move into a black neighborhood and, in Calvin's view, are ruining it. Thus, the subtext of the show's logline is that each episode's individual enigma will be based on the clash of cultures between white Midwesterners and black Los Angelenos—the standard sitcom "fish out of water" trope. That clash is repeatable and ultimately unresolvable, which makes it useful to the sitcom form. Sitcom form requires a recurring conflict, one which will not be fully resolved until the series finale (if then). Assimilationist shows' loglines typically ignore matters of race or ethnicity. And pluralist ones can be race agnostic (as in *Family Matters*) or they can engage those matters in separate-but-equal situations where the races barely interact with one another (as in *Girlfriends*). What is distinctively multiculturalist about a show like *The Neighborhood* is that it has two races interacting with one another. The black family does not assimilate into white, Midwestern culture (or vice versa), but, rather, the diversity of the core characters is the source of the humor. In one episode, the white characters are made to understand how racial profiling operates. In another, Dave intrudes into the black barbershop that Calvin feels is his turf. Dave comes to comprehend the sanctity of black barbershops and their community function while Calvin is stunned to find the black patrons like Dave better than him. In both of these episodes, a specific race's experiences and attributes are the source of humor, but it is humor that arises from incongruities and not superiorities. If *The Neighborhood* succeeds as a multiculturalist show it is because the *recurring* nature of the conflict allows it to explore different facets of those contrasting cultures—something that is difficult to accomplish in a single sketch.

Two aspects of sitcom narrative form that nurture a multiculturalist discourse are its large, ensemble cast and, if the show is a hit, its story's extensive length. Conventional sitcoms like *Cheers* (1982–1993), *Friends*, or *The Big Bang Theory* (2007–2019) profit diegetically from their multiple protagonists. Once those characters are established, the writers can spread storylines among them and not worry about spending air time establishing them. Certainly, some characters are more prominent than others, but the number of protagonists allows for a diversity of storylines. One week, character A is featured and the next week it might be character B or C. Multiple protagonists also allow for a diversity of racial or ethnic positions. Subcultures are not monoliths of persons who have identical values, beliefs, and appearances. An ensemble cast facilitates a range of character types within a subculture.

Take *Fresh Off the Boat* (2015–) as an example. The program is about a family that has immigrated from Taiwan—a mother, father, three sons, and the father's mother. These six protagonists have differing attitudes toward their subculture, which is based on race (Asian), ethnicity (Chinese), and national identity (Taiwanese). In many respects, the mother, Jessica (Constance Wu), is the most committed to Taiwanese culture. She speaks English with a Mandarin dialect, encourages her sons to appreciate their Taiwanese heritage, and has numerous traits typically associated with the "tiger mom"— the stereotype of the hyper-disciplined Asian mother who obsessively pushes her children to succeed academically. On the other end of the spectrum, the oldest son, Eddie (Hudson Yang), is fully immersed in American culture (especially African-American culture) and the least invested in his Taiwanese heritage. *Fresh Off the Boat* fits the sitcom convention of a large ensemble cast and uses it to spread stories among the main characters, but it also illustrates how such a large cast enables the program to illustrate the diversity *within* an Asian-American family. And, most importantly to the sitcom form, the array of characters in *Fresh Off the Boat* includes one who resides in between the cultural extremes of Jessica and Eddie. As I've described in *The Andy Griffith Show* and *Sex and the City*, sitcoms use in-between characters to mediate between opposing positions—Andy and Samantha, respectively. In *Fresh Off the Boat*, the father, Louis (Randall Park), serves this important function. He both enthusiastically embraces American culture and he retains his reverence for Taiwanese heritage, which enables him to form a cultural bridge between the extremes of Jessica and Eddie. In-between characters are an essential component of the sitcom form and they help clear the path for multiculturalist discourse.

Further, the length of sitcom narratives and the development of characters over many episodes/seasons permits the writers and showrunners to construct three-dimensional characters, even from ones that began as two-dimensional stereotypes. Consider, for example, how a character like the white bigot, Archie Bunker, in *All in the Family*, became more multidimensional as the years went by. In *Fresh Off the Boat*, you might expect that the boys' grandmother, Jenny (Lucille Soong), would be the most stereotypically associated with Taiwanese culture, especially since she speaks very little English (preferring Mandarin, which is presented with subtitles). However, as the seasons progressed, the show played against that stereotype by revealing her to be a huge fan of Garfield, the cartoon cat, and other elements of American culture, and, in season four, she secretly takes English as a second language (ESL) classes. Because six characters are used to represent a subculture in the show, it can afford to include traits that are not stereotypical and which even derail stereotypes, and this can be baked into a character's long-term development.

A Very Brief History of Race-Based Sitcoms

One can identify a sitcom's discourse or discourses—assimilationist, pluralist, and multiculturalist—by closely examining the humor strategies the sitcom employs (superiority or incongruity) and its implementation of the genre's narrative components (recurring problematic, multiple protagonists, and long storylines). This is true of any ideological component, but it is particularly notable when thinking about race, ethnicity, and national origin. It is possible to find these discourses scattered over the history of comedies that represent subcultures, but they have not been equally represented in every era of American television. It is useful, therefore, to put these discourses into historical context and recognize how they have evolved. I have alluded to some of this history as I've presented the three discourses, but in piecemeal fashion. To sum up the representation of race and ethnicity in the sitcom, I will briefly explain how the eras of the "black situation comedy" developed. I suspect that similar eras could be found in the representation of other races and ethnicities. Indeed, the following outline might apply to *most* races and ethnicities.

Several scholars have delineated the black sitcom's history. Robin R. Means Coleman drew upon work by Cedric Clark and Angela Nelson to develop her list of six eras:[16]

1. 1950–1953: TV Minstrelsy
2. 1954–1967: Nonrecognition
3. 1968–1971: Assimilationist
4. 1972–1983: Social Relevancy and Ridiculed Black Subjectivity; aka, the Lear Era
5. 1984–1989: Black Family and Diversity; a.k.a., the Cosby Era
6. 1990–1998: Neo-Minstrelsy

The "minstrelsy" era demarcates the time of *Amos 'n' Andy* (the TV version) and *Beulah*, when superiority humor reigned and shows were populated with degrading stereotypes that were born in 19th-century minstrel shows and continued in the radio era. As the Civil Rights Movement grew in the 1950s, so did public consciousness about the harmful nature of such stereotypes. The unfortunate result was broadcast networks' near-total erasure of most subcultures from TV screens, which Means Coleman dubs the "nonrecognition" era. Out of fear, perhaps, of alienating viewers, the networks opted to avoid controversy by ignoring it. Black protagonists finally returned to television in 1968, at the start of the "assimilationist" era, as was heralded by *Julia*. Means Coleman and McIlwain contend, *Julia* "offered a racist ideology that Black culture was most prized when it approached the norms and values of Whiteness. These series sent a placating message, presenting Blacks as accommodating, docile, and nonthreatening. For those invested in Blackness, these series carried a message of cultural abandonment and assimilation."[17] In the assimilationist era, race was once again not recognized. There were black actors appearing (rarely) on television, but their roles were not written to acknowledge their blackness.

Means Coleman's era of "social relevancy and ridiculed black subjectivity" began promisingly for African-American representation in the early 1970s when producer Norman Lear led the charge to make the sitcom socially relevant. With *All in the Family*'s success, it appeared that the genre might become an advocate for social progress. Lear followed *All in the Family* with innovative black-cast shows— *Sanford and Son*, *Good Times* (1974–1979), and *The Jeffersons*. Advancing from *Julia*, it was the first time that the African-American experience and black protagonists were central to the narrative problematic. However, these shows were marred, according to Means Coleman, by separate-but-equal pluralism: "African Americans operated in odd worlds marked by knavery and bigotry, and non-Blacks need not take part except to rescue African American youth from its deficient family peril."[18] The pluralist discourse returned in the era of "neo-minstrelsy," which began in 1990. Demeaning, minstrel-era stereotypes made a comeback in the black-cast shows that sprouted on fledgling networks Fox, UPN, and The WB. Although these shows did attract a sizeable black audience and helped establish those new networks, critics decried the negative imagery on which they relied. Means Coleman and McIlwain express dismay that "Sambos, coons, and Sapphires proliferated as racial separation and inequality returned."[19]

Between the eras of ridiculed black subjectivity and neo-minstrelsy, the black sitcom experienced a brief renaissance of shows that approached multiculturalism—an era that Means Coleman titled, the "black family and diversity." In *The Cosby Show* (1984–1992), its spin-off, *A Different World* (1987–1993), and the short-lived *Frank's Place*

(1987–1988), blackness is not erased and the diversity of the black experience is explored. Also, the black characters are not sequestered in their own diegetic ghetto, separate from white characters. Some have criticized *The Cosby Show* for not going further in its representation of the African-American experience and for creating an implausible, bourgeois black family with a doctor for a father and a lawyer for a mother. In its efforts to avoid negative stereotypes, *The Cosby Show* may have worked too hard to present impossibly positive role models. In her 2005 update to her original list of eras, Means Coleman recognizes a few shows that might be opening up television to a *seventh* era, ones that might explore today's multiculturalist discourse: *The Bernie Mac Show* (2001–2006), *The Hughleys* (1998–2002), and *My Wife and Kids* (2001–2005). Debuting in 2014, *Black-ish* continues in this line and for that reason I have chosen it as this chapter's case study.

Case Study: *Black-ish*

To comprehend how race, ethnicity, national origin, and religion work within a specific sitcom, it is helpful to examine a single show that foregrounds characters of a subculture. We can then ask, how are those characters fit into the sitcom form? Does the program's logline take race into consideration? And, most importantly, how does, or does not, the show implement the discourses of assimilationism, pluralism, and/or multiculturalism? Several comedies today place a subculture front and center, but they are often ones produced by smaller cable networks or SVOD platforms and they anticipate a narrowly defined audience. One exception to this is *Black-ish*. It is notable, and a bit surprising, that a conventional broadcast network (ABC) green-lit *Black-ish*, whose title trumpets the fact that it will address African-American issues and which was created by black writer-producer Kenya Barris. Even in the 21st century, it is still uncommon for minority producers to create a program that is accepted by a broadcast-television network.

Black-ish is represented as being an autobiographical representation of Barris's life as a successful black man, with a family of six kids.

Barris observed his own kids growing up in a privileged environment that was much whiter than that of his own youth. For him, "the best story I knew was a family which was absolutely black, living in a world that was changing around them."[20] The program has focused on racial politics from the very beginning, which has earned it both fans and detractors. No less an African-American luminary than President Barack Obama has called it his "favorite show."[21] In contrast, conservative white politician Donald Trump, before he was president, suggested that *Black-ish* unfairly privileges the black experience. He tweeted, "How is ABC Television allowed to have a show entitled 'Blackish'? Can you imagine the furor of a show, 'Whiteish'! Racism at highest level?" Trump's tweet—filled with grammatical errors—qualifies the charge of "racism at the highest level" by adding a question mark at the end, but his comment still falls in line with white supremacists' claim that black-oriented TV shows, films, and affirmative-action programs are "reverse racism." Soon after Trump became president, *Black-ish* devoted an episode to the election ("Lemons," January 11, 2017). Written and directed by Barris, it tried to sort through feelings about this polarizing public figure. Obviously, *Black-ish* is not shy about addressing racially charged issues that are in today's news. Despite Trump's and others' criticism of it, it has established itself over five seasons (at the time of this writing, summer 2019). And it has been popular enough to spawn two spin-offs: *Grown-ish* (2018–) and *Mixed-ish* (2019–). The latter continues *Black-ish*'s attention to race in America by focusing on the travails of a mixed-raced family.

Black-ish's Logline, Its Narrative Problematic

When *Black-ish* was developed in 2014, it was advertised with this official logline: "Centers on an upper-middle-class black man (Anthony Anderson) who struggles to raise his children with a sense of cultural identity despite constant contradictions and obstacles coming from his liberal wife, old-school father and his own assimilated, color-blind kids."[22] From this logline we can see that the program's narrative problematic is based on the racial identities of the family members. Each week, some obstacle—often rooted in a racial issue—is confronted by the family. And each week, the family comes to some sort of understanding of that obstacle, without ever completely surmounting it. To do so would mean the end of the series. Of course, it would also mean the end of racial conflict in America and that, too, seems unlikely to occur.

The pilot episode clearly established the program's premise. In a voiceover by Andre "Dre" Johnson (Anthony Anderson), he breaks the fourth wall and speaks to the viewer. He introduces himself as "your standard old, incredibly handsome, unbelievably charismatic black dude" and his wife, Rainbow "Bow" Johnson (Tracee Ellis Ross), as a "pigment-challenged mixed-race woman." Further exposition explains that Dre was a child from "the hood" that became a successful advertising executive. In the pilot, the race-related narrative enigma centers on Dre's desire to become his advertising firm's first black senior vice president (SVP). The narrative catalyst is framed as a racial issue of breaking the color barrier. Dre's father, Earl "Pops" Johnson (Laurence Fishburne), says he should have joined a black firm, where he could have advanced more quickly; but Dre wants to prove a point by succeeding at a predominantly white firm. Thus, the show's narrative problematic could be configured in the form of a question: if a black person seeks success in a historically white profession, will they have to compromise their racial identity? In the episode, Dre is disappointed to learn that his boss has appointed him as SVP of the company's "urban division," effectively relegating Dre to deal with advertising solely for black consumers. As he asks in voiceover, "Wait. Did they just put me in charge of black stuff?" And Pops castigates him as, "head puppet of the white man." To reaffirm his black identity, Dre pitches an exaggerated video for the "LA Tourism Account" that contains images of radical black activism—including the 1992 LA riots, the police pursuit of O.J. Simpson's white Bronco, and Malcolm X. The montage ends on an image from the riots of a business displaying a sign to dissuade looters from attacking it: "BLACK OWNED THANKS." Over this image, text appears ("Keepin' it real") that is shot with bullet holes. His white boss and colleagues react with stunned silence and he is nearly fired. The episode's enigma is thus brought to a climax, forcing an answer to "Should one compromise one's authentic identity in order to succeed?" The episode resolves this question by having Dre come up with a new campaign where he emphasizes the mixing of diverse racial aspects without erasing them. As he says to the audience at the episode's conclusion, "Urban can mean hip, cool, and colorful. Just like my family." He continues, "Funny thing is, I didn't feel urban. I just felt like a dad who was willing to do whatever he had to for his family. And isn't that the American dream?"

As is conventional in sitcom narrative structure, this *Black-ish* episode has found a resolution to an immediate problem (the pitch for the LA Tourism Account) that only partially resolves the show's overarching narrative problematic (sustaining one's cultural identity). That is, one "obstacle" is overcome, but larger questions of racial identity are not fully resolved. This enables the show to continue raising new issues each week, all of which fall under the umbrella of asserting racial identity. For example, *Black-ish* has worked through stories about:

- Dr. Martin Luther King Jr. and the history of the civil rights struggle
- Police violence against African-American men and white fear of black men
- Racial stereotyping and segregation of public facilities (in an episode about pool parties)
- Interracial romance
- Colorism within the black community
- The n-word in black and white contexts

In many episodes, the larger ideological or political question is expressed through concrete experiences of a family member—as with Dre's being limited to the urban advertising market. And in each case, the episode ends with a *partial* resolution of that question. Dre finds a compromise in his ad campaign, but the larger question of whether black professionals should be restricted to working on urban projects is not definitively answered. Such is the conventional narrative structure of the sitcom.

Discourses of Race

The ways in which *Black-ish* handles its race-infused stories determine how it employs racial discourse (or discourses). The show is overall multiculturalist, even though individual characters espouse assimilationist or pluralist perspectives. As the show's logline suggests, *Black-ish*'s children are "*assimilated*, color-blind kids" (emphasis added). The "old-school" Pops comes from the days of separate-but-equal pluralism when African Americans had to fight to establish the validity of their own culture. He doesn't trust assimilation because he believes that it inevitably leads to the watering down of black culture. He's disgusted with the color-blind kids' attitude and would definitely agree with those who oppose color-blind TV casting—holding that when race is ignored in casting, the characters functionally become white. Pops' wife and Dre's mother, Ruby Johnson (Jenifer Lewis), shares Pops' pluralist view. The show began with her as a "recurring" character, but elevated her to the main cast in season two as Pops' role diminished. Thus, these characters serve a similar discursive function in the program.

In between the assimilated kids and the old-school parents, the central character, Dre, must negotiate the pressures to assimilate—resisting the tempting rewards of assimilation and repeatedly reasserting his racial identity. Dre is the literal voice of *Black-ish* because it is he who narrates the episodes and thus his in-between-ness defines the program—as does Carrie's narration of *Sex and the City* episodes. Moreover, Dre resembles Andy and Louis—in *The Andy Griffith Show* and *Fresh Off the Boat*, respectively—in that they all perform a similar mediating position among opposing discursive factions. For Andy, the factions include "big city" values (e.g., feminism) conflicting with "small town" ones. And for Louis, the factions are his Taiwanese heritage clashing with contemporary American popular culture.

Dre's wife, Bow, is another mediating, in-between figure. Her in-between-ness stems from having a white father and a black mother (as does the actress who plays her, Tracee Ellis Ross). Her position as a mixed-raced woman is often played for incongruous humor, as when her mother-in-law calls her "half-rican" instead of African American. Barris commented about Bow, "when you're black and white, it puts you right in the middle. In society there are two opposing forces and the people you love the most in your life are on either side of that, so where does that place you?"[23] Bow cannot lay claim to the "authentic" blackness of Dre because she did not grow up in the 'hood. She identifies as black, but she is implicitly and explicitly criticized by Dre and his parents for not being "black enough." This is established early in the show's history when, in the pilot, Dre and Bow argue about the authenticity of the promotional campaign on which Dre is working:

Bow: You gotta keep it real.
Dre: Keep it real? All this coming from a biracial or mixed or omni-colored complexion or whatever-it-is-they're-calling-it-today woman, who, technically, isn't even really black.
Bow: Okay, well, if I'm not really black then could somebody please tell my hair and my ass!

In some respects, Bow fulfills the stereotype of the "tragic mulatto," the mixed race person doomed to an unhappy life alienated from both white and black society. She must negotiate the pressure to assimilate in different ways than Dre does, which can be seen in the pilot episode when she tells him he's going too far when he pushes his black attitude in his white boss' face. In this episode, she is presented as the voice of reason who helps Dre understand that he has gone overboard in his rejection of assimilation. Both she and Dre are characters in the middle, bringing together two extreme discourses on race (assimilationism and pluralism), but doing so in a slightly different fashion. Bow's biracial position became increasingly important to *Black-ish* storylines, resulting in an entire episode, titled "Bow-racial," being devoted to it and the launching of a spin-off, *Mixed-ish*, in 2019. *Mixed-ish* is a prequel to *Black-ish* that shows a young Bow growing up in a mixed-race family.

The Humor of *Black-ish:* Incongruity

As Dave Chappelle's "stereotype pixie" incident illustrates, creating humor out of race is a very tricky proposition. Humor can function as an instrument of power, as a way that subcultures are derided and suppressed. As Means Coleman's timeline shows, degrading minstrel stereotypes did not die with *Amos 'n' Andy*. They resurrected in the 1990s and they could come back today. *Black-ish* studiously avoids slipping into superiority-grounded minstrel humor. The characters are not mocked for their racial attributes. Although Dre does do things that the more levelheaded Bow labels stupid, they are generally not stereotypically buffoonish, as is Chappelle's stereotype pixie. Instead of superiority humor, the majority of *Black-ish*'s humor is based in incongruity.

Black-ish is a single-camera show, not a multicamera sitcom shot with an audience. This allows it to control editing more precisely, which can pay dividends in its ability to generate incongruity humor. Specifically, the show often builds humor through juxtaposition—especially of the past and the present. When it begins the episode "Dr. Hell No" with footage of the notorious Tuskegee syphilis experiment (1932–1972) and then cuts to Dre's prostate exam it constructs humor by contrasting the terrible damage done to African-American men in Tuskegee, Alabama, with his own minor, modern-day medical concerns. Further, the visual contrast between the black-and-white footage from Tuskegee and the color images of Dre makes the viewer aware of the cinematographic differences between the two. This humor could only be achieved through the viewer's awareness of a TV/film technical aspect (B&W vs. color cinematography), which thus makes it televisual humor. *Black-ish* is also fond of another editing technique that is uncommon in multicam shows: the quick flashback vignette of just two or three shots, which often interrupts a scene. Both modes of TV production can certainly include scenes set in the characters' past, but *Black-ish*, *Dream On* (1990–1996), and other single-camera sitcoms often cut a few shots into a scene as a way of briefly and incongruously contrasting the past with the present. In "Dr. Hell No," for instance, Dre, in voice-over, boasts about how he goes to the doctor on a regular basis, unlike during his childhood when his father found excuses not to take him for treatment. Four quick shots from his childhood show his father saying, "He'll be fine" and "Walk it off," even when Dre is coughing violently or his leg is obviously broken. Dre continues bragging in voice-over about how well he takes care of himself, but short shots belie his claims. He says, "I take care of myself by going to the doctor regularly, exercising [cut to a shot of him throwing a toy basketball in his office], watching what I eat [cut to him returning one piece of candy to a bowl after taking a dozen others], and getting more sleep [cut to him napping in a committee meeting]." In each case, humor is prompted via editing and, in the latter instance, humor arises through a combination of image and sound editing that brings together incongruous significations. That is, sound claims one thing while image incongruously and ironically shows the opposite.

Black-ish Case Study: Conclusion

Black-ish illustrates how racial multiculturalist discourse plays out in two ways. First, it is built upon a narrative problematic (a logline) that fundamentally incorporates race into the construction of its storylines. Second, at its core, the show is *about* assimilation, but it does not approach it in an assimilationist manner. Rather, it is about one family's difficulty with assimilating and their desire to maintain a black identity. Characters in the show express assimilationist and pluralist views, but the storylines use them to illustrate the problems with those views. The diversity of perspectives thus qualifies *Black-ish* as a predominantly multiculturalist discourse. Finally, although race often intersects with power in ugly ways, *Black-ish* does not rely on superiority humor targeting a subcultural stereotype. It depends instead on clever, unpredictable dialogue and interesting stylistic flourishes to make the viewer laugh.

Notes

1 Michael Omi and Howard Winant, *Racial Formation in the United States: From the 1960s to the 1990s* (New York: Routledge, 1994).
2 For more on stereotyping, the other, and essentialism, see Stuart Hall, "The Spectacle of the 'Other,'" in *Representation*, 2nd edition, edited by Stuart Hall, Jessica Evans and Sean Nixon (Thousand Oaks, CA: Sage Publications, 2013), 215–271.
3 Quoted in Melvin Patrick Ely, *The Adventures of Amos 'n' Andy: A Social History of an American Phenomenon* (Charlottesville, VA: The University Press of Virginia, 2001), 78.
4 Herman Gray, *Watching Race: Television and the Struggle for "Blackness"* (Minneapolis, MN: University of Minnesota Press, 1995).
5 Ibid., 84.
6 Ibid., 84–91.
7 Gray maintains that the pluralist shows did not address black issues and that they were essentially conventional sitcom stories/tropes with a black cast. The impact of race on characters, for Gray, is only engaged in the multiculturalist shows. My slightly different approach is to include any show with a principally subcultural cast in the pluralist category, even if it does include storylines rooted in the black experience. Multiculturalist shows, in my view, are ones that include a diverse cast of many races (including white) and ethnicities, respect the individual characteristics of those races/ethnicities, and still steer clear of demeaning stereotypes.
8 Gray, 85.
9 Kristen J. Warner, "Plastic Representation," *Film Quarterly* 71, no. 2 (Winter 2017), https://filmquarterly.org/2017/12/04/in-the-time-of-plastic-representation/, accessed June 7, 2019. Warner expands her position in *The Cultural Politics of Colorblind TV Casting* (New York: Routledge, 2018).
10 Dave Itzkoff, "It's Not 'The Office.' The Boss Is a Woman," *New York Times*, March 26, 2009, https://www.nytimes.com/2009/03/29/arts/television/29dave.html, accessed May 20, 2019.
11 Gray, 88.
12 Ibid., 90.
13 "Chappelle's Story," *Oprah*, http://www.oprah.com/oprahshow/chappelles-story/, accessed May 30, 2019. The sketch itself is available online on Comedy Central's Website: http://www.cc.com/video-clips/s191yw/chappelle-s-show-stereotype-pixies---black-pixie---uncensored.
14 Ibid.
15 Lesley Goldberg, "TV Pilots 2018: The Complete Guide to What Lives, Dies and Still Has a Pulse," *Hollywood Reporter*, January 22, 2018, www.hollywoodreporter.com/live-feed/tv-pilots-2018-complete-guide-1076193, accessed May 30, 2019.
16 Robin Means Coleman originally mapped out these eras in *African American Viewers and the Black Situation Comedy: Situating Racial Humor* (NY: Garland, 1998), 84–147. Means Coleman draws on Cedric C. Clark, "Television and Social Controls: Some Observations on the Portrayals of Ethnic Minorities," *Television*

Quarterly 8, no. 2 (1969): 18–22; and Angela Nelson, "From Beulah to the Fresh Prince of Bel-Air: A Brief History of Black Stereotypes in Television Comedy," unpublished manuscript, 1991. And she slightly revised her eras five years later in Robin R. Means Coleman and Charlton D. McIlwain, "The Hidden Truths in Black Sitcoms," in Mary M. Dalton and Laura R. Linder, *The Sitcom Reader: America Viewed and Skewed* (Albany, NY: State University of New York Press, 2005).

17 Means Coleman and McIlwain, 130.
18 Ibid., 132.
19 Ibid.
20 Khaleeli, Homa. "Obama Loves It, Trump Called It Racist: Why *Black-Ish* is TV's Most Divisive Show." *The Guardian*, Feb. 25, 2017, https://www.theguardian.com/tv-and-radio/2017/feb/25/series-creator-kenya-barris-on-abc-sitcom-black-ish, accessed September 13, 2019.
21 Ibid.
22 Lesley Goldberg, "TV Pilots 2014: The Complete Guide to What Lives, Dies and Still Has a Pulse," *Hollywood Reporter*, January 6, 2014, https://www.hollywoodreporter.com/live-feed/tv-pilots-2014-complete-guide-667314, accessed June 7, 2019.
23 Jim Halterman, "*black-ish*: Rainbow Being Biracial Isn't (Always) a Laughing Matter, *TV Insider*, www.tvinsider.com/104092/blackish-rainbow-biracial-kenya-barris-interview/, accessed June 5, 2019.

6

COMEDY, TELEVISUALITY, AND CONVERGENCE

Most situation comedies construct narrative worlds that are hermetically sealed. That is, their episodes build a consistent diegesis for their characters to inhabit—strictly governed by what the industry calls the show's narrative "bible." Characters live in these worlds without acknowledging themselves as fictional constructs, with viewers watching them. In this regard, they're much like characters in 19th-century novels, conventional plays, and the classical cinema. One can see this in most of the sitcoms I have examined in detail to this point, including three of my case studies: *I Love Lucy* (1951–1957), *The Andy Griffith Show* (1960–1968), and *Sex and the City* (1998–2004). Lucy, Andy, and Carrie are unaware of themselves *as fictional TV characters*. They are wholly submerged within their diegeses. True, Lucy does go to Hollywood in a series of episodes and encounters movie stars such as John Wayne, William Holden, and Eve Arden. And Andy has a similar experience where he participates in the filming of a movie about his life. But Lucy and Andy remain in character in these episodes and the real-life actors, Lucille Ball and Andy Griffith, are never recognized as such. Additionally, the programs make few self-referential allusions to themselves *as* television programs. Nothing in the dialogue breaks the fourth wall and highlights the fact that these are TV episodes about making movies. That is, the programs do not acknowledge themselves *as programs*. And these three case studies are also unaware of other television programs in the sitcom genre. They seldom refer out to other contemporary programs or to the history of the sitcom as a genre. And if they do invoke another program, the characters still remain within that program's diegetic world—much like how the Marvel Cinematic Universe (MCU) can share superheroes among numerous TV shows and movies—and do not address the viewers outside that diegesis in the "real world." The viewer observes the characters in these worlds without them acknowledging they're being watched, as if we were on a successful bird-watching outing where the birds never realized we had trained our binoculars on them.

Despite the predominance of consistent narrative worlds in the genre, there has always been an element that threatens to transgress this fictive premise and calls attention to itself *as fiction*. We can see this, for example, in the *Scrubs* episode that is a parody of a multicam sitcom, as mentioned in Chapter 1. The humor of such an episode depends upon the viewer's recognition of its similarity to, but difference from, previous sitcom instances and draws the viewer's attention to the conventions of the genre. In so doing, the episode potentially critiques those conventions and makes fun of the values presented by the earlier shows. The critiquing function of parody carries with it the potential to change our attitudes toward an individual program or, indeed, toward an entire TV genre. Some critics have said that such parodies mark the decline of a genre, of an indication that the genre has run out of fresh ideas and thus must cannibalize itself for humor. The rise and fall and rise again and fall again of the sitcom disprove the notion that genres behave in so tidy and predictable a fashion, but the reference of one show to another show or a show's breaking of the fourth wall to refer to itself certainly disrupts the diegetic homogeneity found in most sitcoms. And this disruption has led critics to make claims that some shows are "postmodern" disturbances of television's formulaic stagnation.

In short, this chapter examines the premise that sitcoms can be self-reflexive and intertextual (alluding to other programs) and that they may engage in transmedia storytelling (building stories across several media). I will also return to John Caldwell's related concept of "televisuality" (alluded to in Chapters 1 and 2) and include David Bordwell's premise of "intensified continuity." And I will offer some thoughts on how the 21st-century blending of film, television, and online media in seemingly unpredictable ways—labeled "convergence"—may encourage the staid sitcom to embrace these disruptive changes and innovation. Debuting in its half-hour format in 1989, *The Simpsons* (1989–) arrived just when broadcast and cable networks were proliferating. In fact, it virtually single-handedly established the newly created Fox network as a viable competitor to ABC, CBS, and NBC. Against all odds, *The Simpsons* proved that adults would watch an animated comedy program during prime time. One proof of its success and impact is that it now holds the record for the longest-running American narrative-TV program. *The Simpsons* is my choice for this chapter's case study because it relies heavily upon self-reflexivity and intertextuality and because it continues to thrive during the post-network, convergence era of television.

The Televisual Sitcom: TV *about* TV

The sitcom has long had a reputation for having a simplistic, barren style. This reputation stems from the multicam sitcom's pedestrian camerawork, set design, and lighting—necessitated by shooting in a studio in front an audience. The presence of an audience tips us off to the fact that multicam sitcoms are essentially theatrical presentations. The shows could be performed on a stage in a theater with a proscenium arch in much the same fashion as they are presented for the three or four cameras on a sound stage—the cameras remaining outside the stage's virtual proscenium. The humor of shows such as *2 Broke Girls* (2011–2017), *Mom* (2013–), and *Mike and Molly* (2010–2016) is firmly grounded in their dialogue and the performances of their cast, and they have been since the days of *I Love Lucy* and other multicam sitcoms such as *Cheers* (1982–1993), *Friends* (1994–2004), and *The Fresh Prince of Bel-Air* (1990–1996). In these shows, cameras are there not to create funny compositions or angles, but, rather, to accurately document the actors' performances. And sound design isn't supposed to be humorous in its own right; the microphones are just there to capture accurately the dialogue. It often feels like the camera operators and sound technicians are recording an event, which, in fact, is what they were doing during the early, live broadcasts of sitcoms.

It's not surprising therefore that most multicam shows' showrunners are writers of dialogue and not directors choosing camera angles, lighting, and actors' blocking. Compared to even low-budget films of the latter-half of the twentieth century, the visual and sound style of the multicam sitcom shows very little panache. Nonetheless, multicam sitcom style does use many of the conventions of classical film—particularly those that evolved into the so-called "continuity system" during the first 10 or 15 years of the cinema's history. (The term refers to a cinematic storytelling mode that creates the illusion of a seamless, *continuous* series of shots and actions.) However, the sitcom's use of the continuity system is so basic that it lessens the impact of that mode of production. Continuity-system elements such as the 180-degree rule and shot-reverse shot remain foundational to the multicam approach, but you typically do not see visual extravagances that heighten the impact of these conventions and neither do you see visual style used in a decorative fashion—beautiful for the sake of beauty. Multicam production is simple and functional, qualities of what John Caldwell calls "zero-degree style."[1] He singles out so-called "quality" multicam sitcoms of the 1970s—many produced by Norman Lear—for ignoring the medium's stylistic potential: "There were no flourishes, canted camera angles, videographic ecstasies, or even bracketed montages. The sets were just that: spaces where quality actors could perform live."[2] Even the single-camera productions of the 1960s through the 1990s were relatively modest in their stylistic aspirations, as can be seen in shows as varied as *Get Smart* (a spy comedy, 1965–1970), *M*A*S*H* (set in the Korean War, 1972-1983), and *Doogie Howser, MD* (a medical comedy, 1989–1993).

However, some TV shows of the 1980s and 1990s broke from the tradition of zero-degree style. In 1995 Caldwell argued that a more "cinematic" strain of TV production had evolved in the previous 15 years, in shows such as *Hill Street Blues* (1981–1987), *Miami Vice* (1984–1989), *Twin Peaks* (1990–1991), and *My So-Called Life* (1994–1995). His examples were known for breaking from TV's norm of attenuated style and adopting stylistic traits more commonly associated with films destined for theaters. These shows, he argues, contain "excessive style," by which he means they embrace visual and sound aspects that go beyond the functional telling of a story.[3] This is the form of television expression that he labels "televisual." Notably, there are very few humorous shows in Caldwell's televisual examples. Aside from the sketch comedy, *The Tracey Ullman Show* (1987–1990); the movie-mocking show, *Mystery Science Theater 3000* (1989–1999; 2017–); and the music video-mocking show, *Beavis and Butt-head* (1993–1997), Caldwell finds only one contemporary narrative comedy that might qualify as televisual, *The Simpsons*. Nonetheless, I contend that his concept of televisuality can help us understand the sitcom beyond *The Simpsons*.

A working definition of televisual comedy is that it generates humor through the medium of television itself—using camera angle and framing, sound effects, odd lighting, and so on, to trigger laughter. Further, televisual humor can be divorced from a show's narrative drive. The visual and sound gags need not move the story along and, indeed, they may even interrupt narrative progression. Consider the show *Parker Lewis Can't Lose* (1990–1993), which ran during the original televisual period that Caldwell discusses and laid the foundation for subsequent comedies such as *The Larry Sanders Show* (1992–1998), *Arrested Development* (2003–2006), *The Office* (US: 2005–2013), *My Name Is Earl* (2005–2009), *30 Rock* (2006–2013), and *The Goldbergs* (2013–). The program was known for its expressive use of lighting, camera angles, sound effects, and other stylistic techniques—especially at the hands of frequent director, Bryan Spicer. In the "Close But No Guitar" episode, high school students Parker (Corin Nemec) and Mikey (Billy Jayne) fear punishment from principal Grace Musso (Melanie Chartoff). In one scene, Spicer initially has Musso lit from behind and once she walks into a close-up, the lighting brightens *in the middle of the shot*, and the camera comes to rest on her in a low-angle close-up. The lighting expressively portrays her as mysteriously powerful and the low angle emphasizes her domination of the boys. Spicer is following the conventional industry practices to employ style (back light, low-angle camera) to communicate aspects of the characters' narrative situation (the ominous power of the principal and impending punishment). In fact, it's a bit audacious of him to change the lighting mid-shot and thus one could argue that he has "intensified" continuity style principles—as David Bordwell has identified in theatrical films from the 1960s onward.[4] In some instances, visual/sound style becomes so intensified in *Parker Lewis Can't Lose* that it briefly interrupts narrative flow. When a camera angle or a sound effect is so far outside the norms of TV production that it demands we notice it and thereby draws attention away from the story, then style is no longer invisible. It is now referring to itself as style.

We can observe this form of narrative interruption in the pilot episode of *Parker Lewis Can't Lose*. In one scene, Parker is menaced by Kubiac (Abraham Benrubi) for sitting on his lunch. We hear Parker, in voiceover, say, "Why is it that people like me have been running way from people like him all of our lives? Because they're a lot bigger." Parker's voiceover is a constant element in the program. It remains within the show's diegetic world (and should not be classified as extra-diegetic) because it is clearly supposed to represent the character's thoughts and not the comments of actor Corin Nemec or an omniscient third party. Many TV shows employ diegetic voiceovers (see *Malcolm in the Middle* for examples); they normally don't disrupt classical cinema conventions. But in this *Parker Lewis Can't Lose* scene, the voiceover becomes part of a self-reflexive joke that draws attention to the voiceover itself as a television technique. The first self-reflexive element of this scene occurs when Kubiac enters the gym, snorting and expressing his anger with Parker. He exhales in a tight close-up and the lens fogs up—thus breaking the fourth wall by drawing attention to the camera lens used to record the scene. Then, when Parker asks Kubiac if he can forgive his transgression, Kubiac responds by quoting Parker's recent voiceover, "No, because people like you have been running away from people like me all of our lives." Parker recognizes that his subjective voiceover line—which Kubiac could not have heard—has been quoted verbatim. He looks directly at the camera and says, "Whoa!" His exclamation takes the viewer out of the story for a split second, because it is directed to them and not to the other characters in the scene. Parker's line asks the viewer to recognize that one character is using precisely the same line as another character. It thereby undermines our suspension of disbelief, if only for a moment. And it illustrates how a comic text such as *Parker Lewis Can't Lose* can reflect back upon itself.

Direct address such as Parker's and a program's interruptive self-reflexivity often depend upon one another. An early master of television self-reflexivity was George Burns, who had been a star of vaudeville and radio before transferring his and his wife's, Gracie Allen's, act to television as *The George Burns and Gracie Allen Show* (1950–1958). Burns brought to television the notion of the performer talking directly to the audience, as he had done in stage shows during vaudeville's waning years. And he explicitly referred to the machinery necessary to broadcast the program. In the 1951 episode "The Income Tax Man," he appears in front of a stage curtain and explains to both the studio audience and viewers at home:

> You see, in television, there are three cameras. And each camera has a red light. And when the red light is on, you know that that camera is working. So you face that camera and you smile. Watching the red light gets to be a habit and whenever I see it I give it all my personality. And last night I smiled at a man's taillight all the way in to the movies.

A few seconds later, he notices that a cameraman's cigarette needs a light. He walks over, revealing a camera, or TV "paraphernalia," as he calls it, and provides a match. Returning to his spot in front of the curtain, he explains to the in-studio audience and us at home, "He's the man who's watches my close-ups. [And then to the cameraman:] I'll work on your nails later, Bob." Shortly afterward, the kitchen set appears behind George as he continues to stand in front of the curtain, outside the diegetic space. Gracie, in character, enters the kitchen and George, still out of character, looks at her there. She, however, cannot see him as he is not yet part of the diegesis (see Figure 6.1).

Figure 6.1 While standing outside the set of *The George Burns and Gracie Allen Show*, George looks in on his wife. She is in the story world already and can't see him. He must walk around the set and enter the diegesis through a set door.

George is among a limited number of actors/characters who can make the rather curious, but seamless, transition from a self-reflexive, extra-diegetic figure (the actor, George Burns, who knows about camera lights) to a diegetic figure sealed within the narrative world (a character who has fictional adventures). In this particular episode, the actor George is joking with the audience when he looks to the left and sees "Mr. Miller" approaching his fictional house. The camera cuts to Miller going through the door and we hear George, off-camera, bid him to come in. What follows is a scene between in-character George and Mr. Miller. Thus, the actor George has figuratively crossed the proscenium threshold and become the character George. Decades later, Garry Shandling took this peculiar form of crossover between diegetic and extra-diegetic spaces even further in his self-reflexively titled multicam sitcom, *It's Garry Shandling's Show* (1986–1990). Its theme song humorously establishes the show's deeply rooted self-reflexivity: "This is the theme to Garry's show, / The opening theme to Garry's show. / This is the music that you hear as you watch the credits." Much like Burns's cigarette-lighting bit, *It's Garry Shandling's Show* often reveals the TV cameras and the studio audience (see Figure 6.2). Strangely, the in-character Garry *knows that he's in a weekly sitcom*; he knows that we're watching him. He frequently makes comments about the show itself, such as, "I hope you enjoyed tonight's show, because its explosive issue was chaperoning. And the lesson we learned was, I'm no good at it. And next week's explosive issue is, 'Pen pals, do we really need to know what they look like?'" And he jokes about dream sequences and other television tropes. *The George Burns and Gracie Allen*

Figure 6.2 Shattering the fourth wall, Garry Shandling shows his diegetic date around the set of *It's Garry Shandling's Show*. He drives an electric car from set to set and reveals the studio audience and members of the show's crew.

Show is notable for its ability to flip back and forth between diegetic and extra-diegetic spaces in humorous ways, but *It's Garry Shandling's Show* utterly obliterates the boundary between the two. Aside from some of the later animated shows, no television sitcom has been more radical in its assault upon television's diegetic "rules."

Clearly, self-reflexivity can manipulate playfully the boundary between diegetic and extra-diegetic spaces. The examples above illustrate how three levels of self-reflexivity function in the sitcom. The first, and least disruptive, self-reflexivity level is embodied in the references to the world of television that are made by fictional characters without them breaking out of their diegetic space. Aside from several shows about producing newscasts and comedy programs (e.g., *Sports Night* [1998–2000] and *Murphy Brown* [1988–1998; 2018–2019]), there are numerous programs in which fictional characters encounter real-world celebrities. These can be special story arcs, as we saw with *I Love Lucy* and *The Andy Griffith Show*, or behind-the-scenes shows such as *Episodes* (2011–2017) and *The Comeback* (2005; 2014), which deal with the production of sitcoms and other fictional programs. In each of these instances, the fictional character does not recognize themselves as an element of a diegesis; they don't know they are in a story on which we are eavesdropping. A second, more precarious level of self-reflexivity is when diegetic characters lay bare the production apparatus of the show they are in while they are in it. This happens less frequently, but can be seen in the diegetic slippage in *The George Burns and Gracie Allen Show* and *It's Garry Shandling's Show*. The third form of self-reflexivity is an ambiguous one. There are times in sitcoms when the *character* looks directly at us, breaking the fourth wall, and talks to us as if it were the *actor* talking and yet it simultaneously seems to still be the character who is looking at us. Parker's exclamation of "Whoa" is one such instance. It seems that he's speaking *as Parker* and not as the actor Corin Nemec, and thus the line is diegetic. But, on the other hand, the other characters in the scene do not hear him say, "Whoa," and thus it is extra-diegetic.

The only clear-cut instances of a sitcom actor speaking *as an actor*— that is, wholly extra-diegetically—are the extremely rare instances of when an actor blows their line on sitcoms that are broadcast live. This happened to Jamie Foxx when he appeared in *Live in Front of a Studio Audience: Norman Lear's* All in the Family *and* The Jeffersons on May 22, 2019—a stunt broadcast event in which an all-star cast recreated episode scripts from over 40 years ago. Foxx stuttered on a line, paused and said to the camera, "It's live! Everyone sitting at home just thinks their TV just messed up." The studio audience laughed, and his fellow cast members struggled to keep straight faces, but he regained his composure, the scene continued, and the suspension of disbelief returned. Sitcoms and other comic forms are not overly concerned with logical consistency. And we viewers, as we watch these shows and experience their diegetic anomalies, are not typically troubled by them.

Intertextuality

To this point, we've considered texts that refer back to themselves and their own fictional constructs. Now we must consider how sitcom texts derive humor by referring outward to a broad variety of cultural products: other TV shows, yes, but also commercials, films, comics, novels, poetry, artwork, pornography, textbooks, philosophical treatises, social-media memes, religious symbols, and on and on. Almost any cultural text can be grist for comedy's mill—resulting in quotations, allusions, homages, imitations, and even plagiarism and other unauthorized borrowing.

Some have argued that extreme intertextuality can be a radical art form. For postmodern theorist Julia Kristeva, who coined the term, intertextuality characterizes artworks that are in such radical conversation with other works that they themselves have no one unified voice. Imagine a TV show that is entirely comprised of clips from other TV shows—an assembly of short bits. These fragments rely upon associations with their original texts for meaning. A montage such as this could juxtapose fragments in interesting, even humorous, ways to communicate an idea or just to make us laugh; but if the montage has no organizing principle, then it reaches a state of cacophony, of fragments at war with each other. This radical form of montage is what Peter Wollen had in mind when he proposed the idea of a "counter cinema" in 1972 and found intertextuality to be an aspect of Jean-Luc Godard's films that increased during the 1960s:

> It becomes more and more impossible to understand whole sequences and even whole films without a degree of familiarity with the quotations and allusions which structure them.
> ... Godard's own voice is drowned out and obliterated behind that of the authors quoted.

Conventional, classical cinema and, by extension, conventional television, produce texts that are, in Wollen's words "self-contained object[s], harmonized within [their] own bounds." *Counter* to that is Godard's avalanche of allusions, which creates "open-endedness, overspill, intertextuality."[5]

Wollen's perspective dovetails with those of contemporary proponents of postmodern theory, especially Fredric Jameson's and Roland Barthes's. Wollen, Jameson, Barthes, and Kristeva, among others, maintained that the state of art, literature, film, TV, and architecture in the late 20th century was necessarily allusive and foundationally fragmented. They extolled the virtues of parody and intertextuality as reflective of the human condition in dizzyingly splintered times. They also contended that such cultural splintering was emblematic of the "death of the author," by which they meant that a text is best understood as the intersection of texts that came before it and that the reader constructs sense from the text by making associations among the text and others to which it alludes. For postmodernists, the "vision" or "intention" of an individual author is less important than the meaning-making that the reader does when they comprehend the text in a network of other texts.

Scholars who find intertextuality to be a disruptive cultural force generally do not focus their attention on humorous texts. One supposes this may be part of the general dismissal of comedy as inconsequential, as "just a joke." However, we may find ways that comic intertextuality can provide cutting criticism of cultural texts and the social mores that support them. There are two major, closely related forms of comic intertextuality that I will consider: parody and bricolage. Both may engage with the humor principle of incongruity. A parody is, generally speaking, a work that takes the form of another individual work or uses the established form of a group of works (e.g., multicam sitcoms) and twists it in such a way as to critique that original form in a humorous manner. Thus, a parodic work takes on the outward appearance of one thing, but then surprises us by incongruously distorting that thing. My sense of the term bricolage stems from the structural anthropology of Claude Lévi-Strauss.[6] Broadly, it identifies a work that has been assembled from previous works—a mash-up or something that borrows from something else and puts it to a new use. Bricolage lends itself to comedy, because assembling disparate odds and ends can often lead to humorous incongruity.

To understand parody better, consider the false documentary that is *The Office*—both the first, British version (2001–2003) and its American remake (2005–2013). *The Office* employs the conventions of the documentary form (handheld camera, awkward framing, subjects speaking to the camera, etc.) but applies them to a fictional narrative. It implicitly makes fun of those conventions and has been labeled a "mockumentary," both because it is a fake, "mock" documentary and because it gently mocks or ridicules the form itself. In separate essays, Brett Mills and Ethan Thompson have also dubbed it "comedy vérité," thus incongruously splicing "comedy" together with a term for French documentaries that originated in the 1960s, "*cinéma vérité*" (literally, "cinema truth").[7] Mills argues that *The Office* plays with the documentary form in order to subvert it and thereby critiques the notion that documentaries can present unmediated truth. The seeming verisimilitude of documentary is undermined when actors in a scripted comedy can perform a false version of truthfulness. Comedy vérité poses the question to the viewer, "How can you be certain that the next documentary you see—which might look and sound like *The Office* does—is truthful or authentic?" Perhaps it's all just "truthiness," as satirist Stephen Colbert characterized "news" items on his parody of TV news, *The Colbert Report* (2005–2015).[8]

Further, Mills contends that the obvious impact that the cameras have on the characters in *The Office* illustrates the fundamental ways that cameras in all documentaries provoke responses from the people being filmed that might be quite different from their "natural" behavior. The office manager (David Brent [Ricky Gervais], in the UK version; Michael Scott [Steve Carell], in the US) incessantly mugs for the cameras, performing as if he were on stage or in his own sitcom, and many of the workers are obviously uncomfortable with the cameras' presence. One clear message of both programs is that the cameras have affected the behavior of these office workers. Mills links this to the original *cinéma vérité* films, which sometimes confronted the people they were filming. *Cinéma vérité* was not a purely observational, fly-on-the-wall documentary approach. Rather, its filmmakers often pointedly confronted its subjects. Jean Rouch and Edgar Morin's *Chronicle of a Summer* (1961) is a key example of this self-questioning, self-reflexive approach. In the film, Rouch and Morin deliberate the state of French society with a group of individuals (not actors or pundits), but before doing so they converse with them about the difficulty of behaving "naturally" in front of cameras. Do cameras necessarily provoke a false performance from people, evoking an inauthentic version of themselves? At the end of the film, we see the participants watch parts of it in which they appear, and another conversation is had about how much "truth" (*vérité*) the footage contains.

For Mills, *The Office* continues the same interrogation of the documentary form that a film such as *Chronicle of a Summer* began some 30 years previously. *Chronicle of a Summer* achieves its critique directly, through frank conversations between filmmakers and participants. *The Office* illustrates how a parody might also comment on a preexisting text and subtly undermine it, though not so directly as in *Chronicle of a Summer*. We don't see *The Office* characters react to the film made of their lives, although one episode portrays a reunion of them where they talk about the film's impact on them. There are thus limits to how much *The Office* borrows from *cinéma vérité* in order to render a continuing, fictional story. Other television shows have taken the documentary style even further—culminating in *Documentary Now!*

(2015–), which duplicates the original documentaries remarkably closely. *Documentary Now!* poses as an authentic documentary series, complete with earnest introductions by esteemed actress, Helen Mirren. At the start of its *third* season, the credit scene shows clips from genuine films and she intones in false seriousness, "Hello, I'm Helen Mirren and you're watching *Documentary Now!* season 52." This season began with an episode, "Batshit Valley," that hews so closely to the target of its parody—the Netflix documentary, *Wild Wild Country* (2018)—that it's possible to mistake it for the real thing. *Documentary Now!* is comic parody, but it is not a sitcom, because it does not feature characters in a continuing story. It does, however, illustrate the extremes to which parody of documentary can be taken.

In addition to comedy vérité, it is possible to identify sitcom parodies of many other forms and genres of television and film—including newscasts, musicals, Westerns, gangster films, and so on. In most cases, parody playfully deconstructs aspects of those preexisting texts, deriving humor from the disjunction between the original text and the parody's rendering of it. Numerous examples exist in which a sitcom parodies the genre itself. Possibly the most audacious of such genre parodies is a *Scrubs* episode tellingly titled "My Life in Four Cameras" (February 15, 2005).

For nine seasons, *Scrubs* was produced as a single-camera show, without a studio audience or a laugh track. In one episode, however, a main character, J.D. (Zack Braff), fantasizes about life being like a multicam sitcom. As we hear him express this fantasy in voiceover, the show cuts to a sitcom set with four cameras and a studio audience.[9] Suddenly, the lighting changes; the actors' performances are broader; and the camera angles replicate multicam visual style. And there's now a laugh track, which *Scrubs* does not otherwise use. There is diegetic motivation for this shift in style (a character's fantasy), but it also breaks the fourth wall and self-reflexively parodies the conventions of multicam sitcom productions. It even quotes the voiceover introduction used by *Cheers*: "J.D.'s sitcom fantasy is filmed before a live studio audience." As we saw in *The Office*'s parodic, implicit critique of documentary form, *Scrubs* is also finding fault with the text it is parodying. Moreover, "My Life in Four Cameras" is more explicit in its criticism of the multicam sitcom than *The Office* is of documentary. The *Scrubs* episode comes to a sad conclusion as one of J.D.'s patients dies. He explains, "Unfortunately, around here things don't end as neat and tidy as they do in sitcoms. ... [N]ice people don't always get better." The specific lesson of the episode is that sitcoms are disconnected from the realities of hospitals and terminally ill patients, but the more general point of this parody is that conventional multicam sitcoms' worlds contain implausible, superficial stories and that they are told through a hyperbolic humor style. The episode encourages the viewer to contrast the fantasy's multicam presentation style with the single-camera production that defined the program. The episode does end with J.D. extolling the comfort provided by multicam sitcoms as he watches a *Cheers* episode, but all of *Scrubs'* other single-camera episodes encourage the viewer to reject multicam sitcoms as old-fashioned and shallow.

Thus, we can see parody at work in slightly different fashions in *The Office*, *Documentary Now!*, and *Scrubs'* "My Life in Four Cameras." The first two implicitly critique an entire form of filmmaking and the latter explicitly critiques an incarnation of the genre within which it itself resides: the sitcom. In all three cases, however, the parody takes the form of a preexisting text and points out its flaws, in humorous fashion. Parody thus contains two core components: (1) an implicit or explicit critique of the parodied text and (2) a reliance on mimicry or resemblance. Bricolage functions a bit differently from parody, although both depend on other texts for the humor they generate and the meanings they signify. Bricolage, however, need not contain an element of critique and is more commonly rooted in reference and assembly instead of resemblance.

Animated TV comedies are particularly prone to bricolage. In *Bob's Burgers*, for example, the credit sequence often employs this technique. The credits change every episode to include a pun in the names of the store next to Bob's restaurant and the exterminators' van that arrives to cope with a vermin infestation. One week (March 26, 2017), the store assumed the name, "Pro-Pain Accessories Dominatrix Supplies," and the exterminator was "Dale's Dead-Bug." Both names allude to a previous animated program, *King of the Hill* (1997–2010). In that show, the main character, Hank Hill, is proud of selling "propane and propane accessories," as he repeatedly explains his job. And another character, Dale Gribble, owns Dale's Dead-Bug exterminators and drives a van with a deceased bug on the roof. These references to *King of the Hill* are perhaps unsurprising because Jim Dauterive was associated with that show as a producer and a frequent episode writer, and he later developed *Bob's Burgers* with Loren Bouchard. The continuation of Dale's Dead-Bug from one show to the other may possibly be explained as transmedia storytelling—where characters and storylines from one text continue in another—but "Pro-Pain Accessories Dominatrix Supplies" is an example of pure bricolage. *Bob's Burgers* is here re-using something from one text ("propane accessories"), but it is incongruously manipulating it to create a humorous pun drawing on the language of sado-masochism ("Pro-pain Accessories Dominatrix Supplies"). The pun is not a transmedia continuation of *The King of the Hill* story in *Bob's Burgers*. And it does not parody *King of the Hill*. It is not mimicking "propane accessories" in order to critique it, as can be seen with my *Scrubs* and *The Office* parodies, but instead it offers the knowing viewer a joke based in wordplay. If one knows the *King of the Hill* catchphrase, "propane accessories," then "Pro-pain Accessories Dominatrix Supplies" is an unexpected and amusingly incongruous twist on the phrase's original meaning.

Comedic bricolage relies upon an original text for humor and significance, but that original is recombined with other textual fragments to create something new. It works much like a tile mosaic, which can contain hundreds of small fragments. If you look at a single fragment in isolation, it has little significance, but when combined and re-contextualized among other fragments, it can participate in the formulation of some new text, even a new artwork. In the realm of the sitcom, bricolage means nothing if the viewer cannot connect an intertextual element of a TV program with its previous text; but when it works correctly it can provide a deeper sense of humor, one in which the viewer has figured out a semiotic puzzle and is rewarded with an incongruity that may make them laugh. Comedy writers constantly work as bricoleurs, as anthropologists call persons who practice bricolage. They bring together images and words in ways that are both familiar and strange.

This process is not limited to animated programs. Among the earliest live-action shows to capitalize extensively on bricolage was *Dream On* (1990–1996). The show centers on Martin Tupper (Brian Benben), a young book editor who—as we see in the opening credits—spent many of his formative years fascinated with television and movies. Its episodes follow Martin through various dating mishaps, which are punctuated by short clips from films and TV programs when he is emotionally distressed. For instance, in one episode, Martin's mother dies of a heart attack. As Martin watches the paramedics fail to revive her, the show cuts to a soldier playing, "Taps." When he cries in grief later, despite the difficult relationship he had with her, it cuts to a three-second clip from *Imitation of Life* (1959) in which a young woman named Sarah Jane (Susan Kohner) exclaims, "Mama, I did love you!"

The *Imitation of Life* clip illustrates various ways that bricolage functions. First and most obviously, we are supposed to recognize the clip as being from another, older media text—a film released some 30 years before *Dream On*. The show's producers further emphasize the clip's connotation of "old movie" by converting *Imitation of Life*'s original color image into black-and-white. In bricolage, an element that is incorporated into a new context still retains its identity as belonging to its old context. That is, even if we don't know the film, *Imitation of Life*, as we watch this *Dream On* scene, we still recognize that these three seconds are from a different and markedly older film. Just as in a stew where we can still taste the separate elements, the ingredients of a bricolage stand out as individual components.

Second, by wrenching Sarah Jane's exclamation out of its *Imitation of Life* context and juxtaposing it with Martin's anguish, the original denotative meaning of the clip (a woman expressing guilt for disavowing her mother) is transformed into an expression of Martin's inner thoughts. That is, Sarah Jane and Martin *share* an expression of regret for their alienation from their mothers. And the Sarah Jane clip comes to stand in for, and to amplify, Martin's feelings. Returning to my stew analogy, it is similar to how flavors in a stew come to change one another as they blend together. In this case, Sarah Jane's feelings blend with Martin's and heighten the representation of his.

A third facet of bricolage illustrated by this instance is that some aspects of the original meaning of the clip are lost in its combination with new images. In *Imitation of Life*, Sarah Jane deserts her mother, because she (Sarah Jane) is a light-skinned African American who wishes to "pass" for white and her mother makes that impossible. Obviously, this racial component is not part of Martin's complicated relationship with his own mother. And viewers of *Dream On* are unlikely to carry the connotations of racial injustice from *Imitation of Life* into this episode. So we can see that bricolage is based in similarity and difference. In this case, the similarity of emotion (grief mixed with guilt) between two characters and the difference in the sources of the characters' guilt.

Fourth, and finally, if bricolage makes the viewer of a sitcom laugh, it is because of the humor principle of incongruity. Bricolage can introduce elements into a text that we are not expecting and that are incongruous with the text we are viewing. In this *Dream On* scene, the *Imitation of Life* clip interrupts color shots of a young man crying at a wake with a black-and-white shot of a woman weeping on her mother's casket. Martin is emotional in this scene, but Sarah Jane's emotion feels hyperbolic in comparison. The intensity of her emotion does not fit the level of his. It is incongruous and, thus, it is potentially funny—despite the fact that this is a scene of sadness. *Dream On* often uses clips in this incongruous fashion. The main character's thoughts and feelings are denoted through the clips, but there is always something that marks the inserts *as disruptions*, as elements that do not fit with what preceded them, as humorous incongruities.

Television bricolage was not invented in the 1990s, but the wealth of allusions and gags definitely ramped up as the 20th century came to a close. The allusion avalanche was facilitated by an evolution in the technology used to watch and, notably, to record television. Until the

1980s and the introduction of videocassette recorders for consumer use, television was an extremely ephemeral medium—one that could only be experienced live, at the time that a program was broadcast. If you wanted to view an episode more than once, then you had to catch it when it was rerun during the summer or in syndication. What this meant specifically for comedies was that the humor of a joke or a visual gag had to trigger a laugh when one first saw it. Television comedy was less like a humorous essay where one could read and reread a passage in order to savor a joke and more like a comic film in a theater where you had just one chance to catch a joke and uproarious audience laughter might even obscure a follow-up joke. The VCR changed viewers' relationship with television in many ways—especially in the introduction of time-shifting—and it had a specific impact on comedy in that it allowed viewers who had recorded a program to rewind a comic bit and re-experience it. And, if you missed a line, you could always go back and watch a portion of the episode again. This encouraged comedy producers such as the people behind *South Park* (1997–) to pack more gags and intertextual allusions into episodes, on the assumption that at least some viewers would video-record them and use their VCRs to painstakingly and slowly step through parts of the program.

The possibility of joke re-viewing escalated further in the late 1990s when the DVD and the TiVo digital video recorder (DVR) were released to consumers. Even though VCRs did permit multiple viewings of episodes, the quality of the tape-recorded video image and the primitive, distorted slow motion and pausing made it difficult to scrutinize visual jokes in depth. If, for example, there was a visual pun such as the "Pro-pain Accessories" storefront in *Bob Burgers*, you might not be able to read it even if you could pause a videocassette at a key point. In the early 2000s, DVRs were incorporated into most cable- and satellite-TV tuners and TV shows began to be released on DVDs, giving humor fans tools for dissecting visual gags in much greater detail.

This did not go unnoticed by comedy writers. Mitchell Hurwitz, the creator of *Arrested Development* (2003–2006, 2013, 2018), contended in 2005, "We often feel that we're really making a show for the new technology here. We're making a show for TiVo, and we're making a show for DVD, and it really becomes part of our objective in making this thing."[10] He felt that these new technologies freed him and his writers to accelerate the rhythm of the jokes and to layer joke upon joke, creating a comic density that would have been incomprehensible in television's network era and on the movie screen. The ability to clearly freeze and slow down television comedies, to interrupt their flow, is particularly important to intertextual humor. In the *Arrested Development* episode titled "The Immaculate Election" (March 20, 2005), we find an intertextual example that could profit from freezing and re-viewing. In that episode, teenage George Michael (Michael Cera) is embarrassed by a video he made of himself brandishing a *Star Wars* lightsaber in his garage. The video is humorous on one level because he looks goofy and overly serious as he waves it around. On a second level, his video makes intertextual reference to a viral YouTube clip, generally known as *Star Wars Kid* (2003), in which a high school student clumsily imitates Darth Maul's use of a lightsaber in *Star Wars: Episode 1 – The Phantom Menace* (1999). Thus, the *Arrested Development* visual gag is an intertextual reference to a viral video that is itself an intertextual references to a *Star Wars* film. The ability to freeze this scene and research its origin allows one to appreciate its intertextuality in a way that would have been difficult or impossible in the years before the DVD/DVR and Google searches. Moreover, the intertextuality of George Michael's video did not end with "The Immaculate Election." The video makes an appearance in three more *Arrested Development* episodes! The program was known for weaving self-reflexive references such as this throughout its episodes, which, again, can profit from the viewer's ability to slow or pause a scene in order to consult an *Arrested Development* fan wiki.[11] Further, George Michael's video has earned an intertextual life of its own as excerpts from it have been converted into memes and animated GIFs.[12] And in 2018, the *Star Wars* YouTube channel continued the show's connection with *Star Wars* by creating a mash-up where Ron Howard, the *Arrested Development* narrator, summarizes the story of *Star Wars: A New*

Hope in the style of *Arrested Development*.[13] Thus, this short segment of George Michael *as* the Star Wars Kid *as* Darth Maul illuminates how today's media landscape thrives on intertextuality and a density of layered allusions.

Media Convergence and Its Impact on the Sitcom

Thus far in this chapter, I have considered how sitcoms allude to themselves (self-reflexivity) and to other texts through parody and bricolage (intertextuality). I turn my attention now to texts that both refer to and *extend* other texts. Such texts do so to construct a diegetic world that continues across numerous media—as one can witness in the comic book-based "universes." The Marvel Cinematic Universe (MCU), for instance, is populated with its super heroes—Spider-Man, the Hulk, Black Widow, et al.—that originated in comic books. They can now be found in movies, TV shows, graphic novels, video games, action figures, and other media. On a much smaller scale, television sitcoms have fabricated their own universes for decades. Most often, these universes have existed solely within the medium of television. But the converging of television with theatrical film and online services in the 21st century has demanded new ways of thinking of sitcoms across different media—bordering on what has come to be called transmedia storytelling.

Spin-offs and Sequels

Beginning in the network era, the simplest way for a television comedy to extend its diegetic world was through the spin-off. One (or more) character from a successful program can be extracted from a show and inserted into a slightly different situation on a new program. Typically, the extracted character(s) exits the original show, returning only for special episodes. During the network era, the single most fertile source of sitcom spin-offs was *All in the Family*, from which no less than seven programs were directly or indirectly created: *Maude* (1972–1978), *Good Times* (1974–1979), *The Jeffersons* (1975–1985), *Archie*

Bunker's Place (1979–1983), *Checking In* (1981), *Gloria* (1982–1983), and *704 Hauser* (1994). Some were forgettable one-season shows; indeed, *704 Hauser* lasted only five episodes. But the others ran for multiple seasons to respectable ratings. Thus, during the network era of television, spin-offs were a convenient shortcut to developing new television shows, hoping to capitalize on the success of the originals.

In terms of intertextuality and narrative structure, the network-TV spin-off is usually a one-way street. Spin-offs expand the original program's story, but they soon become detached from it and have little on-going impact on the original story arcs. And, similarly, the original show's characters make infrequent appearances on the new, spun-off show. In comedy shows, it's rare for the original show and the spin-off to have storylines that crossover on an ongoing basis, but it did occur in the world of two drama series: *Homicide: Life on the Street* (1993–1999) and *Law & Order* (1990–2010). Thus, most sitcom spin-offs begin with a strong sense of intertextuality but that quickly diminishes as the spin-off's storylines develop on their own. Moreover, some spin-offs are not even contemporaneous with the original program—taking place years after or years before, or starting when the old program ends—which makes crossover impossible. We can see this in the narrative lines of two recent spin-offs. *Schooled* (2019–) chronicles Lainey's (AJ Michalka) challenges as a teacher approximately ten years after her time as a high school student in *The Goldbergs* (2013–); and *Young Sheldon* (2017–) portrays the adult Sheldon character (Jim Parsons) from *The Big Bang Theory* (2007–2020), starting when he was nine (portrayed by Iain Armitage). This break in the characters' timelines allows viewers to find out what happened to Lainey and provides more of Sheldon's backstory, but in neither case do the characters affect the story lines in their original programs. And, in a strange twist of casting, Mary Cooper, Sheldon's mother, is portrayed by two actresses who are themselves mother and daughter. Laurie Metcalf plays the older Mary in *The Big Bang Theory* and her daughter, Zoe Perry, fills the role of the younger version of the character in *Young Sheldon*. Time-shifted spin-offs most clearly illustrate the way that later shows detach themselves from their host.

Shows that start when one show ends—such as *Frasier*'s debut as *Cheers* concluded (1993)—operate much like movie sequels. They borrow exposition from the texts that launched them and continue their stories, but there is no earlier text still on the air for them to crossover with on a weekly basis. Some shows were popular enough that they jumped from the small screen to the large one and inspired theatrical sequels. *Sex and the City* (1998–2004), for example, has seen its characters' stories continued in two movie sequels: *Sex and the City* and *Sex and the City 2*. The *Sex and the City* movies are a continuation of the storylines begun in the TV series and they began when the original show ended—much like *Frasier* and other spin-offs. Other TV shows that inspired notable theatrical-movie sequels include: *The Addams Family* (1964–1966) and *The Addams Family* (1991) and *Addams Family Values* (1993); *The Brady Bunch* (1969–1974) and *The Brady Bunch Movie* (1995); *The Monkees* (1966–1968) and *Head* (1968); and *Police Squad!* (1982) and three sequels, *The Naked Gun: From the Files of Police Squad!* (1988), *The Naked Gun 2 ½: The Smell of Fear* (1991), and *Naked Gun 33 1/3: The Final Insult* (1994). The list is a relatively short one, however, because most movie sequels of TV shows have been pale imitations of their originals and have not endeared themselves to audiences or critics. Drama TV shows, especially science-fiction ones, have had the greatest success, as can be seen in the many sequels to *Star Trek* (1966–1969).

The Impact of Video Streaming on Comedy Content and Form

Spin-offs and movie sequels of TV series have been joined by new methods for distributing "television" content in the 21st century. We've discussed earlier the ways that the DVD and DVR created the opportunity for denser, more intertextual comedies. These technological advances were quickly followed by a rapid shift to on-demand services and the rise of the internet, which have disrupted how media are delivered and consumed. And new, inexpensive digital production tools have also prompted a revolution in how media are made. In 2006, Henry Jenkins attempted to stabilize these shifting media sands in an influential book, titled *Convergence Culture: Where Old and*

New Media Collide.[14] Network-era television, along with newspapers, paper books, and motion-picture theaters, are major examples of "old media." "New media" refers to websites, networked applications (iTunes, weather/mapping apps, etc.), video and social-media platforms (YouTube, Facebook, Twitter, Instagram, etc.), gaming platforms (including Nintendo Switch and VR gaming rigs), e-books, digital art installations in museums, and so on. At the time of Jenkins's book, however, the category of new media did not yet include SVOD services, because the first notable SVOD success, Netflix, didn't start streaming video until 2007. Even before Netflix, Jenkins found that the collision of old and new media had opened a space for new forms of storytelling: "A transmedia story unfolds across multiple media platforms, with each new text making a distinctive and valuable contribution to the whole."[15] Jenkins spends a chapter on the Wachowskis's *Matrix* franchise as a case study, explaining how elements of its story have been woven together from live-action movies, animation, video games, and comic books—not to mention fiction written by fans that extrapolates stories from the canonical characters.

Convergence culture and the new media underpinning it have had an undeniable impact on the sitcom in the 21st century, but enduring changes to one of television's sturdiest genres are difficult to ascertain. The sitcom's future is impossible to predict, but, as I write this chapter in the summer of 2019, it feels certain that major disruptions to the network-era sitcom have occurred and will continue to occur until a new equilibrium may be reached. Two major factors are fueling this disruption: (1) *consumers'* access to SVOD "portals," notably including Netflix, Amazon, and Hulu; and (2) *producers'* free or cheap access to online distribution systems such as YouTube and Vimeo.[16] The rise of SVOD portals in the 2010s has enabled viewers to "cut the cord"—discontinuing their cable/satellite subscriptions. And the new distribution systems have allowed content creators to release their works to the world without approval from the restrictive content gatekeepers of both television networks and SVOD portals.

Considering first the ramifications of SVOD portals, we must account for changes in both content and form. First, in terms of comedy content, portals carry programs that would blatantly violate network standards and FCC indecency laws. A show such as *Big Mouth* (2017–), which was picked up by Netflix, makes frequent, vulgar references to masturbation and genitalia, which would not be permitted on network TV or basic cable, although it might find a home on premium cable networks such as HBO. In recent years, cable television, which is not governed by the FCC in the same way that broadcast television is, has released transgressive comedy material on the order of *Rick and Morty* (2013–) on Adult Swim, but basic cable still does not enjoy the freedom allowed premium cable networks. Several SVOD portals initially depended on broadcast TV shows to attract customers. NBC and Fox, for instance, are partners in Hulu and that SVOD service relies heavily on reruns of sitcoms from those networks. However, as portals have ventured into the realm of producing their own original content—as opposed to simply licensing it—they have sought to distinguish themselves from network TV comedies. They've obviously been inspired by HBO shows such as *Girls* (2012–2017), *Veep* (2012–2019), and *Silicon Valley* (2014–) in the frankness of their representations of sexuality (including nudity), the audacity of their satire, and their liberal use of profanity. Some notable SVOD-produced comedies include:

- Amazon: *Orange Is the New Black* (2013–2019), *Red Oaks* (2014–2017), *Transparent* (2014–2019), *One Mississippi* (2015–2017), *The Marvelous Mrs. Maisel* (2017–), *Forever* (2018–)
- Hulu: *Difficult People* (2015–2017), *Casual* (2015–2018), *The Mindy Project* (Fox, then Hulu, 2015–2017)
- Netflix: *Bojack Horseman* (2014–), *Unbreakable Kimmy Schmidt* (NBC development, then Netflix, 2015–2019), *Grace and Frankie* (2015–), *Master of None* (2015–2017), *GLOW* (2017–), *Santa Clarita Diet* (2017–2019), *Dear White People* (2017–), *Big Mouth* (2017–), *Russian Doll* (2019–)

It's not just the content of these programs that differ from network sitcoms. They have also evolved the format of television comedy—modifying the conventions of network-era, single-camera sitcoms to suit the needs of SVOD distribution. For instance, even though portals provide video on-demand 24 hours-a-day and thus don't have to work within a broadcast-TV grid of time slots, their comedies still conform to the network-era standard of half-hour episodes—with only a few exceptions. There is more flexibility in the length of episodes, however. Network shows, after subtracting the commercials, cold opens, and tags, clock in at a compact 21 minutes of actual narrative. SVOD-produced episodes typically run 25–35 minutes and can go longer, if the story demands it. It might appear to be a small difference, but it allows scriptwriters and directors the freedom to adapt the running time to the story instead of the story to the running time.

It does seem curious, perhaps, that portals stick to the premise of a half-hour for comedy episodes and an hour for drama episodes. (Shows that incorporate humor into essentially dramatic plots can also run an hour, as in *The Marvelous Mrs. Maisel* and *Orange Is the New Black*.) It is also curious that SVOD portals bother to adhere to the concept of individual episodes, since so many portals release a program's entire season in one fell swoop—allowing viewers to binge eight or nine hours at once. As Allie Volpe has pointed out, there are things going on behind the scenes that encourage portals to stick with half-hour episodes for comedy.[17] Chief among these is portals wanting to keep their options open when it comes time to lease or syndicate their properties—in the USA and in foreign markets. If *Master of None*, for example, were to be leased to a broadcast or cable network, it would need to fit into a programming grid that expects comedies to be approximately 30 minutes long. A second incentive to stay within 30 minutes is the rules of the Emmy Awards when it comes to categorizing comedies and dramas. The rules don't try to distinguish between shows intended to be amusing and those that are not. Rather, they state:

> Any series where the average episode length is approximately thirty (30) minutes is eligible to enter in the Comedy

Series category; any series where the average episode length is approximately sixty (60) minutes is eligible to enter in the Drama Series category.[18]

The Emmys no longer have the prestige or clout that they did in the network era, but they remain the most significant award show for television productions. SVOD portals need to win Emmys to solidify their position as producers of legitimate competitors to broadcast/cable networks.

One final aspect of industry practices that encourages half-hour comedy episodes is how union members are paid. The Writers Guild of America (WGA), for example, represented union scriptwriters in negotiating an agreement in 2017 with what they call "high budget subscription video on demand" (HBSVOD) services—specifically, Amazon, Hulu, and Netflix. The minimum payments ("compensations") to scriptwriters were set for episodes at certain maximum running times: 15 minutes, 30 minutes, and 60 minutes. At this writing, the minimum compensation for a "teleplay" (a script for a single episode) is $10,180 for a 30-minute show and $19,728 for a 60-minute show.[19] Thus, the HBSVOD portals have a financial incentive to structure comedy narratives as individual episodes that run under 30 minutes.

Despite the persistence of the half-hour running time in SVOD original comedy programs, their storytelling format does indeed depart from the narrative structure that dominated the network era. If you compare scripts of, say, *Casual*, *Master of None*, or *Russian Doll* with those created for broadcast networks, you'll notice that the story in an SVOD show is not segmented into conventional "acts." The reason for this is simple enough. Just like programs on premium cable, SVOD comedy shows are not interrupted by commercials. Consequently, although SVOD shows have conventional scenes, they have no acts and they don't need to create mini-cliffhangers just before commercial breaks to attempt to hold viewers' attention. Because SVOD episodes are not segmented, the story arcs can develop in unconventional rhythms. For example, the "Free Churro" episode (September 14, 2018) of *Bojack Horseman* (2014–) is presented as one long monologue—a eulogy that Bojack delivers at what he thinks is his mother's funeral. Thus, episodes for SVOD shows are more like miniature movies or chapters in a novel than sitcoms. The cause–effect chain of such a show can be constructed much like one is in a movie/novel, without regard for the end of an act and the beginning of a commercial break.

Unlike theatrical films, however, half-hour SVOD episodes are conceptualized as one chunk within a larger narrative—similar, again, to a chapter within a book. After all, viewers may binge-watch an entire season of a show—episode after episode—if they so desire. When contrasted with the conventional network-era sitcom, this leads to a different function of an episode's beginning and end. During the peak of the network sitcom, storylines in sitcom episodes were only loosely connected to each other. What happened to, say, Andy Taylor (Andy Griffith) in a single *Andy Griffith Show* episode did not depend heavily on his history in previous episodes and did not lead directly into future episodes' storylines. There were exceptions to this, but, generally speaking, episodes could stand on their own as completed stories. The impetus for this was to simplify the broadcast of episodes in summer reruns and, if the show were successful, in syndication. Since one episode did not continue a story from a previous one and since it did not expect viewers to see the next one, episodes could be watched in virtually any order. Sitcoms from the 1950s to the 1970s generally were not serialized, continuing stories, which were the province of the daytime soap opera. Network-era broadcasters wanted viewers to stay in the flow of an evening's programming, but they did not anticipate that viewers could be led into another episode of a sitcom *immediately* after finishing the previous one. Network-era viewers could binge on an evening's worth of various shows on a single network, but they could not binge-watch a particular program in an evening.

Amazon's, Hulu's, and Netflix's all-encompassing desire to battle against competing options—YouTube, social media, human interaction—and lock a viewer into viewing its service has led to an increased serialization of the sitcom form. Most SVOD comedy episodes have open endings, raising questions that might be answered in following episodes. And all SVOD interfaces automatically roll the viewer into the next episode unless they take some specific action to stop it. If you want to read the end credits, you'd better hit a button on your remote quickly! Thus, the default of the SVOD comedy-watching experience is binge watching, not individual-episode watching. This has forced the half-hour comedy to adapt and serialize its narrative structure. SVOD shows will often still start with a cold open, but the opening credits have become superfluous. Those credits may be skipped with the press of a button on Netflix's interface. For comedy episodes, this means that the story starts more quickly and exposition is abbreviated to the bare minimum. And the ending of an episode functions to lure the viewer into the next episode in their binge. The post-credit tag scene has become a casualty of the rollover to the following episodes. In the network era, the tag was used to maintain viewer interest during the credits. Because Netflix hopes to entice the viewer to move on to the next episode directly after the story ends, the tag has become superfluous and few SVOD comedy programs have them anymore. The ending of an episode of *GLOW* provides an example. Sam Sylvia (Marc Maron) is a struggling film/TV director, trying to launch a low-budget TV wrestling show. In the "Liberal Chokehold" episode he learns that one of the wrestlers, Justine Biagi (Britt Baron), is his daughter. This is revealed in the episode's final scene, causing him to yell at her, "What the fuck do you want? Do you want money? Do you want bone marrow?" She runs from the room and the episode concludes with Sam sitting on a hotel bed, alone. His (and the viewer's) questions aren't answered and, in four seconds, Netflix flows into the next episode, where they just might be.

YouTube and the Webisode

Since its launch in 2005, YouTube has had a profound impact on the distribution and consumption of video and music. It has provided a distribution platform to virtually anyone with a camera in their phone.

And a generation of TV watchers born around the time that YouTube launched has grown up spending more time with it than with either broadcast/cable networks or SVOD portals. What YouTube and other online video-distribution systems like Vimeo will mean for comedy on screens over the long haul has yet to be determined. But, in the short term, a few observations are in order.

YouTube thrives on short videos and this is particularly true for comedy. In the early years of YouTube it was thought that original half-hour Webisodes could be produced to compete with conventional broadcast and cable programs. But major media conglomerates quickly found it was difficult to make a success of such Webisodes and that videos under five minutes were much more popular. And the humorous videos that went viral and attracted the biggest audiences were typically short skits, comedy bits performed by stand-up comedians, or clips from network TV programs. Nick Marx notes, "As producers (and their parent companies) of original Web video have increasingly sought cross-platform mobility, comedy—short, cheap, and accessible across media—has become their preferred genre, providing a cost-effective format for experimentation and immediacy."[20] Moreover, professionally produced, scripted comedy with recurring characters has often been surpassed in popularity by videos shot by amateurs of their pets' or kids' funny antics. You can, of course, find sitcom episodes on YouTube, many of which have been posted in violation of US copyright law, but the most successful comedy on YouTube is typically not "situation" comedy. That is, the most widely shared viral videos are not powered by humor created by the situations in which fictional characters find themselves. Instead, they are gag- or joke-centered comedy. In some respects, comedy on YouTube is reminiscent of comedy in the early years of radio, when gags born in Vaudeville were competing with the situation-based humor of *Amos 'n' Andy* and *The Goldbergs*.

Nonetheless, YouTube has provided a platform for short-form situation-comedy series that have had modest success and made stars of their performers. One example is *Broad City*, created by and starring Ilana Glazer and Abbi Jacobson. *Broad City* began as a series of approximately three-minute Webisodes distributed online between 2009 and 2011. With the help of conventional sitcom supporters such as Amy Poehler (star of *Parks and Recreation*), the Web series was developed into a half-hour show for Comedy Central in 2014 and ran through 2019. Glazer and Jacobson's transition from Web series to cable-network series illustrates how short-form online video is used in the 21st century as a source for program content by broadcast and cable networks, much as the networks have recruited comedians from improv troupes and stand-up comedy clubs.

In addition to providing a talent pool, broadcast/cable networks view online video mostly as a way to expand a program's brand and drive viewers back to the TV shows where the real money is made selling advertising. For example, during *The Office*'s run in the USA, the scripts were written so that they were intentionally longer than 21 minutes. The producers wanted excess footage of some of the minor characters so that it could be repurposed online. You could learn more about Phyllis (Phyllis Smith) or Stanley (Leslie David Baker) if you went to the show's website, but those storylines had no impact on the story arcs of the main characters. They were merely a way to get viewers interested in the show's plot developments so that they'd watch more episodes on TV—and view more commercials. Thus, they qualify as transmedia storytelling, but only in a limited sense. They transpose characters from one medium (broadcast TV) to another (the web), but do the web clips, as Jenkins advocates, "mak[e] a distinctive and valuable contribution to the whole"? In this instance, there is not a whole, expansive universe of *Office* storylines to which both the TV program and the web clips contribute—influencing one another. Rather, it's the TV program's universe and the web clips are spin-offs from it—expanding that universe, but not influencing its core elements. As Marx phrases it, "Hit television shows from many genres presently provide abundant ancillary content in the form of Webisodes, character blogs, and interactive games at their network web sites. But the flow of content in the opposite direction—from the Internet to established, 'old' media like television—has been decidedly less prominent."[21]

Case Study: *The Simpsons*

This chapter has discussed how the sitcom wrings humor out of self-reflexivity, intertextuality, and transmedia extensions of television texts in an era of on-demand, converged media. *The Simpsons* offers an exemplary case study of the disruption of network-era television practice. For many scholars, it epitomizes self-reflexive and intertextual comedy, and the pervasiveness of transmedia texts—having appeared in a film, comic books, video games, a Universal Studios theme-park ride, and dolls and other merchandise that are too numerous to name.[22] Perhaps paradoxically, *The Simpsons* wreaked havoc on many of television's conventions—especially conventions of the sitcom—at the same time that it virtually singlehandedly established the viability of a new over-the-air television network when Fox was just beginning. And despite its ridiculing of some central tenets of American middle-class ideology (Christian religion, the family, the work ethic, and so on), it has been embraced by the mainstream American viewing audience for a very long time—becoming the longest running scripted program on prime-time American television, both in terms of the number of seasons it has run and the number of episodes it has produced.

Self-reflexivity

I will begin with *The Simpsons*'s many self-reflexive aspects. As I have argued above, comic television self-reflexivity functions in three ways: references to the world of TV by characters within a diegesis; characters laying bare the production of the show they are in, but still remaining in character; and actors seeming to break out of their characters, shatter the fourth wall, and address us *as actors*.

First, we can see how Homer, Marge, Lisa, Bart, and Maggie stay in character while they encounter cartoon versions of real-life TV actors and other celebrities playing themselves. The list of such guest appearances is exceedingly long and varied. It includes Jennifer Garner, Mister T, Paul Newman, Jon Stewart, and Betty White, as well as musicians Blink-182, Green Day, Ludacris, Metallica, the

Dixie Chicks, "Weird Al" Yankovic, and more. There have even been episodes in which the producers of *The Simpsons* (Matt Groening and James L. Brooks) have appeared on the show in cartoon form. When a *Simpsons* character meets a celebrity, they do so as their character, drawing the real-world person into the fictitious world of "Springfield," whose exact location has never been revealed. In these instances, the diegetic space of the characters blurs with real-world spaces such as Hollywood. The show slyly alludes to the people who make TV, but without breaking Homer, et al. out of their diegetic universe.

The second self-reflexive form, where the actual apparatus of television-making is laid bare, has the potential for being more diegetically disruptive. *The Simpsons* often makes jokes at its own expense and invites viewers to share in the joke, urging them to stop suspending disbelief and recognize this TV show *as* a TV show. As Lisa might say, it often "goes meta." It thus qualifies as a strikingly televisual show, too. For example, one episode was done in the style of *The LEGO Movie* (2014), converting the characters into LEGO blocks. At the very beginning, Homer wakes up protesting, "It's not selling out! It's co-branding! Co-branding!" His remarks make little sense within the diegetic world of the show, but rather refer to criticisms of *The Simpsons* selling out and giving into marketing demands. A few moments later, at breakfast and under the opening credits, the LEGO version of Bart comments that something feels odd. Marge explains, "You're right, there *is* something different about the Simpsons today," seeming to recognize their LEGO kitchen and to be speaking about the program itself and not just the Simpsons family; but then she continues, "Your father is wearing a tie!" Bart accepts her mother's answer: "Oh, that's what's different!" And Lisa confirms her answer: "That's the one and only thing!" Obviously, the metacritical humor of this interchange relies on the viewer recognizing *The Simpsons* as a TV show that might promote *The LEGO Movie* or LEGO products. (And, in fact, a *Simpsons* LEGO set and video game were made available concurrent with this episode.)

Few sitcoms have incorporated apparatus-revealing self-reflexivity as extensively as *The Simpsons*. It often shatters the fourth wall in its opening credit sequence. In lieu of a cold open, the program established in its first season that it would change the credits virtually every week: in what appears to be after-school detention, Bart writes different texts on a blackboard (beginning with "I will not waste chalk"); Lisa riffs a unique saxophone solo; and, when Homer arrives home in his car, the entire family gathers on their couch, in front of a television. The latter "couch gags" quickly became an identifying element of the show. Since they are not part of the main storytelling and have no impact on an episode's events, they can directly comment on the making of TV comedy—as in one particularly morbid couch gag imagined by graffiti artist Banksy that portrays the animation of *The Simpsons* as occurring in an Asian sweatshop where miserable workers toil in an underground dystopia, *Simpsons* dolls are filled with shredded kittens, and the holes in *Simpsons* DVDs are popped out by an emaciated unicorn. The final image in this couch "gag" is a 20th Century Fox compound surrounded by barbed wire, as if it were a prison. Fox has been remarkably tolerant of the ridicule the program aims at it. In one episode, Homer has an idea for a reality-TV show and phones Fox. The automated answer he receives is a sharp needling of the network's programming: "You've reached Fox. If you're pitching a show where gold-digging skanks get what's coming to them, press 1. If you're pitching a rip-off of another network's reality show, press 2. Please stay on the line. Your half-baked ideas are all we've got."

The third form of self-reflexivity I discussed above is actors looking into the camera and directly addressing us *as actors*—for instance, actor George Burns speaking as George Burns. Despite all the fourth-wall breaking in which *The Simpsons* revels, the show's voice actors do not speak to us as "themselves": Dan Castellaneta (Homer), Julie Kavner (Marge), Nancy Cartwright (Bart), and Yeardley Smith (Lisa), among others. Any direct address, such as when the characters introduce the annual "Treehouse of Horror" Halloween show, is done as the character, not as the actor—which is similar to how direct address works in sitcoms such as *Parker Lewis Can't Lose* (discussed earlier), *Malcolm in the Middle*, and *The Bernie Mac Show*. It's not clear why *The Simpsons* does not incorporate this form of self-reflexivity. Perhaps it's more diegetically complicated for voice actors to break through the fourth wall—especially considering the disjunction between their characters' and the actors' physical appearances. For example, a ten-year-old schoolboy (Bart) is voiced by a middle-aged woman (Nancy Cartwright).

Intertextuality

I argued earlier that intertextuality is best understood in terms of parody and bricolage. Moreover, I contended that both of these phenomena refer outward to other texts, but that parody may be distinguished from bricolage because it carries with it an implicit critique of the text which it resembles. Bricolage, in contrast, can allude to other texts without resembling them or making fun of them.

In terms specifically of previous sitcom texts, *The Simpsons* mocks its host genre at the same time it still remains essentially a sitcom. Through self-parody, it critiques fundamental aspects of the genre such as timeworn narrative tropes, insipid catchphrases, and conservative discourse. The entire program can be viewed as a parody of early television sitcoms with their bumbling husband and caring, smart wives—which is made explicit in a 2009 credit sequence that replicates the openings of *The Honeymooners* (1955–1956), *The Dick Van Dyke Show* (1961–1966), *The Brady Bunch* (1969–1974), and *Cheers* (1982–1993). Of course, it's not just sitcoms that *The Simpsons* parodies. Virtually every episode is poking fun at some element of contemporary culture. "The Simpsons Spin-Off Showcase" episode, for instance, debuts three spin-offs of *The Simpsons* that never existed: *Chief Wiggum, P.I.*, *The Love-matic Grampa*, and *The Simpsons Family Smile-Time Variety Hour*.[23] The segments directly parody *Magnum, P.I.*, fantasy-based sitcoms, and insipid variety shows, respectively. Hosted by unctuous character Troy McLure, the episode ends with him falsely teasing *The Simpsons* upcoming season: "How do you keep *The Simpsons* fresh and funny after eight long years? Well, here's what on tap for season nine: magic powers, wedding after wedding after wedding. And did someone say, 'long lost triplets'?" *The Simpsons* again turned the parody inward—making fun of itself and other long-running sitcoms—when the show passed *Gunsmoke* (1955–1975) as broadcasting the most episodes in a scripted TV series (in 2018, after 636 episodes). Its opening sequence mocks Western's shoot-outs at high noon. Maggie faces down a stereotypical cowboy in a Western street. He snarls, "Can't let you do it. Can't let you break my record" and draws his gun. Maggie draws and shoots him. Then, Western style credits follow with a cameo of each Simpsons saying a catchphrase associated with them—including Bart shouting, "Ay, caramba!"

The cultural references are so thick that often a viewer must pause and rewind an episode to catch all the gags, or refer to lists of references on the Simpsons Archive, the Simpsons Wiki, or similar online reference sites. Each episode is chock-a-block with references to other media texts—from other sitcoms to old and new movies to sculpture and painting to avant-garde art to cable-news channels to video games to comics to literature and so on, seemingly ad infinitum. I quoted Mitchell Hurwitz above and his comment in 2005 regarding *Arrested Development*; he asserted that the proliferation of DVRs in the 2000s allowed its writers to stuff jokes into episodes at a rate that necessitated pausing and re-viewing video to catch all these evanescent gags. In truth, *The Simpsons* pioneered this sort of humor overload a good 15 years earlier in the pre-DVR era, when videocassettes allowed a primitive form of freeze framing. Its online fans delved into these semi-hidden gags, calling it "freeze-frame fun."

Chris Turner, writing in 2004, maintains that the "most elaborate example of Freeze Frame Fun in the show's history" comes from a 1994 episode, "Homer Badman."[24] In an acerbic parody of tabloid-news TV shows, the episode presents a sleazy program titled *Rock Bottom*, which must address erroneous claims it previously made. The Simpsons family watches their TV set as 35 correction statements scroll rapidly up the screen in less than two seconds—impossible to read unless you freeze the image. They include: "Cats do not eventually turn into dogs" and "Bullets do not bounce off of fat guys."[25] One line even breaks the fourth wall to tweak fans engaging in freeze-frame fun: "If you are reading this you have no life." And the scroll ends with a self-deprecating line, "The people who are writing this have no life." Another, more recent example, occurs in an episode filled with allusions to Netflix's *Stranger Things* (2016–), Homer browses made-up Netflix titles of "Scandinavian crime dramas with full nudity"— including *Bøøben*, *The Girl with the Dragon Ta-tas*, *Stockholm Sin-Dome*, and *Finnish Already*. Nine movie thumbnails appear on-screen for just three seconds. These punning titles would be impossible to read in the time they're visible. A viewer must have their finger on the pause button if they wish to catch this brief parody of Netflix's programming.

The Simpsons's extreme intertextuality can be critical of the texts it targets, as we saw in these two parodies of tabloid journalism and SVOD platforms, but it is not always so. Oftentimes *The Simpsons* humorously blends media texts for the sheer amusement born of incongruous mash-ups. If we narrowly define parody as requiring an element of criticism, then these blends don't quite qualify. They are more bricolage than pure parody. For example, in that same *Stranger Things* episode, *The Simpsons* sneaks in a quick visual and sound quotation of Francis Ford Coppola's epic movie, *Apocalypse Now* (1979). Bart, Milhouse, and Ralph are participating in a contest called "Krusty's Toy Trample!" where they are racing through the "Hello Krusty" toy store. The title of the store is itself a passing allusion to Hello Kitty products, and the allusion to the Coppola film comes when Ralph falls into a barrel of Krusty Slime, whose parodic warning label reads, "Fun for kids! Toxic for pets!" Ralph slowly emerges from the slime, with only his eyes visible, much like the iconic image of Captain Willard (Martin Sheen) in *Apocalypse Now*, and the nondiegetic music shifts to notes seemingly from the Doors' "The End," which is used in the film. This scene is an intertextual mix of parody and bricolage. The Krusty Slime label makes fun of unhelpful warning labels in a quick parody of them. But the allusions to Hello Kitty, *Apocalypse Now*, and "The End" are more bricolage than parody, because they are not denigrating the original texts. If the viewer is amused by the shot of Ralph extricating himself from the Krusty Slime barrel, it is because they have recognized the original sources of this image and its accompanying song and have found it amusing to having their original meaning shifted by this incongruous change of context. That is, a young boy in a toy contest is a very different context from a soldier in a Vietnam swamp. There is an incongruity between the original source (an anti-war war film) and its appearance in *The Simpsons*. This relatively simple scene thus has a wealth of allusions in it. Viewers of *The Simpsons* have become accustomed to unpacking the show's dense visuals to discover amusing bricolage bits such as these.

The Simpsons Copes with Convergence

Debuting in 1989, *The Simpsons* was definitely not originally designed for an era of internet-based on-demand video and SVOD portals. After all, the internet as we know it today barely existed at that time and the browser that most popularized the Web, Mosaic, wasn't released to the public until four years later. However, *The Simpsons* has thrived in the 21st century, despite continuing to rely on a conventional two-act structure, segmented by commercials and limited to 21 minutes of story time. Even though it has faced strong competition from animation on SVOD services, its narrative structure has not been made more serial to accommodate binge viewing. This is evident in the way that most episodes' stories are self-contained, without much continuation of storylines. Thus, in many ways, *The Simpsons* seems stuck in the 20th century, but the heightened transmedia opportunities of the current media environment have allowed its narrative to be expanded in new ways and have certainly benefitted the program financially.

The Simpsons comics have been available since 1993—including titles such as *Bartman*, *Radioactive Man*, and *Itchy & Scratchy Comics*. In fact, many of the characters, the narrative premises, and the overall visual design of *The Simpsons* television show were essentially formed in the comic Groening created in 1977, titled *Life in Hell*. As the cartoon on the cover of the 1987 compilation *School Is Hell* illustrates, the *Life in Hell* character Bongo, a one-eared rabbit, was essentially a forerunner of Bart—down to his detention chalkboard. In that book cover, Bongo writes repeatedly and rather darkly on the blackboard, "I must remember to be cheerful and obedient." And in Figure 6.3,

Figure 6.3 As *The Simpsons*' 25th season started, Bart was still in detention. His blackboard writing here refers back to the program's longevity.

which appears at the start of the 25th season's first episode, Bart defiantly and self-reflexively scrawls on his chalkboard, "25 years and they can't come up with a new punishment." Bongo and Bart are close to the same age and share a rebellious attitude toward school authorities. Many of the panels in *School Is Hell* contain the seeds of *The Simpsons* episodes.

Starting with the release of *Bart vs. the Space Mutants* in 1991 for the Nintendo Entertainment System, there have been over 25 *Simpsons*-related video games. And *The Simpsons Movie* came along in 2007. In addition, *The Simpsons* Ride opened at Universal Studios Florida and Universal Studios Hollywood theme parks in 2008. Of course, the amount of *Simpsons* merchandise (dolls, T-shirts, etc.) is quite staggering. These extensions of *The Simpsons* universe allow fans to see the characters in new narratives, but they don't influence the core, canonical *Simpsons* storylines presented on Fox TV stations. In other words, the TV program has spawned many media texts, but those texts have not had an impact on the original program. Consequently, it cannot be said that *The Simpsons* has attained the transmedia ideal that Henry

Jenkins theorized in 2006, when he proposed that the texts of different media could affect one another across a franchise's universe. Still, taken as a whole, all of *The Simpsons*' many media texts work together to create *Simpsons* tropes that have circulated broadly in international popular culture.

Although not quite conforming to the transmedia ideal, there have been many ways that contemporary, internet-based media have had an impact on *The Simpsons*. There are thousands of *Simpsons* clips on YouTube. Although their legality is questionable, Fox does not seem to be in a hurry to have them taken down. One video compiling couch gags, for example, has garnered almost nine million views.[26] Presumably, Fox believes that these clips do more good than harm—luring viewers back to the original program where the commercials are aired. Fox and *The Simpsons* producers have long resisted licensing episodes to a subscription VOD service. For many years, SVOD giant Netflix has delivered *Simpsons* DVDs through its dwindling DVD-subscription service, but it has never streamed the show. Fox itself does offer on-demand access to all seasons through SimpsonsWorld.com. However, at the time of this writing (summer 2019), you cannot simply subscribe to this service. Fox requires users to sign in with credentials from a cable or satellite TV service and even after doing so, one must sit through commercials while an episode streams. The situation changed in 2019 when one of the largest media mergers of the 21st century occurred: the acquisition of Fox by Disney. Now, Disney owns the Fox television properties and has launched its own streaming service, Disney+, which will be the only SVOD service to carry *Simpsons* episodes. In typically self-reflexive manner, *The Simpsons* producers ridiculed their new owners in a promotional video in which Homer proclaims, "I for one salute our new corporate overlords," while standing in front of a "Welcome Synergy" sign and statues of Darth Vader and Disney head, Bob Iger (see Figure 6.4). A picture of Fox founder Rupert Murdoch appears in a trash can.

The internet has nourished various other forms of user-generated *Simpsons* material. Thousands of memes have been created using images from the show—as static JPEGs and animated GIFs. Three

COMEDY, TELEVISUALITY, AND CONVERGENCE

Figure 6.4 On the occasion of *The Simpsons*'s parent company being acquired by Disney, Homer cheerfully proclaims, "I for one salute our new corporate overlords!"

Simpsons fans created an online service in 2016 to freely create both static memes and animated GIFs. Inspired by *The Simpsons* character, Professor Frink, the Frinkiac service offers millions of screenshots from *Simpsons* episodes and automates the process of selecting an image and displaying text over it—in *The Simpsons* font, no less. In a basic act of bricolage, one might even recontextualize such an image to imagine Frink pontificating about the sitcom (see Figure 6.5). Frinkiac users may share their bricolage creations on social media, perhaps hoping they'll go as viral as other *Simpsons* memes have in the past. Once again, Fox and the producers of *The Simpsons* seem to accept the free publicity that such efforts generate and have not sent a cease-and-desist letter to Frinkiac. Fan fiction has also been generated by individuals who are not associated with the show. On fanfiction.net, for example, there are over a thousand fan-authored stories about *The Simpsons* characters. One popular example, "Bart Simpson: Attorney at Law," runs 93,216 words over 20 chapters. Its summary reads, "Seventeen years in the future Bart Simpson, is now a successful attorney in East Springfield. He has everything, and is happy.

COMEDY, TELEVISUALITY, AND CONVERGENCE

Figure 6.5 The Frinkiac service makes it easier to construct memes and GIFs from *The Simpsons* images—encouraging fans to create new use of the show's characters and tropes.

That is going to be challenged when some women reenter his life."[27] Fan fiction existed before the internet, but in those pre-internet days it lacked an effective distribution system. Sites like fanfiction.net enable a transmedia experience in which fans themselves expand a program's diegetic universe—taking the characters into the future, as in this example, or re-imagining the characters in different ways.

Clip compilations, meme bricolages, and fanfiction are creative extensions of a text, but they are not the only way that the fans connect to that text in this networked era. A voluminous amount of information about the program has been shared online by fans with no official input from Fox. In fact, *The Simpsons* was an early instance of crowd-sourced data on the Internet. In March 1990, just four months after the show debuted in its half-hour format, a fan who was a computer-science student created the alt.tv.simpsons newsgroup (abbreviated as ATS), an online place for posting information and opinions about *The Simpsons*.[28] It was initially shared across the Usenet network and may now be found on Google Groups.[29] ATS data also inform simpsonsarchive.com and other online resources. For example, the *Simpsons Wiki* is a user-generated encyclopedia with over 20,000 pages of Simpson-iana.[30]

ATS and its successors offer fans a community of like-minded viewers and their debates about *Simpsons* characters and stories are a transmedia experience—as their networked conversations shape their understanding of the *Simpsons* universe. And there have been some limited instances of ATS affecting the show's storylines and character development. For example, Comic Book Guy's catchphrase, "Worst. Episode. Ever." comes from an ATS post by John R. Donald, who hated the "Itchy & Scratchy: The Movie" episode and groused, "I thought this was easily the worst episode ever." In a subsequent *Simpsons* episode, the writers parodied obsessive fans like Donald. Showing Comic Book Guy posting to a Usenet newsgroup, he rants, "Last night's *Itchy & Scratchy* was, without a doubt, the worst episode ever. Rest assured I was on the Internet within minutes registering my disgust throughout the world." It's impossible to say with any certainty how often *The Simpsons* writers were influenced by online commentary. More likely, their attitude toward fans poring over *Simpsons* in excruciating detail was similar to that of Matt Groening, who once said of ATS users, "Sometimes I feel like knocking their electronic noggins together."

Through both products officially sanctioned by Fox and unsanctioned user-generated material, *The Simpsons* has managed to find new, digital means of expression in the SVOD-dominated 21st century. Its roots in 20th-century network-era television are occasionally evident, but many of *The Simpsons* texts that circulate today could not exist in the pre-digital, pre-internet days.

The Simpsons Case Study: Conclusion

There are many ways in which *The Simpsons* is unlike any other sitcom—notably in its record-setting longevity—and yet it is still a prime example of what the genre has become in recent times. There is more self-reflexive and intertextual humor in a single *Simpsons* episode than there is in an entire season of *The Big Bang Theory*. It may even be more densely packed with allusions than animated shows such as *South Park* and *Family Guy*, which are themselves known for breaking the fourth wall and referring out to today's popular-culture tropes and memes. Moreover, despite its roots in the network era, *The Simpsons* has actively engaged with crowd-sourced and on-demand culture in an era that some have declared "post-network." *The Simpsons* no longer provokes the cultural outrage that it used to in many circles and its audience has definitely declined since its peak years, but still it just keeps motoring along. With each episode, it sets a new record for longevity and finds innovative techniques to build self-reflexive and intertextual humor.

Notes

1 John Thornton Caldwell, *Televisuality: Style, Crisis, and Authority in American Television* (New Brunswick, NJ: Rutgers University Press, 1995), 56. Jeremy G. Butler, *Television Style* (New York: Routledge, 2010), 81–87.
2 Caldwell, 56.
3 Caldwell titles the first chapter of his book, "Excessive Style: The Crisis of Network Television." Caldwell, 3–31.
4 David Bordwell, *Figures Traced in Light: On Cinematic Staging* (Berkeley, CA: University of California Press, 2005), 23.
5 Ibid., 85.
6 Claude Lévi-Strauss, *The Savage Mind* (Chicago, IL: University of Chicago Press, 1966). Originally published as *La Pensée sauvage* in 1962.
7 Brett Mills, "Comedy Vérité: Contemporary Sitcom Form," *Screen* 45, no. 1 (Spring 2004): 63–78; and Ethan Thompson, "Comedy Vérité? The Observational Documentary Meets the Televisual Sitcom," *The Velvet Light Trap* 60 (2007): 63–72.
8 Colbert debuted the term on the first episode of *The Colbert Report* (October 17, 2005).
9 See discussion and illustrations in Jeremy G. Butler, "Televisuality and the Resurrection of the Sitcom in the 2000s," in *Television Style* (New York: Routledge, 2010), 173–76.
10 David Bianculli, "Mitch Hurwitz, Creator of 'Arrested Development,'" *NPR*, February 10, 2006, https://www.npr.org/templates/story/story.php?storyId=4987832. Quoted in Thompson, 63–72.
11 "Arrested Development Wiki," *Fandom*, https://arresteddevelopment.fandom.com/wiki/Main_Page, accessed June 12, 2019.

12 George Michael video GIFs are collected here: https://giphy.com/gifs/arrested-development-michael-cera-george-7kpQyA3qn2bVC
13 *Arrested Development: Star Wars with Ron Howard!*, Star Wars Channel, May 2, 2018, YouTube, https://youtu.be/o6XERmXsP-U, accessed April 28, 2019.
14 Henry Jenkins, *Convergence Culture: Where Old and New Media Collide* (New York University Press, 2006).
15 Ibid., 95–96.
16 For an explanation of the term, "portals," see Amanda D. Lotz, *Portals: A Treatise on Internet-Distributed Television* (Ann Arbor, MI: Michigan Publishing, University of Michigan Library, 2017), http://dx.doi.org/10.3998/mpub.9699689.
17 Allie Volpe, "The One thing That Isn't Evolving with Netflix & Hulu's Takeover of TV," *Thrillist*, 16 October 2017, https://www.thrillist.com/entertainment/nation/netflix-episode-length-streaming-services-traditional-tv, accessed February 27, 2019.
18 Television Academy, "71st Primetime Emmy Awards 2018-2019 Rules and Procedures," 22 Feb 2019, http://www.emmys.com/sites/default/files/Downloads/2019-rules-procedures-v4a.pdf, accessed February 27, 2019.
19 Writers Guild of America, "Schedule of Minimums," 2017, *Writers Guild of America*, https://www.wga.org/uploadedfiles/contracts/min2017.pdf, accessed February 28, 2019.
20 Nick Marx, "'The Missing Link Moment': Web Comedy in New Media Industries," *The Velvet Light Trap* no. 68 (Fall 2011), 15.
21 Ibid.
22 See, for example, Jonathan Gray, *Watching with The Simpsons: Television, Parody, and Intertextuality* (New York: Routledge, 2006).
23 Discussed in Jason Mittell, *Genre and Television: From Cop Shows to Cartoons in American Culture* (New York: Routledge, 2004), 193.
24 Chris Turner, *Planet Simpson: How a Cartoon Masterpiece Defined a Generation* (Boston, MA: Da Capo Press, 2004), 286.
25 "[2F06] Homer Bad Man," *The Simpsons Archive*, July 21, 1996, https://www.simpsonsarchive.com/episodes/2F06.html, accessed April 9, 2019.
26 Angry Baby, *Couch GAGs in season 11–20*, YouTube, August 3, 2017, https://www.youtube.com/watch?v=V0tIrNXgoQM, accessed March 26, 2019.
27 Quick-n-Popular, "Bart Simpson: Attorney at Law," *fanfiction*, September 17, 2006, https://www.fanfiction.net/s/3157288/1/Bart-Simpson-Attorney-at-Law, accessed March 26, 2019.
28 Alan Siegel, "Best Message Board Ever," *Slate*, September 26, 2013, https://slate.com/culture/2013/09/the-history-of-simpsons-message-board-alt-tv-simpsons.html, accessed April 9, 2019.
29 "alt.tv.simpsons," *Google Groups*, https://groups.google.com/forum/?hl=en#!forum/alt.tv.simpsons, accessed June 12, 2019.
30 "Simpsons Wiki," *Fandom*, https://simpsons.fandom.com/wiki/Simpsons_Wiki, accessed June 12, 2019.

QUESTIONS FOR DISCUSSION

Chapter 1: Understanding the Sitcom

1. How would you describe the storytelling conventions of the sitcom? Identify the following parts of sitcom narrative in an episode you've seen: cold opening, act I, act II, tag. Does your episode have A and B stories? If the episode you picked doesn't have all of these parts, what is it missing and why? What do you imagine your show's logline would be?
2. Evan S. Smith labels some common sitcom "predicaments" and "character mixes." Have you seen them employed in TV shows you watch? What are some other tropes you can identify?
3. Do you like to watch shows with laugh tracks? Why or why not?

Chapter 2: A Critical/Cultural History of the Sitcom

1. Which aspects of the sitcom did *Amos 'n' Andy* establish when it was on radio? Which humor category does the use of "blackvoice" and racial stereotypes put the show in: superiority, release/relief, or incongruity?
2. What was innovative about *I Love Lucy*'s mode of production? Is that mode still being used today and, if so, in which shows?
3. Many critics and industry insiders felt that the sitcom genre would not survive into the 21st century, but it has. What changes have there been in the genre that have allowed it to persist into the post-network, digital era?

QUESTIONS FOR DISCUSSION

Chapter 3: Comedy, Family, and Small Towns

1. What current television shows depict a "nuclear family" and which ones have characters that stray from this model? What do they suggest about changing values regarding families?
2. What distinguishes urban, suburban, and rural sitcoms? How do differences in settings lead to differences in types of stories that are told?
3. How do sitcom women balance the demands of career and motherhood? Does the genre seem to favor specific roles for women? Is this different now than it was in the 1950s?

Chapter 4: Comedy, Sex, and Gender Identity

1. What milestones have there been in the inclusion of LGBTQ characters in sitcoms? What negative and positive attributes have accrued around LGBTQ characters?
2. Can you think of a current sitcom that expresses the values of third-wave feminism? How do its characters do so? How are they different from second-wave feminists?
3. In what sense is gender "performative" rather than biological? How are gender traits determined more by culture than physical attributes? Which sitcoms or individual sitcom characters play with gender roles?

Chapter 5: Comedy, Race, Ethnicity, and Religion

1. Which program's loglines (their "narrative problematics") seem to take race and/or ethnicity into consideration? How are racial themes woven into sitcom stories?
2. Consider a show with a cast that is predominantly made up of minority characters. Does the show implement the discourses of assimilationism, pluralism, and/or multiculturalism?
3. The "stereotype pixie" in Dave Chappelle's sketch comedy show raises uncomfortable questions about the reception of comedy

based in race and ethnic humor. How can we understand his dilemma in terms of the theories of humor? And do sitcom episodes have the same issues as short sketches?

Chapter 6: Comedy, Televisuality, and Convergence

1. Sitcoms released since the advent of the DVD and DVR are able to pack episodes with intertextual references. What examples can you provide of humor based on obscure references in TV shows? Which shows seem to rely most heavily on intertextuality?
2. Parody and bricolage are two very similar concepts. How would you distinguish them? Can you think of examples of bricolage that are not also examples of parody?
3. The Marvel Cinematic Universe is an extremely successful example of transmedia storytelling. Sitcoms have not been able to replicate that level of success, but there have been instances in which sitcom storytelling has travelled from one medium to another. How does this change the way that stories can be told in the era of digital and online media?

VIDEOGRAPHY

In chronological order.

Amos 'n' Andy (radio, 1928–1960; TV, 1951–1953)
The Goldbergs (radio, 1929–1946; TV, 1949–1957)
Lum and Abner (radio, 1931–1954)
The Eddie Cantor Show (radio, 1931–1949)
Easy Aces (radio, 1932–1945)
Ed Wynn, The Fire Chief (radio, 1932–1936)
The Jack Benny Program (radio, 1932–1955; TV, 1950–1965)
Fibber McGee and Molly (radio, 1935–1959; TV, 1959–1960)
The Aldrich Family (radio, 1939–1953; TV, 1949–1953)
The Great Gildersleeve (radio, 1941–1958; TV, 1955–1956)
Mary Kay and Johnny (1947–1950)
My Favorite Husband (radio, 1948–1951; TV, 1953–1955)
Mama (1949–1957)
The Life of Riley (1949–1958)
Beulah (1950–1952)
The George Burns and Gracie Allen Show (1950–1958)
The Hank McCune Show (1950)
I Love Lucy (1951–1957)
Our Miss Brooks (1952–1956)
The Adventures of Ozzie and Harriet (1952–1966)
Private Secretary (1953–1957)
The Danny Thomas Show (1953–1964)
Topper (1953–1955)
Father Knows Best (1954–1960)
The Bob Cummings Show (1955–1959)
The Honeymooners (1955–1956)
The Phil Silvers Show (1955–1959)
Bachelor Father (1957–1962)
Leave It to Beaver (1957–1963)
The Real McCoys (1957–1963)
The Donna Reed Show (1958–1966)
Dennis the Menace (1959–1963)
The Many Loves of Dobie Gillis (1959–1963)
My Three Sons (1960–1972)
The Andy Griffith Show (1960–1968)
The Flintstones (1960–1966)
Mister Ed (1961–1966)
The Dick Van Dyke Show (1961–1966)
McHale's Navy (1962–1966)
The Beverly Hillbillies (1962–1971)
The Jetsons (1962–1963; 1985–1987)
The Lucy Show (1962–1968)
My Favorite Martian (1963–1966)
Petticoat Junction (1963–1970)
Bewitched (1964–1972)
Gilligan's Island (1964–1967)
Gomer Pyle, U.S.M.C. (1964–1969)
My Living Doll (1964–1965)
The Addams Family (1964–1966)
The Munsters (1964–1966)
Get Smart (1965–1970)

VIDEOGRAPHY

Gidget (1965–1966)
Green Acres (1965–1971)
Hogan's Heroes (1965–1971)
I Dream of Jeannie (1965–1970)
My Mother, the Car (1965–1966)
Family Affair (1966–1971)
It's About Time (1966–1967)
The Monkees (1966–1968)
The Flying Nun (1967–1970)
Julia (1968–1971)
Mayberry R.F.D. (1968–1971)
The Ghost and Mrs. Muir (1968–1970)
The Bill Cosby Show (1969–1971)
The Brady Bunch (1969–1974)
The Courtship of Eddie's Father (1969–1972)
The Mary Tyler Moore Show (1970–1977)
The Odd Couple (1970–1975)
The Partridge Family (1970–1974)
All in the Family (1971–1979)
*M*A*S*H* (1972–1983)
Maude (1972–1978)
Sanford and Son (1972–1977)
The Corner Bar (1972–1973)
Good Times (1974–1979)
Happy Days (1974–1984)
Rhoda (1974–1978)
Barney Miller (1975–1982)
One Day at a Time (1975–1984; 2017–2019)
Phyllis (1975–1977)
The Jeffersons (1975–1985)
Alice (1976–1985)
Laverne & Shirley (1976–1983)
Three's Company (1976–1984)
What's Happening!! (1976–1979)
Soap (1977–1981)
Diff'rent Strokes (1978–1986)
Taxi (1978–1983)
WKRP in Cincinnati (1978–1982)
Archie Bunker's Place (1979–1983)
Checking In (1981)
Love, Sidney (1981–1983)
Cheers (1982–1993)
Family Ties (1982–1989)
Gloria (1982–1983)
Police Squad! (1982)
Silver Spoons (1982–1986)
Kate & Allie (1984–1989)
Night Court (1984–1992)
The Cosby Show (1984–1992)

Who's the Boss? (1984–1992)
The Golden Girls (1985–1992)
Designing Women (1986–1993)
It's Garry Shandling's Show (1986–1990)
Frank's Place (1987–1988)
Full House (1987–1995)
Married... with Children (1987–1997)
The Days and Nights of Molly Dodd (1987–1991)
The Tracey Ullman Show (1987–1990)
The Wonder Years (1988–1993)
Murphy Brown (1988–1998; 2018–2019)
Roseanne (1988–1997; 2018)
Doogie Howser, M.D. (1989–1993)
Coach (1989–1997)
Seinfeld (1989–1998)
The Simpsons (1989–)
Dream On (1990–1996)
In Living Color (1990–1994)
Parker Lewis Can't Lose (1990–1993)
The Fresh Prince of Bel-Air (1990–1996)
Home Improvement (1991–1999)
Roc (1991–1994)
Mad About You (1992–1999; 2019–)
Martin (1992–1997)
The Larry Sanders Show (1992–1998)
Beavis and Butt-Head (1993–1997; 2011)
Frasier (1993–2004)
Living Single (1993–1998)
The Nanny (1993–1999)
The Sinbad Show (1993–1994)
704 Hauser (1994)
Ellen (1994–1998)
Friends (1994–2004)
Sister, Sister (1994–1999)
South Central (1994)
Caroline in the City (1995–1999)
NewsRadio (1995–1999)
The Drew Carey Show (1995–2004)
The Parent 'Hood (1995–1999)
The Wayans Bros. (1995–1999)
Everybody Loves Raymond (1996–2005)
Moesha (1996–2001)
Suddenly Susan (1996–2000)
The Jamie Foxx Show (1996–2001)
The Steve Harvey Show (1996–2002)
Ally McBeal (1997–2002)
King of the Hill (1997–2010)
South Park (1997–)
Veronica's Closet (1997–2000)
The Hughleys (1998–2002)

VIDEOGRAPHY

Sex and the City (1998–2004)
Becker (1998–2004)
That 70s Show (1998–2006)
The King of Queens (1998–2007)
Will & Grace (1998–2006; 2017–2020)
Sports Night (1998–2000)
Family Guy (1999–)
The Parkers (1999–2004)
Curb Your Enthusiasm (2000–)
Girlfriends (2000–2008)
Malcolm in the Middle (2000–2006)
The World According to Jim (2000–2009)
My Wife and Kids (2001–2005)
One on One (2001–2006)
Reba (2001–2007)
Scrubs (2001–2010)
The Bernie Mac Show (2001–2006)
The Office, UK (2001–2003)
Arrested Development (2003–2006; 2013–)
Two and a Half Men (2003–2015)
Weeds (2005–2012)
My Name Is Earl (2005–2009)
The Comeback (2005; 2014)
The Office, US (2005–2013)
30 Rock (2006–2013)
The New Adventures of Old Christine (2006–2010)
The Big Bang Theory (2007–2019)
The Sarah Silverman Program (2007–2010)
Community (2009–2015)
Cougar Town (2009–2015)
Modern Family (2009–2020)
Parks and Recreation (2009–2015)
The Middle (2009–2018)
Louie (2010–2015)
Mike & Molly (2010–2016)
2 Broke Girls (2011–2017)
Bob's Burgers (2011–)
Episodes (2011–2017)
New Girl (2011–2018)
Suburgatory (2011–2014)
Whitney (2011–2013)
Girls (2012–2017)
Don't Trust the B---- in Apartment 23 (2012–2014)
The Mindy Project (2012–2017)
Veep (2012–2019)
Mom (2013–)
Orange Is the New Black (2013–2019)

Rick and Morty (2013–)
The Carrie Diaries (2013–2014)
The Goldbergs (2013–)
Transparent (2014–2019)
Black-ish (2014–)
Bojack Horseman (2014–)
Broad City (2014–2019)
Jane the Virgin (2014–2019)
Red Oaks (2014–2017)
Silicon Valley (2014–)
Younger (2015–)
Casual (2015–2018)
Crazy Ex-Girlfriend (2015–2019)
Difficult People (2015–17)
Documentary Now! (2015–)
Fresh Off the Boat (2015–)
Grace and Frankie (2015–)
Master of None (2015–2017)
One Mississippi (2015–2017)
The Carmichael Show (2015–2017)
Unbreakable Kimmy Schmidt (2015–2019)
Insecure (2016–)
Lady Dynamite (2016–2017)
Dear White People (2017–)
She's Gotta Have It (2017–2019)
Big Mouth (2017–)
GLOW (2017–)
Santa Clarita Diet (2017–2019)
The Marvelous Mrs. Maisel (2017–)
Young Sheldon (2017–)
Forever (2018–)
The Conners (2018–)
Russian Doll (2019–)
Schooled (2019–)

BIBLIOGRAPHY

Akass, Kim and Janet McCabe, eds. *Reading Sex and the City*. London: I. B. Tauris, 2006.

Attallah, Paul. "The Unworthy Discourse: Situation Comedy in Television," in *Interpreting Television: Current Research Perspectives*. Edited by Willard D. Rowland, Jr. and Bruce Watkins, 222–249. Beverly Hills, CA: Sage, 1984.

Becker, Christine. "Acting for the Cameras: Performance in the Multi-Camera Sitcom." *Mediascape* (Spring 2008): 1–11.

Butler, Jeremy G. "Redesigning Discourse: Feminism, the Sitcom and *Designing Women*." *Journal of Film and Video* 45, no. 1 (Spring 1993): 13–26.

Butler, Jeremy G. "Televisuality and the Resurrection of the Sitcom in the 2000s," in *Television Style*, 173–222. New York: Routledge, 2010.

Caldwell, John Thornton. *Televisuality: Style, Crisis, and Authority in American Television*. New Brunswick, NJ: Rutgers University Press, 1995.

Carroll, Noël. *Humour: A Very Short Introduction*. Oxford: Oxford University Press, 2014.

Clark, Cedric C. "Television and Social Controls: Some Observations on the Portrayals of Ethnic Minorities." *Television Quarterly* 8, no. 2 (1969): 18–22.

Dalton, Mary M. and Laura R. Linder, eds. *The Sitcom Reader: America Viewed and Skewed*. Albany, NY: State University of New York Press, 2005.

Desjardins, Mary. *Father Knows Best*. Detroit, MI: Wayne State University Press, 2015.

Diffrient, David Scott. *M*A*S*H*. Detroit, MI: Wayne State University Press, 2008.

Dyer, Richard. *Pastiche*. New York: Routledge, 2007.

Eaton, Mick. "Television Situation Comedy." *Screen* 19, no. 4 (Winter 1978): 61–90.

Ellis, John. *Visible Fictions: Cinema:Television:Video*. Boston, MA: Routledge, 1992.

Ely, Melvin Patrick. *The Adventures of Amos 'n' Andy: A Social History of an American Phenomenon*. Charlottesville, VA: The University Press of Virginia, 2001.

Feuer, Jane, Paul Kerr and Tise Vahimagi, eds. *MTM 'Quality Television'*. London: BFI Publishing, 1984.

BIBLIOGRAPHY

Fiske, John. *Television Culture*, 2nd ed. New York: Routledge, 2011.

Gray, Herman. *Watching Race: Television and the Struggle for "Blackness."* Minneapolis, MN: University of Minnesota Press, 1995.

Gray, Jonathan. *Watching with the Simpsons: Television, Parody, and Intertextuality*. New York: Routledge, 2006.

Hall, Stuart. "The Spectacle of the 'Other,'" in *Representation*, 2nd ed. Edited by Stuart Hall, Jessica Evans and Sean Nixon, 215–271. Thousand Oaks, CA: Sage Publications, 2013.

Haralovich, Mary Beth. "Sitcoms and Suburbs: Positioning the 1950s Homemaker." *Quarterly Review of Film and Video* 11, no. 1 (May 1989): 61–83.

Hilmes, Michele. *Only Connect: A Cultural History of Broadcasting in the United States*, 4th ed. Boston, MA: Wadsworth, 2014.

Jenkins, Henry. *Convergence Culture: Where Old and New Media Collide*. New York University Press, 2006.

Jermyn, Deborah. *Sex and the City*. Detroit, MI: Wayne State University Press, 2009.

Jones, Gerard. *Honey, I'm Home!: Sitcoms: Selling the American Dream*. New York: Grove Weidenfeld, 1992.

Kalviknes Bore, Inger-Lise. "Laughing Together: TV Comedy Audiences and the Laugh Track." *Velvet Light Trap* 68 (2011): 25–26.

Landay, Lori. *I Love Lucy*. Detroit, MI: Wayne State University Press, 2010.

Lavery, David and Sara Lewis Dunne, eds. *Seinfeld, Master of Its Domain*. New York: Continuum, 2006.

Liebman, Nina C. *Living Room Lectures: The Fifties Family in Film and Television*. Austin, TX: University of Texas Press, 1995.

Lotz, Amanda D. "Sex, Careers, and Mr. Right in Comedic Dramas: The 'New' New Woman of *Ally McBeal* and *Sex and the City*," in *Redesigning Women: Television After the Network Era*, 88–117. Urbana, IL: University of Illinois Press, 2006.

Marc, David. *Comic Visions: Television Comedy and American Culture*. Boston, MA: Unwin Hyman, 1989.

Marc, David. "The Situation Comedy of Paul Henning: Modernity and the American Folk Myth in *The Beverly Hillbillies*," in *Demographic Vistas: Television in American Culture*, Revised Edition, 39–64. Philadelphia, PA: University of Pennsylvania Press, 1996.

Marx, Nick and Matt Sienkiewicz, eds. *The Comedy Studies Reader*. Austin, TX: University of Texas Press, 2018.

Means Coleman, Robin R. *African American Viewers and the Black Situation Comedy: Situating Racial Humor*. New York: Garland, 1998.

Mellencamp, Patricia. "Situation Comedy, Feminism, and Freud: Discourses of Gracie and Lucy," in *Star Texts: Image and Performance in Film and Television*. Edited by Jeremy G. Butler, 316–332. Detroit, MI: Wayne State University Press, 1991.

BIBLIOGRAPHY

Mills, Brett. "Comedy Vérité: Contemporary Sitcom Form." *Screen* 45, no. 1 (Spring 2004): 63–78.

Mills, Brett. *Television Sitcom*. London: BFI Publishing, 2005.

Mittell, Jason. *Genre and Television: From Cop Shows to Cartoons in American Culture*. New York: Routledge, 2004.

Morreale, Joanne. *Critiquing the Sitcom: A Reader*. Syracuse, NY: Syracuse University Press, 2003.

Nelson, Angela. "From Beulah to the Fresh Prince of Bel-Air: A Brief History of Black Stereotypes in Television Comedy," unpublished manuscript, 1991. Cited in Means Coleman, Robin R. *African American Viewers and the Black Situation Comedy: Situating Racial Humor*. New York: Garland, 1998.

Newman, Michael Z. and Elana Levine. *Legitimating Television: Media Convergence and Cultural Status*. New York: Routledge, 2012.

Pugh, Tison. *The Queer Fantasies of the American Family Sitcom*. New Brunswick, NJ: Rutgers University Press, 2018.

Rowe, Kathleen. *The Unruly Woman: Gender and the Genres of Laughter*. Austin, TX: The University of Texas Press, 1995.

Smith, Evan S. *Writing Television Sitcoms*. New York: Perigee, 2009.

Smith-Shomade, Beretta E. *Shaded Lives: African-American Women and Television*. New Brunswick, NJ: Rutgers University Press, 2002.

Thompson, Ethan. "Comedy Vérité? The Observational Documentary Meets the Televisual Sitcom." *Velvet Light Trap* 60, no. 1 (Fall 2007): 63–72.

Tropiano, Stephen. *The Prime Time Closet: A History of Gays and Lesbians on TV*. New York: Applause Theatre & Cinema, 2002.

Turner, Chris. Planet Simpson: How a Cartoon Masterpiece Defined a Generation. Boston, MA: Da Capo Press, 2004.

Vidmar, Neil and Milton Rokeach. "Archie Bunker's Bigotry: A Study in Selective Perception and Exposure." *Journal of Communication* 24, no. 1 (Winter 1974): 36–47.

Warner, Kristen J. *The Cultural Politics of Colorblind TV Casting*. New York: Routledge, 2018.

INDEX

Page numbers in *italics* refer to figures. Page numbers in **bold** refer to tables.

2 Broke Girls 37, 133–134, *134*, 153, 157, 199
30 Rock 23, 33, 24, 91, 138, 139, 201
60 Minutes 77
704 Hauser 219

Adams, Don 39
Addams Family, The (movie) 220
Addams Family, The (show) 71, 220
Addams Family Values 220
Adventures of Ozzie and Harriet, The 67, 98, 103–104
African Americans: in 1970s sitcoms 76; in 1980s sitcoms 78; in 1990s sitcoms 84; absence of 112–113; "black laughs" and 31; black sitcom history and 185–187; *see also* race; *individual actors*; *individual shows*
Aldrich Family, The 58, 60, 61, 62, 64
Alice 111, 137
Allen, Gracie 203, *204*
Allen, Woody 30
All in the Family 37, 71, 72–74, 104, 106, 108, 109, 122, 123, 140–142, 184, 186, 218–219
Ally McBeal 137, 149
Altman, Robert 75

Amazon Prime Video 93, 221, 222, 225–226
Amos 'n' Andy 58–59, 60–61, 62, 66, 67–68, 76, 163, 165–166, 172–173, 185, 193, 227
Andy Griffith Show, The 1, 11, 16, 21, 69, 96–97, 107, 112–125, *114*, 134, 184, 191, 197, 206
Annie Hall 30
Ansari, Aziz 169–170
Apocalypse Now 234
archetypal characters 26–28
Archie Bunker's Place 218–219
Arden, Eve 135, 197
Arnaz, Desi 65, 66, 68
Arrested Development 34–35, *35*, 91, 92, 93, 201, 216–218, 233
assimilationist discourse 167–171, 182
assimilationist era 185–186
A stories 17–18
audience-response track 30–33
Azzari, Tom 87

Bachelor Father 110
Bakhtin, Mikhail 7, 127
Ball, Lucille 65–66, 197
Barney Miller 79

INDEX

Barr, Roseanne 39, 78–79, 99–100, *100*, 133
Barris, Kenya 7, 187–188, 192
Barthes, Roland 208
Beavis and Butt-head 201
Becker 137
Behrs, Beth 133
Berg, Gertrude 99, 166
Bernie Mac Show, The 50, 92, 103, 105, 110, 167, 187, 231
Better Things 111
Beulah 185
Beverly Hillbillies, The 69, 96, 107–108
Bewitched 70, 71, 140
Big Bang Theory, The 17–23, 24, 25, 27, 28, 31, 33, 90, 183, 219, 241
Big Mouth 222
Billboard, The 57–58
Billingsley, Barbara *100*
black-cast sitcoms 171, 172;
 see also African Americans; race; *individual shows*
Black Entertainment Television (BET) 172
black family and diversity era 186–187
Black-ish 7, 11, 16, 50, 95, 165, 167, 187–194
black sitcom history 185–187
blackvoice 165–166
blended families 110
blocking 39–40, 47
Bloodworth-Thomason, Linda 80
Blount, Jason 48
Bob Cummings Show, The 67
Bob's Burgers 83, 95, 102, 106, 212–213
Bojack Horseman 222, 224–225
Bordwell, David 198, 202
Bore, Inger-Lise Kalviknes 33
Bosom Buddies 1
Boston Public 169
Bouchard, Loren 213
Brady Bunch, The 110, 220, 232
Brady Bunch Movie, The 220
bricolage 209, 212–215, 232, 234–235, *238*

Broad City 138, 139, 227–228
Brooks, James L. 72
Brown v. Board of Education 171
B stories 17–18
Buffy the Vampire Slayer 41
Burns, George 203–204, *204*, 231
Burrows, James 84
Bushnell, Candace 146–148
Butler, Judith 129–130, 145–146, 164

Caldwell, John 29, 43–44, 198, 200–201
Cantor, Eddie 61
Carmichael, Jerrod 39, 45–46, *45*
Carmichael Show, The 44–47, *45*, *46*, 51, *52*, *53*, 104, 167
carnivalesque 7, 127
Caroline in the City 137
Carrie Diaries, The 146
Carroll, Noël 8, 9
Carsey, Marcy 77
Cartwright, Nancy 231
Castellaneta, Dan 231
Casual 222, 224
catchphrase 61–62
Cattrell, Kim 157
cause–effect chain 19, 25–26, 225
Chappelle, Dave 180–181, 193
Chappelle's Show 180–181
character mixes **27**
Checking In 219
Cheers 77, 79, 84, 137, 183, 199, 211, 212, 220, 232
child-narrated programs 103
children *see* families; family sitcoms; parent–child relations
Childress, Alvin 173
Cho, Margaret 133
Chronicle of a Summer 210
cinematography **36**, 43–51
cinéma vérité 209–211
civil rights movement 68, 71, 112–113, 185
Clark, Cedric 185
close-ups 47, 49, *49*

253

INDEX

CK, Louis 3
Coach 77, 80
Cohen, Gerry 45, *45*, 47
Colbert, Stephen 209
Colbert Report, The 209
cold openings 17
color-blind casting 169, 171
colorism 176–178, *177*, *178*
Comeback, The 138, 206
Comedians in Cars Getting Coffee 86
Comedy Central 228
comedy *vérité* 91, 209, 211–212
Commedia dell'Arte 26
commercials, breaks for 15, 17, 23, 60–61
Community 37, 44, 50, 91
Conners, The 79
continuity 52–53, *52*, *53*, 200
convergence 11, 199, 218–228, 235–240
Convergence Culture (Jenkins) 220–221
Coppola, Francis Ford 234
Corner Bar, The 140
Correll, Charles J. 58–59, 61, 165, 173
Cosby, Bill 78, 84
Cosby Show, The 77–78, 102, 105, 106, 108, 186–187
Cougar Town 41–42, 102
Courtship of Eddie's Father, The 110
"cringe-worthy" comedy 88–89
Crowley, Pat *100*
Crystal, Billy 142
Curb Your Enthusiasm 23, 89, 92
CW network 84, 175

Daniels, Greg 169
Dauterive, Jim 213
David, Larry 86, 89
Days and Nights of Molly Dodd, The 92, 149
Dear White People 222
DeGeneres, Ellen 143–144, 145
Dennings, Kat 133
Dennis the Menace 102, 118
depth of field 46

Descartes, René 4–5
Designing Women 80, 137, 167
Desilu Productions 65
Desjardins, Mary 98
Dick Van Dyke Show, The 70, 74, 140, 232
Different World, A 186–187
Difficult People 222
Diff'rent Strokes 72, 110
Diller, Phyllis 133
discursive strategies 166–167
Disney+ 237
divorce 96, 110, 137
Documentary Now! 210–211, 212
Donald, John R. 240
Donna Reed Show, The 67, 111, 123
Donner, Richard 40, *41*, *42*, 43
Doogie Howser, MD 200
Dream On 193, 214–215
Drew Carey Show, The 137
Dubin, Charles 75
DuMont network 57, 63
Dunham, Lena 138–139
DVDs 216–217
DVRs 216–217, 233

Easy Aces 59
Eaton, Mick 16
Eddie Cantor Show, The 61
editing **36**, 52–55
Ed Wynn, The Fire Chief 61
Ellen 137, 143–144
Ellis, John 16
Ellis, Peter B. 53–54
Emmy Awards 223–224
emotional incongruity 9–10
Engler, Michael 154
ensemble casts 183–184
Episodes 206
episode structure 15–23, 25, 224–225
ethnicity: introduction to 163–165
Everybody Loves Raymond 33, 92, 105

families: non-traditional 110–112; parent–child relations in 102–104;

socioeconomic class and 104–110; traditional 97–102
Family Affair 110, 112
Family Guy 83, 99, 241
Family Matters 173, 174–175, 182
family sitcoms 77–79, 95–125; *see also individual shows*
Family Ties 77, 104, 105
fan fiction 238–239
Father Knows Best 67, 70, 78, 98, 107, 123, 174
female gaze 152–156, *155*, *156*, 159
Fey, Tina 39, 93
Fibber McGee and Molly 60, 61, 62
film noir 41
Flintstones, The 32, 71, 83, 98
Flying Nun, The 70
fourth wall 40, 44, 103, 197, 202–206, *205*, 211, 230–232, 241
Fox network 82–83, 84, 199, 231, 237
Foxx, Jamie 207
Foxx, Redd 39
Frank's Place 92, 167, 186–187
Frasier 84, 105, 108, 172, 220
Freaks and Geeks 170
freeze-frame fun 233–234
Fresh Off the Boat 95, 103, 183–184, 191
Fresh Prince of Bel-Air, The 37, 167, 199
Freud, Sigmund 5–6, 127, 130, 153
Freund, Karl 66
Friends 1, 33, 81, 84–85, 88, 105, 137, 143, 171, 172, 183, 199
Frinkiac service 238, *239*
Full House 77, 110

gag comedy 2, 132–133, 153
Game of Thrones 41
gay parents 145
gaze theory 130, 153, 159–160
Gelbart, Larry 75, 76, 90
gender: in cinema and TV studies 129–134
gender identity 129–134
gender roles 96, 97–103, 108, 111–112, 115–118, 120–122, 127–128, 134–139

generation gaps 96, 102–104, 118–123
George Burns and Gracie Allen Show, The 203–204, *204*, 205–206
Get Smart 200
Ghost and Mrs. Muir, The 70, 111
Gidget 103
Gilligan's Island 40, *41*, 42–43, *42*
Girlfriends 84, 138, 167, 175–179, *177*, *178*, 182
Girls 23, 132, 138–139, 222
Glazer, Ilana 227–228
Gleason, Jackie 39
Gloria 219
GLOW 222, 226
Godard, Jean-Luc 208
Goldberg, Whoopi 133
Goldbergs, The (contemporary) 24, 34, 47–50, *48*, 53–54, 103, 201–202, 219
Goldbergs, The (on radio/early television) 59, 60–61, 67–68, 99, 106–107, 163, 166, 227
Golden Girls, The 137, 167
Gomer Pyle, U.S.M.C. 69, 74
Good Times 50, 72, 76, 111, 186, 218
Gosden, Freeman F. 58–59, 61, 165, 173
Grace and Frankie 2, 222
Gray, Herman 166–167, 168, 173, 179
Great Gildersleeve, The 110
Green Acres 96, 107–108
Grey's Anatomy 25
Griffith, Andy 197
Groening, Matt 235, 240
Groundhog Day 21
Grown-ish 188
Gunsmoke 233

"half-hour comedy" 23–26
Hall, Stuart 13
Handler, Chelsea 133
Hank McCune Show, The 66
Happy Days 1, 77
Harris, Neil Patrick 32
Harris, Susan 142
Hayes, Sean 144–145

INDEX

Head 220
high-key lighting 38–39, *38*, 41–42
Hill, Anita 80
Hill Street Blues 200
Hobbes, Thomas 4–5
Hogan's Heroes 71
Holden, William 197
Home Improvement 99
Homicide: Life on the Street 219
Honeymooners, The 98, 106, 107, 110, 232
Howard, Ron 217
Hughleys, The 187
Hulu 221, 222, 225–226
humor: theories of 4–11
Hurwitz, Mitchell 216–217, 233
Hutcheson, Francis 8

I Dream of Jeannie 70
I Love Lucy 1, 11, 14–15, 33, 57, 64–68, 88, 95, 107, 108, 110, 197, 199, 206
image-of-woman approach 129–130
Imitation of Life (1959) 214–215
incongruity theories of humor 4, 179–180, 181, 193
In Living Color 84
Insecure 139
intensified continuity 198, 202
intertextuality 198, 199, 207–218, 232–235, 241
I Remember Mama 64
It's About Time 70
It's Garry Shandling's Show 204–206, *205*

Jack Benny Show, The 67
Jacobson, Abbi 227–228
Jameson, Fredric 208
Jamie Foxx Show, The 137
Jane the Virgin 139
Jeffersons, The 31, 72, 76, 108, 167, 186, 218
Jenkins, Henry 220–221, 228, 236–237
Jennings, Alex *48*
Jermyn, Deborah 154, 158
Jetsons, The 71

Jokes and Their Relation to the Unconscious (Freud) 5
Jones, Jill Marie 177
Jones, Rashida 169–170
Jordan, Jim and Marian 60
Julia 111, 168–169, 179, 186
"jump the shark" 1

Kate & Allie 111, 137
Katzenberg, David 48–50, 54
Kavner, Julie 231
Key & Peele 7
kinescope 64, 65
King, Michael Patrick 157
King of Queens, The 99, 109
King of the Hill 83, 213
Kristeva, Julia 207
Kwapis, Ken 23

Landay, Lori 110
Larry Sanders Show, The 89, 91, 137, 201
Lassie 107
laugh track 30–33, 61, 66, 75, 92
Laverne & Shirley 77
Law & Order 219
Lear, Norman 72–74, 76, 80, 104, 136, 140, 186, 200
Leave It to Beaver 67, 70, 98, 103, 105, 107, 108, 111, 123
LEGO Movie, The 230
Leibman, Nina 105
Lévi-Strauss, Claude 209
LGBTQ discourse 156–158
LGBTQ representation 85, 108, 128–129, 139–146
Life in Hell 235
Life of Riley, The 98
lighting 38–39, *38*, 41–43, 201
Live in Front of a Studio Audience 207
Living Single 84
Lockhart, June *100*
Loeb, Philip 68
loglines 15–16, 113, 147–150, 182, 188–191
Lorre, Chuck 17, 31
Lotz, Amanda D. 149

INDEX

Louie 3, 111
Love, Sidney 142–143
low-key lighting 41
Lucy Show, The 110, 137
Lum and Abner 59

M*A*S*H 37–38, 74–76, 90, 92, 200
Mad About You 108, 143
Magnum, P.I. 232
Make Room for Daddy 67
Malcolm in the Middle 37, 92, 103, 106, 109, 202, 231
male gaze 130–132, 153–154
Mama 58, 64, 67–68, 99
Many Loves of Dobie Gillis, The 103
Married … with Children 82–83, 84, 98, 106
Marshall, Garry 77
Martin 84
Marvel Cinematic Universe (MCU) 198, 218
Marvelous Mrs. Maisel, The 222, 223
Marx, Nick 227, 228
Mary Kay and Johnny 57, 63, 66, 95
Mary Tyler Moore Show, The 37, 71–72, 74, 102, 108, 136–137
Master of None 170, 222, 223, 224
Matrix, The 221
Maude 72, 108, 218
Mayberry R.F.D. 21, 117
McCormack, Eric 144
McHale's Navy 74
McIlwain, Charlton D. 186
Means Coleman, Robin R. 185–187, 193
Metcalf, Laurie 219
Miami Vice 44, 200
Michalka, AJ *48*
Middle, The 95, 102, 106, 109
middle-class family sitcoms 105–106, 108–110
Mike & Molly 109, 199
Mildred Pierce 135
Millet, Kate 128
Mills, Brett 209–210

Mindy Project, The 138, 167, 222
minstrelsy era 185
Mirren, Helen 211
mise-en-scene 35–43, **36**
mismatched narrative knowledge 10
Mister Ed 70
Mixed-ish 188, 192
mockumentaries 50, 91–92, 209
Modern Family 4, 5–10, 14, 24, 27–28, 33, 44, 50–51, *51*, 92, 95, 96, 103, 105, 145, 146, 164
Moesha 84
Molaro, Steven 17
Mom 24, 95, 105, 106, 199
Monkees, The 220
Moore, Mary Tyler 71, 136
Morin, Edgar 210
MTM Enterprises 71, 136
multiculturalist discourse 167, 179–184, 186–187
multiple camera (multicam) production 24–25, 29–30, 35–47, **36**, 50, 52–55, 66, 67, 74, 199–200, 211–212
Mulvey, Laura 153
Munsters, The 70
Murphy Brown 77, 80, 111, 137, 206
music 34–35
My Favorite Husband 66
My Favorite Martian 70
My Living Doll 70
My Mother, the Car 70
My Name Is Earl 92, 201
My So-Called Life 200
Mystery Science Theater 3000 201
My Three Sons 98, 110, 112
My Wife and Kids 187

Naked Gun, The 220
Naked Gun 2 1/2, The 220
Naked Gun 33 1/3 220
Nanny, The 110, 112
narrative problematic 15–18, 20–21, 25, 55, 61, 69–70, 73, 75, 78, 83, 85, 88, 95, 101, 104, 106, 108, 113,

INDEX

123, 125, 147–149, 159, 174, 178, 182, 186, 188–190, 194
Neighborhood, The 182–183
Nelson, Angela 185
Nelson, Ozzie and Harriet 103–104
Nelson, Ricky 103–104
neo-minstrelsy era 186
Netflix 90, 93, 221, 222, 225–226, 234, 237
network era: end of 81–82
New Adventures of Old Christine, The 111, 138
NewsRadio 137
Nielsen, Arthur C. 58, 64
Night Court 80
Nixon, Cynthia 157
non-diegetic music 34–35
nonrecognition era 185
non-traditional families 110–112
Notaro, Tig 39, 133
nuclear family 97–102, 108

Obama, Barack 188
Odd Couple, The 28, 140
Office, The 24, 33, 50, 92, 170, 201, 209–210, 211, 212, 228
Omi, Michael 164
One Day at a Time 111, 137
One Mississippi 222
One on One 110
Oprah Winfrey Show, The 144
Orange Is the New Black 145, 222, 223
Orrantia, Hayley 48, 49
Our Miss Brooks 67, 135–136

parent–child relations 96, 102–104; *see also* families; family sitcoms
Parent 'Hood, The 84
Parker, Sarah Jessica 157
Parker Lewis Can't Lose 91, 103, 201–203, 206, 231
Parkers, The 84
Parks and Recreation 50, 92, 167, 169–170
parody 209, 211–212, 232–233, 234–235

Partridge Family, The 111
patriarchal ideology 150–152, 159
Perry, Zoe 219
Petticoat Junction 69, 96, 107–108
Phil Silvers Show, The 67, 74
Phyllis 108
physical comedy 2–3
pluralist discourse 167, 171–179, 182, 186
Poehler, Amy 228
point-of-view editing 54
Police Squad! 220
postmodernism 207–208
Prady, Bill 17
Pratt, Carroll 31
predicaments **27**
Private Secretary 67, 135–136
production modes 23–26, 29, 64–68
product placement 60

queer culture 158; *see also* LGBTQ discourse; LGBTQ representation

race: assimilationist discourse and 167–171; in cinema and TV studies 165–167; history of sitcoms based on 184–187; introduction to 163–165; multiculturalist discourse and 179–184; pluralist discourse and 171–179
racial essentialism 164
racial formation approach 164
radio 58–63
Real McCoys, The 67, 96, 107
Reba 138
recurring situations 26–28
Red Oaks 222
Reiner, Carl 70
relief/release theories of humor 4, 5–7
religion: introduction to 163–165
repeatability 15
Retta 169–170
Reynolds, Gene 75
Rhoda 108
Rick and Morty 30, 222

Rivers, Joan 133
Roberts, Clete 75–76
Roc 84, 143, 167
role-reversal episodes 100–101, 116–117
Romano, Ray 39
Roseanne 77, 78–79, 99–100, *100*, 109, 143
Rosenstock, Richard 17
Rouch, Jean 210
Rowe, Kathleen 150, 154
rule of three 9
rural sitcoms 107
Russian Doll 21, 222, 224

Sam 'n' Henry 58
Sanford, Isabel *100*
Sanford and Son 72, 73, 76–77, 105, 106, 108, 167, 172, 186
Santa Clarita Diet 222
Saturday Night Live 7
Schooled 219
School Is Hell 235–236
Schumer, Amy 133
Schur, Michael 169
Sconce, Jeffrey 107
scopophilia 153–154, 159
Scrubs 34, 50, 91, 198, 211–212
second-wave feminism 71, 72, 129, 134–135, 136, 138, 141, 146, 150–152, 155, 159
Seinfeld 35, 37, *38*, 39–40, 81, 84–89, 137, 171, 172, 179
Seinfeld, Jerry 39, 86
self-parody 232–233
self-reflexivity 198, 199, 202–206, 211, 217, 229–232, 241
sequels 218–220
sequential incongruity 9
Sergeant Bilko 74
setting 106–107
sex: changing representations of 129–134; as taboo subject 127
Sex and the City 11, 16, 34, 92, 128, 133, 137, 146–160, 184, 197, 220

Sex and the City (movie) 149, 220
Sex and the City 2 (movie) 149, 220
sexual politics 128
Shandling, Garry 204–205, *205*
show bible 21, 197
Sidney Shorr: A Girl's Best Friend 143
Silicon Valley 222
Silverman, Sarah 133
Silver Spoons 110
Simon, Al 66
Simpsons, The 11, 14, 16, 44, 73, 82, 83–84, 89, 91, 99, 102, 118, 199, 201, 229–241, *236*, *238*, *239*
Simpsons Movie, The 236
simultaneity and the illusion of liveness 29
Sinbad Show, The 84
single camera production 24–25, 29, 33–34, **36**, 37–38, 40–43, 47–55, 67, 92, 193–194
single parents 110–112
Single Parents 111
Sister, Sister 84, 111
sitcoms: in 1960s 68–71; in 1970s 71–77; in 1980s 77–81; in 1990s 81–89; in 2000s 89–93; critical/cultural history of 57–93; on early television 63–64; episode parts of 17; family and small towns and 95–125; introduction to 1–11; longevity of 2; perceptions of 1; race, ethnicity, and religion and 163–194; on radio 58–64; resistance to label of 23–26; sex and gender identity and 127–160; sound and image of 28–55; storytelling and 15–28; televisuality and convergence and 197–241; terminology for 2–3; understanding 13–55
Smith, Evan S. 26–28, **27**, 69, 88, 168
Smith, Yeardley 231
Soap 142, 145
social relevancy and ridiculed black subjectivity era 186
socioeconomic class 96, 104–110, 123–125

INDEX

Sopranos, The 147, 158
Sothern, Ann 135
sound characteristics 30–35
sound effects (SFX) 34–35, 63–64
South Central 84
South Park 83, 216, 241
Spicer, Brian 201–202
spin-offs 218–220
Sports Night 137, 206
Standards and Practices departments 140, 173
Star, Darren 93, 147
Star Trek 220
Star Wars Kid 217
Stearns, Mary Kay and Johnny 63
Steve Harvey Show, The 137
Stranger Things 234
studio audiences 30–32, 65–66; *see also* laugh track
subscription video-on-demand (SVOD) services 90, 93, 220–226, 237
suburban lifestyle 96, 104–110, 123–125
suburban settings 107, 109
Suburgatory 109
Suddenly Susan 137
superiority theories of humor 4–5, 7, 59, 111, 132–133, 153, 163–165, 172–173, 179–180, 181, 185
surrogate spouses 112
Sykes, Wanda 133

tag 17, 22, 25, 87, 226
Tarkington, Rockne 113
Taxi 37, 41, 79, 137
teasers 17
televisuality 43–44, 50–51, 91–92, 198, 199–207, 230
Televisuality (Caldwell) 44
That 70s Show 109
third-wave feminism 138–139, 150–152, 155–156, 159
Thomas, Clarence 80
Thompson, Ethan 209
Three's Company 77, 130–132, *131*

Tinker, Grant 71
Tomlin, Lily 133
Topper 67
Tracey Ullman Show, The 201
traditional values 108
transmedia storytelling 198, 213, 218, 228, 236–240
Transparent 93, 145, 222
tropes 26–28, 55, 125, 168, 174, 182, 205, 232, 237, 241
Tropiano, Stephen 140
Trump, Donald 79, 188
Truth or Consequences 66
Turner, Chris 233
TV Land 93
TVTropes.com 26–27
Twin Peaks 200
Two and a Half Men 33, 89, 105, 110–111

Ullman, Tracey 133
Unbreakable Kimmy Schmidt 23, 93, 222
United Paramount Network (UPN) 84, 175
urban settings 106–107, 108–109

VCRs 216
Veep 14, 222
Veronica's Closet 137
Vimeo 221, 227
voice-over (VO) narration 34
Volpe, Allie 223
voyeurism 130, 153

Wachowskis 221
Warner, Kristen J. 169
Watching Race (Gray) 166
Wayans Bros., The 84
Wayne, John 197
webisode 226–228
Weeds 138
Werner, Tom 77
West, Amber Stevens 45–46, *45*, *46*, 52–53, *52*, *53*
What's Happening!! 111

INDEX

White, Persia 177
Who's the Boss? 77
Wild Wild Country 211
Will & Grace 33, 85, 137, 143, 144–145
Williams, Spencer 173
Winant, Howard 164
Winfrey, Oprah 144
Wizard of Oz, The 158
WKRP in Cincinnati 137
Wollen, Peter 208
Wonder Years, The 34, 92, 103
working-class family sitcoms 106, 109–110

workplace sitcoms 37, 60, 67, 70, 79–81, 84–85, 137; *see also individual shows*
World According to Jim, The 99
Writers Guild of America (WGA) 224
Wynn, Ed 61

Young, Alan 170
Young and the Restless, The 25
Younger 93
Young Sheldon 219
YouTube 90, 221, 225, 226–228

zero-degree of style 29, 39, 43, 90, 200